★ ★ ★ ★ ★ ★ ★ ★ ★

Presidential Follies

★ ★ ★ ★ ★ ★ ★ ★ ★ ★ ★ ★ ★ ★ ★

PRESIDENTIAL
Follies ★ ★ ★ ★ ★ ★ ★ ★

THOSE WHO WOULD BE PRESIDENT ★ ★ ★
AND THOSE WHO SHOULD THINK AGAIN

RALPH Z. HALLOW
and BRADLEY S. O'LEARY

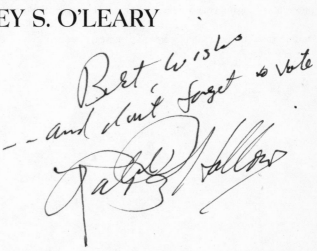

BORU BOOKS

Library of Congress Catalog Card Number 95-080487

ISBN 1-887161-00-7 (cl)
ISBN 1-887161-07-4 (pbk)

Published in the United States by
Boru Publishing, Inc.
33 Spanish Pass Road
Boerne, Texas 78006

Distributed to the trade by
National Book Network
4720-A Boston Way
Lanham, MD 20706

Books are available in quantity for promotional or premium use. Write to
Director of Special Sales, Boru Publishing, Inc., 33 Spanish Pass Road, Boerne,
Texas 78006, for information on discounts and terms, call (800) 447-7118.

Manufactured in the United States of America.

97 96 95 5 4 3 2 1

To my children, Ann O. Weems, Susan Gulla, Lynne Dunnigan, Shannon O'Leary, Erin O'Leary, and McKenzie O'Leary, and my grandchildren, Coy Weems, Stacy Weems, Rebecca Weems, Elizabeth Weems, Kathy Weems, Christina Gulla, Anthony Gulla, Amy Dunnigan, Laura Dunnigan and Stephen Dunnigan, who are my real accomplishments in life. — B.S.O.

* * *

To my wife, Millie, whose ideas infuse much of what I put into this book, whose managerial abilities kept me afloat throughout the writing and whose love sustained me all the while, even when I was less than lovable. And to my son, Ian, who taught me patience and how to keep growing up and learning, and whose work ethic is, well, awesome. — R.Z.H.

✮ ✮ ✮ ✮ ✮ ✮ ✮ ✮ ✮
Acknowledgments

This book could not have been written without Brad O'Leary and myself, so here's a thanks to us from me. Greater thanks still to Millie Hallow, for intellectual input and emotional support; David A. Keene, for anecdotal evidence; Dick Williams, for counter perspective, and Roland Gunn, for straight-from-the-shoulder critiques.

Huggie-type thanks to Ann O. Weems, the president of Boru Books and a woman who edits as if she enjoys it.

Speaking of editing, thanks to the editors at *The Washington Times* — particularly Wes Pruden, Josette Shiner, Fran Coombs and Ken Hanner, Liz Elvin — without whose patience and indulgence I would surely have gone under for the third time; and to *The Washington Times* ace "morgue" staff, particularly Dean Brown, David Dickson (who moved on to write editorials for *The Times*), Clark Eberly and John Haydon.

Punch-in-the-shoulder thanks to John Aquilino, a man's man who has the *write* stuff.

A sounds-like-*pro forma*-but-is-more-than-that thanks to the men and women who serve as aides and advisers to the persons about whom this book is written. Especially those who gave me, with few exceptions — you know who you are — the utmost cooperation.

And, finally, peck-on-the-cheek thanks to Kimberley M. Welter, for her help and to Cindy Clark and Nancy McTaggart at P.M. Consulting for keeping the trains running on time. —R.Z.H.

✶✶✶

* * *

Particular thanks to Ann O. Weems, who took an impossibly rushed project and did what a good editor does — leaned, big time, on the authors to feed her the manuscripts *now*. And then turned the chaotic flow into a recognizable product.

Thanks to Cindy Clark, for being reliably everywhere she is needed all the time and never failing to get the job done.

And special thanks to Erin O'Leary, for research into the psychological background of President Bill Clinton and to Lynne Dunnigan for her insightful input on this chapter.

Finally, thanks to John Aquilino, a writer, editor and critic of considerable excellence, patience and humor — if he would only stop saying, "Big guy." — B.S.O.

✮ ✮ ✮ ✮ ✮ ✮ ✮ ✮ ✮
Contents

✸✸✸

★ ★ ★ ★ ★ ★ ★ ★ ★ ★

Backword

We originally looked forward to writing this foreword to preface the contents of this book. But we left it till last. Till after we had done the heavy lifting, so to speak. That is, written the chapters about the major political figures who are candidates or thinking about becoming candidates for the presidential nominations in 1996 and beyond. And about those who should think again.

By the time we got all that done, and what with the dedications and acknowledgments, and whatnot, it was pretty late in the game. We realized we hadn't decided whether to call it a *foreword* or a *preface*. We dithered. The printer was breathing down the publisher's neck and the publisher was breathing down our necks, as if hot breath on the neck *ever* made *anyone* work faster. It's frankly, well, *distracting*.

Still, we had hoped to say in the preface that our purpose was to create a book that makes politics fun to read about and gives you an insight into the heart and soul of the candidates. We wanted to acknowledge in the foreword that in so many political campaigns you never get to *know* who the candidate really *is*.

We wanted to preface our book by saying that polls show that much of the public feels it can't trust its leaders. One reason for this is that people don't *know* enough about their leaders *before* they vote them into office.

We had hoped to explain in the foreword that we have tried to make this book informative, insightful, *and* humorous because life and politics *are* humorous.

✶✶✶

But by the time we got around to writing the *Hi, reader, here's what we're up to stuff* and realized we hadn't settled beforehand on whether to call it a *foreword* or a *preface*, the publisher told the editor who told us it was too late, already. That we should have done the foreword, or whatever we were going to call it, *first*. And that it was definitely our fault because we wrote the stuff that comes *after* the foreword *before* we wrote the foreword, and so got it *back*ward. Which is what you're just finished reading. The *Backword*.

Now we invite you to go forward and read, laugh, cry, hoot and, above all, *enjoy*.

— The authors

✮ ✮ ✮ ✮ ✮ ✮ ✮ ✮ ✮ ✮
Introduction

We wrote *Presidential Follies* to entertain you and, in the process, to acquaint you with some of your fellow Americans who want to lead our nation. We set out to provide you with humor and new information, sprinkled with what we hope you'll find as insight, about the famous and not-so-famous Americans who would be president. As we say in the subtitle, some of these folks should think again.

Every chapter in this book should be fun to read, or we've failed in our aim. Every chapter should give you a fresh slant on your favorite politicians or maybe an understanding, for the first time, of where some of these folks come down on issues you care about

In using words to draw sketches of Republicans, Democrats and independents who may have an important impact on your life, we hope to provoke you — but we have a nice purpose in mind. We hope to provoke you into saying, "Gee, I've read about so-and-so, seen him on TV — but I never quite looked at him *that* way before." Maybe you don't say "Gee." Maybe you say "Holy moly" or "By gosh." Maybe not. Maybe these short, choppy sentences are beginning to sound like Bob Dole, drifting off into one of his stream of consciousness riffs during a press conference.

Dole has experience, leadership. That's what it's all about. Maybe not. Maybe you won't *believe* how conservative Dole has become. Course, that's what he's afraid of. That you *won't* believe. But as we show you, you're dealing with a new Bob Dole. We compare the new and the old for you. Kind of like *Consumer Reports*. We liked the new

✶✶✶

Bob Dole. He was a friend of ours. Until we wrote the chapter on him.

Same with Phil Gramm. Hey, is *he* a fun guy or what? A bit of a momma's boy. Bet you didn't know that. Bit of a daddy's boy, too. And brains? He must have got himself two helpings. Too bad about the face, though. *Not* a pretty sight. But does Gramm have just the right mix for you, of no-nonsense conservative prescriptions for welfare, immigration, taxes, and spending and a libertarian skepticism about government meddling in anything for any reason at any time? Read and judge for yourself.

We think you'll *love* the Jesse Jackson chapter. We did. We always thought we had a mutual admiration thing going with him, until he found out what we wrote about him. Well, can't blame him. In the Jackson chapter, we explain how he can deny Clinton *and* the House Republicans a victory any time he wants. That's right, the House Republicans. And the Senate Republicans, for that matter. Powerful man, Jesse is. Shame about that rhyming syndrome. Maybe if he sees the right doctor...Then there's Ross Perot. Rich Texan. Doesn't like to be messed with. Gets mad *and* gets even. Ask George Bush. We think you'll like the chapter on Ross. Very carefully done. You write about Ross, you've got to be careful. It's that simple.

And how about that Colin Powell? You'll find the chapter on him a real eye-opener. People want to know. Is he a conservative, is he a liberal, is he in the middle? It's all right there in his chapter. Read it. You'll like it.

You've been wondering who Lamar Alexander *really* is, haven't you? Come on, you've been just a teensie bit curious, right? What's he like up close and in person? You probably remember he was the governor of Tennessee. Maybe you don't know where Tennessee is. Maybe you don't care. Maybe you want to know if he can play the piano. We tell you all that *and* his positions on the issues you care about. How do we know what issues you care about? Because we do.

Ever hear of Arlen Specter? You better have. He used to be a district attorney. He'll prosecute your tail off if you say you haven't heard of him. He put that lyin' woman, Anita Hill, in her place. Remember? No? Read the Specter chapter. Afterward, tell him you read it. Maybe

✳✳

he'll give you a break when you come to his hometown, Philadelphia. Maybe not. Come to think of it, don't tell him you read the Specter chapter. He read it and said he was going to go find a lawyer. Somebody reminded him he *was* a lawyer.

We devote a special section to the two men we regard as the real agenda setters in the waning minutes of the twentieth century. Bill Clinton and Newt Gingrich. Clinton, as you'll learn from the chapter on him, is this nation's first latchkey president. We lay out for you what that means and whether it's good or bad. Some of you may not like Clinton. Sometimes we think there are times Clinton doesn't like Clinton. But can you name three things he's done as president that disqualify him from being president for a second term? Maybe you better read the Clinton chapter.

As for Gingrich, he's a trip and a half. Other Republican politicians have to hire trains and planes and buses and transport people to their events. People hear Gingrich is going to be somewhere and they mob the place. They get there on their own. Pay their own way. Why? What's with this guy they call Newtrino, as if he were some superfast subatomic particle that can smash an atom or a whole army of opposition party politicians?

And what about this black guy Alan Keyes, who turns on the Republican crowds like nobody's business? Would you vote for him? On what basis? We tell you about him and Bob Dornan, who makes friends of enemies and talks a blue streak. Did he have the right stuff? We tell you.

And if you don't read the Buchanan chapter, you'll never forgive yourself. Do you know how many policy positions Clinton and his administration and practically every Republican running or thinking of running sometime have borrowed from Buchanan without so much as a thank you? It's all there, in the Buchanan chapter.

Then there's the chapter on billionaire media mogul Malcolm S. 'Steve' Forbes, Jr., who couldn't decide whether to buy America, or incorporate it and make himself chairman of the board and president. Or spend twenty-five million bucks of his own money to get the Republican nomination. You know Steve is Scottish by descent, so he decided it was cheaper to try to buy a nomination than to buy a whole

✶✶✶

nation. Now *that's* the kind of man we want running the government. Knows the value of a dollar. Knows the value of *billions* of dollars. And knows a bargain when he sees one. He'll ask you if you ever heard the story about the two Scotsmen who took a cab in the rain. If you say no, he'll say: You never will. They walked.

Finally, don't forget about Pete Wilson. Maybe you find it tempting to forget about him. Maybe you don't. He *is* the governor of the most populous and richest state in the union. He has positions on everything. Crime, punishment, "three strikes and you're out," teenage illegitimacy, welfare for noncitizens, affirmative action, taxes, spending, buffered versus nonbuffered aspirins. Mostly they're new positions. He says they're old positions. Why so sensitive? New is good. Or can be. Find out what Pete thinks about all these things, what his background is, schooling, wife's name, Social Security number. No, strike that last item. It wasn't a very interesting Social Security number, so we didn't include it. Otherwise, it's all there, in the Pete Wilson chapter. Too bad he decided to drop out in October, so soon after he had dropped in. Who knows, he may decide to drop back in, sometime soon. Heck, he may re-Pete himself. If not this century, next century.

All in all, we think you'll find that there's more in this book than this brief introduction conveys. Probably even more than meets the eye, though we're not sure, because if it doesn't meet the eye, what does it meet and how do you know it's been met?

If you ever voted in a presidential election or know someone who did, this book is for you. We'd say it's your civic duty to read it, but civic duty was never this much fun. We hope.

PART I

★ ★ ★ ★ ★ ★ ★ ★ ★ ★ ★ ★ ★★ ★ ★★ ★ ★★ ★ ★ ★★ ★ ★ ★

Those Who Think They Should Be President ★ ★ ★ and Some Who Should Think Again

✭ ✭ ✭ ✭ ✭ ✭ ✭ ✭ ✭ ✭
LAMAR ALEXANDER
Two First Names, One Great President?

LAMAR ALEXANDER IS A LEAN-FACED, PLEASANT MAN who looks gentlemanly, almost aristocratic, in a suit and tie. Remarkably, he looks about the same in a plaid lumberjack shirt. This makes it hard to don a lumberjack shirt and look like a lumberjack. But he tried anyway in 1978, walking 1,022 miles across Tennessee in the shirt to show oneness with voters. As luck would have it, Tennesseans had a thing for gentleman-lawyers decked out as lumberjacks. They elected him governor twice.

He wore the shirt again in kicking off his GOP presidential nomination campaign in his hometown of Maryville on the last day in February 1995, his fifty-fifth birthday. By the time his flying road show touched down at the Manchester airport in New Hampshire later that day, he had switched back to suit and tie. Was the sartorial switch a subtle touch, meant to suggest he is a man of conservative principles and traditional values who is not, however, dogmatic and can at times show a certain commendable flexibility? Or were his campaign advisers simply at odds over that most vital of tactical launch decisions: how to dress the candidate on the second stop of the first day of his campaign?*

Showing motional flexibility, Alexander actually began his campaign in 1994 using his foot to put pedal to metal, for a two-month, 8,500-mile campaign drive across thirty-eight states. He said he was

---

*In seeking to explain the curious behavior of a Republican presidential nomination candidate, it is often wise to choose the simple over the subtle.

testing whether enough of his fellow Americans share his prescription for less government, reduced federal spending, wholesale Washington reforms, and a return to strong family and moral values. If he found they did, it might induce him to run for president. Surprise, he found what he wanted to find. America would like what he was about to offer. There's nothing like a two-month drive to focus your ambition.

Alexander, showing yet more flexibility, was again in lumberjack mode in the summer of 1995 as he took to walking once more, this time virtually the length of the state of New Hampshire. He wished to show the commonality of interest, viewpoint, and taste in clothing he shares with Republican voters in the Granite State. Thus would they see him for what he is: a New Hampshirite, in mind and heart. A woodsman, perhaps. Better yet, a man who gets up every morning and says to himself, "Lamar, today you are going to live free or die," as he puts on a plaid shirt.

Actually, there was another, more pressing reason to get out the old tree-felling shirt, khaki trousers, and hiking boots. New Hampshirites, like Iowans and virtually everybody else outside Tennessee, had trouble recognizing his name. A former education secretary during the Bush administration, Alexander isn't necessarily a household name outside his own state, or household, it seems. Still, it was rather annoying that he was stuck in a single-digit rut when it came to New Hampshirites recognizing his name or indicating a preference for him over Bob Dole, or even Phil Gramm, Pat Buchanan, or Pete Wilson. After all, he had been running informally for the nomination for years, just happening with remarkable frequency to find himself in the neighborhood, in key primary and caucus states.

A good question to ask about a potential presidential nominee is, oratorical skills aside, "Can he organize a three-car parade? Or would he spend all his time worrying, say, about where the three cars were made?"

Alexander may be interested in where the cars are made, but he understands the preeminence of organization and planning. Utilizing not only three-car parades, he was on to new-wave, high-tech info-highway politics almost as early as Newt Gingrich. Alexander founded a satellite network centered in Nashville and around himself. The way he ran it was designed to spread the word about the conservative revolution he was identifying with, and to get feedback from viewers (and potential supporters). It also gave him a geographically dispersed network of potential donors and organizers because — how convenient — voters who either own or have access to their own satellite dishes tend to exist on the desirable part of the socioeconomic ladder. Don't forget that satellite dishes were considerably more expensive to buy for the backyard, for the social club, or for the local political or business group, when Alexander ran his network in the late 1980s and early 1990s.

Next, early bird Alexander set out to catch all the best worms or, in his case, much of the best and most expensive talent in the way of GOP campaign advisers in media, policy, communications, fundraising, and management. And he purposely grabbed up the operatives who had the most conservative reputations. He was one of the first to declare formally for the 1996 GOP presidential nomination.

With all this going for him, it just didn't seem right that his Cadillac campaign couldn't seem to get out of first gear. So enter Alexander's brilliant young media consultant, Mike Murphy. Murphy has shoulder-length golden locks and soft blue eyes that lend his cherubic face a certain youthful zest. No one ever mistakes Mike for his client, Lamar, when the two happen to be in the same room. Murphy has the reputation of harboring very conservative thoughts, and preferring, when possible, to hire out to candidates who share his very conservative thoughts.

How to get Alexander's polling numbers up? Murphy toyed with the idea of a combination bumper sticker/radio advertisement jingle to remind inattentive voters that his client is "Lamar Alexander. Two first names. One great president." Fortunately, Murphy was just toying with the idea.

Alexander's peripatetic penchant makes inevitable the comparison of him with that noblest walker in the animal kingdom, the Tennessee walking horse. This high-stepping equine of more than ordinary height and length of spine — Tennessee walkers have an extra vertebra — moves with extraordinary grace and speed. That is how Lamar Alexander would like to high-step all the way to the Republican

National Convention in San Diego, August 1996 — leading the herd. It takes spine for him to think he can do it, what with the obstacles from his past that he has to overcome.

Appearance is not one of them. He may not be a man you'd ever feel comfortable slapping on the back, which may be a plus for a presidential aspirant. Your crazed teenage daughter wouldn't even *think* of asking Lamar Alexander whether he wears boxers or briefs. But you *would* comfortably imagine him doing the ceremonial stuff you expect from a president, and with an American-style grace and dignity. That's definitely a plus.

Lack of musical talent isn't one of them, and that's something Harry Truman fans will appreciate. Alexander plays a mean piano. This is a good thing to have on your résumé if you're applying for the job of Republican presidential nominee. Then you can try to sell folks on the idea that if you make it to the White House, you'll accompany yourself on the piano when you sing your State of the Union speech to Congress. Hell, it's worth a try. In any case, Alexander, an accomplished musician, played the trombone at a Bourbon Street jazz club to help put himself through college. He plays the piano with more passion than he brings to his speeches. Classical, gospel, and country are the types of music he most likes to play, in that order. This appeals to a wider segment of the electorate than George Bush's exclusive preoccupation with miners' daughters' music.

Okay. Alexander is home free on the musical front. So what are his problems? They're definitely not his latest positions on issues that the GOP's conservative activists — the ones who make the difference in presidential preference primaries and caucuses — are about. Alexander doesn't support legislation to grant the demands of homosexual activists for total acceptance in the military, in the Boy Scouts, in the Girl Scouts, and in the public-school classrooms. Nor does he favor "civil rights" legislation protecting homosexuals as a category. But he also thinks homosexuals are entitled to the same protections as anyone else. He'll get no grief from conservatives on this issue. Once considered a limp-wristed centrist, Alexander now calls for the dismantlement of the U.S. Department of Education he once headed. He even favors school vouchers.

✶✶✶

Are we dealing with a dreamboat of the Right Wing, or what? Months before California Governor Pete Wilson got the University of California Board of Regents to deep-six affirmative action, Alexander announced he favors rescinding, or rewording, federal affirmative action laws. He said he wants them to assure only equality of opportunity, not of outcome — in other words, an end to de facto quotas.

Hold on to your seats, ye faithful of the Hard Right, there's more. Alexander opposes open homosexuality in the military. He's dead set against "special protection" under civil rights laws for homosexuals. He opposes putting U.S. forces under United Nations commanders. He favors reducing federal taxes and spending, devolving power from the federal government back to the states and localities and, most of all, to ordinary citizens and their voluntary associations and organizations. And for you champions of the Second Amendment, Lamar opposes gun control.

He favors term limits and warned the new Republican majority in Congress that it too can succumb to Potomac Fever. His motto, developed before 1994's congressional elections that brought Republicans to the majority in both Houses, was: "Cut their pay and send them home." He once said Congress should do its work between January 4 and the beginning of the baseball season and not return until Labor Day, for a brief stint until Thanksgiving. He also advocates cutting members' pay in half, and would let them hold jobs outside of government.

Lamar Alexander is, in short, the very model of a modern major general in Newt Gingrich's Revolutionary Army of the Potomac. One problem is that the two initially top-rated competitors for the nomination, Bob Dole and Phil Gramm, also have staked out these same positions. And don't forget, Pat Buchanan, *Crossfire*'s Irish pugilist and prodigious pundit, also had an early franchise on those and other positions.

So where are the "obstacles" alluded to earlier? And why is it that, initially at least, so many of Washington's political cognoscenti were willing to afford Alexander the status of being, at best, the only other "serious" candidate in a race insiders were predicting would be between Bob Dole and Phil Gramm? For one thing, Alexander is not, on the best of days, a riveting speaker or a commanding presence. Gramm is humorous if not quite commanding. Dole is both funny and commanding. By February of 1995, they all got to show themselves off before the same audience of wingers at the Twenty-second Annual Conservative Political Action Conference in Washington, and what they showed back then didn't change much as the campaign progressed. Gramm wowed the more than 1,000 conservative activists. Dole gave an unfocused speech that nonetheless got a good reception. Alexander, right on all their issues, got a warm but reserved response from the conference participants. And it was one of his better performances.

Oratorical skill alone, of course, does not make a successful candidate. George Bush, for all his educational advantages, seemed to have only a passing acquaintance with spoken English, let alone the finer points of public speaking. Alexander's problem is different. It lurks just below the surface, waiting for his rivals and their henchmen to force it into view. Alexander's dirty little secret: he wasn't a right-winger before being a right-winger was cool. American Conservative Union Chairman David A. Keene, an exponent of traditional conservatism, expresses his skepticism about Alexander with characteristic circumspection and delicacy: "Lamar is not a conservative." Don't mince those words, David.

For one thing, Alexander hasn't been consistent on abortion, although abortion is not a litmus test for conservatism. Many economic conservatives are neutral on the subject, or even pro-choice. Even some who want a president who uses the bully pulpit to emphasize traditional values nonetheless are quite content to leave abortion regulation to state governments. But honesty and consistency of position are dear to the hearts of most conservatives.

Alexander adopts a view similar to that which other pro-choice Republicans adopted in order to make themselves acceptable to the 8 percent of the Republican coalition who take their abortion opposition seriously. These folks are so morally repulsed by what they regard as the taking of an unborn life that they won't vote for a pro-choice candidate, regardless of how he stands on other issues. Alexander is personally against abortion, finds it morally indefensible, but thinks

****

it's a matter for the states, not the federal government, to decide. Alexander may have some kinship on the matter with George Bush. Once a pro-choicer, Bush came to terms with the issue and had his lieutenants retain the uncompromising 1994 GOP platform's anti-abortion language in 1988 and 1992 platforms.

Alexander's states-rights position on abortion will not make him the number-one choice for Pat Robertson's Christian Coalition, or any of the other powerful groups on the Religious Right that want a candidate who has endorsed, or will endorse, a constitutional ban on abortion. Alexander's position is shared, however, by many conservative Christians who oppose abortion, but also believe letting states regulate it is probably the best deal they can settle for in a nation whose voters are severely conflicted over the issue, with the vast majority wanting it regulated but not made totally illegal.

In any case, Alexander's wife, Honey, was active in Planned Parenthood. Embracing Planned Parenthood is about as healthy as sticking your finger in a light socket if you have Republican presidential ambitions. Why? Planned Parenthood thinks a neighborhood without an abortion clinic is like a day without sunshine. Planned Parenthood lobbies for government-funded abortions, and a bit more in the way of "hands on" sex education in the schools, even more than most parents, with the possible exception of what Joycelyn Elders, had in mind.

As governor, Alexander opposed the home schooling bill that his state's legislature passed. Not smart for a man who wants to escape the gravitational pull of Tennessee and go into national orbit on a Republican platform. His home-schooling position angered not only millions of Christian activists, but also traditional conservatives who think freedom from excessive government meddling is more than an empty phrase.

Only a political southpaw (or the kind of Republican who has erotic dreams about hopping into the same shower as members of Americans for Democratic Action) can forget or forgive Alexander for something else. The man from Maryville began his career as a protégé of a *liberal Republican*, Howard Baker, the then-senator from Tennessee. Let's be blunt: Alexander and Baker were buddies. And you know what they say about birds of a feather flocking together. Want more evidence of suspicious behavior? Alexander also served in the *Nixon* administration. Some on the Right have not forgiven Nixon, even in death, for imposing wage and price controls on the economy, or for "selling out" the Republic of China on Taiwan in order to open up relations with the Communist government on the mainland.

Alexander's tenure at the Department of Education was unspectacular from the point of view of conservatives who wanted to see the whole education bureaucracy dismantled. President Bush, who in his 1988 campaign said he wanted to be the "education president" and the "environmental president" as well as the "kinder, gentler" president, named Alexander to be his education secretary to replace the do-nothing Lauro Cavazos. Alexander served as education secretary from 1991 to 1993. Conservatives, who don't think Alexander did much more than Cavazos, find it interesting that Alexander, in his presidential aspirant mode, came to applaud a move that a mid-level black Education Department official, Michael Williams, had made to deny federal funds to colleges and universities that award scholarships based on race. The Bush administration — surprise! — ultimately buckled under pressure from the "civil rights" lobby and the education establishment on the race-based scholarships issue.

Time to bring in the "Mack the Knife" of the conservative movement for the kill. "Lamar was a moderate governor," says Keene. "He was pro-choice [on abortion]. He came out of the moderate wing of the Tennessee party. He was a moderate in the Bush administration, and now is running as more of a populist than a conservative. The bottom line is that he is a very nice and very bright guy, but if you are a conservative, you look at him and you say, 'What's the point?'"

Other Republicans, of course, once took centrist or liberal positions on "litmus test" issues, only to come around to the conservative line — and to be accepted into the fold. Bush is an imperfect example, since he was never fully trusted by conservatives. But Pete du Pont, a liberal-to-centrist in Delaware's legislature and in Congress, then became governor and made the transition to the Right, actually matching words with deeds.

The difference is that Du Pont had a conversion on the road to Damascus. He can tell you why he, as the centrist congressman from

✳✳✳

Delaware, later became the conservative firebrand. The reason, Pete will tell you, is that he experienced what it was all about while governor of Delaware. In fact, Du Pont initiated and carried out what became known as the Reagan supply-side agenda before President Reagan, or anybody else, did. Alexander makes no such claims for his governorship. The contrast leads some profound skeptics on the Republican Right to such crude and cruel jokes as referring to Alexander as "Governor Lamar Baker."

The hard fact of life is that Lamar Alexander didn't start sounding like an exponent of what the liberal press refers to as the "radical Right" until he began contemplating a nomination bid. That doesn't prove the conversion hasn't been genuine. Absent from the Alexander speeches, interviews, and personal conversations, however, is that sneering disdain for Howard Baker-Nelson Rockefeller Republicanism that sounds so mellifluous to conservatives when it comes snarling from the lips of a Phil Gramm or Pat Buchanan. Understandably, Alexander doesn't like the moderate or centrist tag. "I don't know where people get that idea about me." he says. "I've always been a conservative." Well, at least he should be cut some slack for the bad luck of coincidental timing that had him being sworn into office as the governor of Tennessee on the same day in January 1979 as Bill Clinton took the oath as governor of Arkansas.

The Tennessee walker's track record actually isn't all that bad. He, in fact, impressed some conservatives inside Washington's Beltway with his 1984 education reforms. And Alexander takes family values seriously when it comes to his own family. He took half a year off with his wife and children to visit Australia before retiring to become president of the University of Tennessee from 1988 to 1991.

The establishment certainly held him in high regard throughout his career, though this is a mixed blessing. A national magazine once named him the second most effective governor — after the then-governor of Massachusetts, Michael Dukakis. That's a definite *ugh!* Nevertheless, even conservative doubters acknowledge he stood up to the teachers' unions and education establishment. He launched a nationwide crusade for merit pay for teachers and risked political assassination by the teachers' unions when he persuaded his state's

✶✶✶

Democratic legislature to tie incentive pay to teachers' performance.

Something else about the Tennessee walker. He is an honest man for a politician. He admits that as the president of the University of Tennessee he felt compelled to make appointments to key positions in the university based on race and sex, not merit. It was, he says, the climate and pressure of the times. The political climate and times have definitely changed. The Tennessee walker may not have led the changes, but at least he has kept up with them. Can two first names make one great nominee, let alone one great president?

Stay tuned.

✬ ✬ ✬ ✬ ✬ ✬ ✬ ✬ ✬

PAT BUCHANAN

Right from the Start?

PAT BUCHANAN HAS BEEN SAYING from the start that he is right and has a record to prove it. God bless his Irish heart, he does have a record. Some say that's his problem. They say he carries more baggage than the hold of a jumbo jet full of tourists. He's been accused of nativism, racism, anti-Semitism, isolationism, xenophobia and protectionism. And that's only what some fellow Republicans have said about him.

His response, uttered on March 20, 1995, the day he announced for the 1996 Republican presidential nomination: "Well, they haven't invented a name that I haven't been called." Not quite, Pat. Try "president." Or "nominee." Better still, "agenda-setter."

By the summer of 1995, it was clear that Buchanan had indeed set the agenda for the whole field of Republican contenders. He had moved his party and the national dialogue to what he thought was important. And, in many cases, his Republican rivals had come to take positions that Buchanan had first staked out years before. In fact, by the summer of 1995, *"nominee"* is what some influential folks in the Republican coalition thought they might *want* to call him. He already had achieved what the political professionals had said would be impossible. Patrick J. Buchanan had tied such heavyweights as Senator Phil Gramm of Texas and California Governor Pete Wilson for second place behind Senate Majority Leader Bob Dole of Kansas in national polls. These were guys operating with twenty times more money than he had raised, with professionally staffed campaign organizations that reflected their affluence.

✶✶

"I can envision Pat Buchanan emerging as the conservative alternative to Bob Dole by the time of the New Hampshire primary," confided Gary Bauer, president of the powerful Family Research Council and the former chief domestic policy adviser in Ronald Reagan's White House.

Bauer and a number of similarly influential leaders of the religious conservative movement, antiabortion organizations, and moral-values groups were discussing the possibility of formally endorsing Buchanan for the nomination.

How could all this be? For one thing, Buchanan has, as they say, "real personality." Call it a tough guy/nice guy charm. He'll disagree with you, but you never mistake it for a personal attack. He'll tell you why your ideas are full of it, then smile as if to take the edge off. His brown eyes, set in an Irish street-fighter's face, laugh with you, never at you. His whole face crinkles up when he chortles, making you think for a split second that you now know what a six-foot-plus leprechaun in a dark suit and plain-toed laced-up dress shoes (he never wears loafers) would look like, if there were such a being.

Buchanan habitually speaks in the first person singular *and* plural in the same sentence. Again, charming. Even quaint and amusing. And a bit annoying at times. Example: "I think we are more revolutionary than Newt." Translation: Pat Buchanan thinks that Pat Buchanan is more of a revolutionary than House Speaker Newt Gingrich.

How so, Pat? "Take term limits. The only one worth supporting is three terms in the House and two in the Senate. *We* want congressional legislation that says the states of the union have the right to set limits on the terms their representatives serve in both houses of Congress," Buchanan says [emphasis added].

"*My* rivals are all too often arguing which one is the real economic conservative. *My* agenda is much broader and deeper. *We* embrace cultural issues, moral issues, a new foreign policy, protection of American sovereignty, economic patriotism, and no more unfair trade deals for the American worker.

"In this race, *we*'re challenging Dole and Gramm, and *I* am not going to come off as a sweetheart. But I don't think any of them is meaner. It's all perception."

****

Like others whose talents lie in thinking up ideas and communicating them, Buchanan suffers a sometimes profound separation between what he says and what he does. Take the Mercedes-Benz he owned during his 1992 nomination challenge of Bush. He claimed he bought the German luxury import for his wife, Shelley, which in his mind somehow made it okay.

Some workers in Detroit and elsewhere didn't think it was okay. One local union even barred him from a scheduled visit to an auto plant, even though he was campaigning in 1992 against imports and the exportation of American jobs abroad, while actively seeking the support of auto workers and other union members.

You can just hear the *I* and *we* having it out in the Buchanan left frontal lobe. "So *we* spread the buy-American, protectionist, anti-import word? What's that got to do with *me* owning a totally foreign-made car? After all, *I'm* the consumer, aren't *we*?

More than a year after the 1992 presidential election, he pulled up to a reunion with his campaign staff at a hotel in Virginia, across the Potomac from the White House. And, yes, he was driving that Mercedes. Asked about it when he began his latest presidential nomination campaign in February 1995, he said, "The Mercedes? I sold it." Hey, better late than never, as they say.

Still and all, Buchanan may be the least thin-skinned candidate seeking his party's nomination. He has been called everything in the book, and as often as not, by persons he, his wife, Shelley, and his sister Angela "Bay" Buchanan had regarded as close family friends. Take, for example, William Bennett, the former Reagan education secretary and Bush drug policy administrator. Bill Bennett twice publicly accused Buchanan of flirting with anti-Semitism and Naziism — first during Buchanan's audacious Right-Wing challenge of George Bush for the 1992 GOP presidential nomination, and again in the summer of 1995. No accusation, not even racism, is more damaging in American political life today. Both times, however, Buchanan turned the other cheek, refusing to call Bill Bennett names in return.

But Buchanan as a serious possibility for nomination to the highest elected office in the land? A pundit, scribe, and TV personality who has never known the heat of legislative battle? Who never has had to

****

compromise to get something done? Never had to stand lonely at the helm of executive leadership of a city, let alone a state or a nation? Buchanan's answer is as ready as his Irish smile: "I don't think you will find that too many career politicians have the revolutionary ardor it will take to restore our country."

For years, Buchanan has been sorting out who he is and what niche he could stake out in the increasingly crowded field of claimants to conservative-movement leadership. The sorting out began in the 1960s and 1970s, when he served first in Richard M. Nixon's White House as speechwriter and confidant, and then in Gerald Ford's White House, again as speechwriter and adviser.

Richard Nixon, frustrated by an economy that was afflicted with both stagnation and inflation, imposed wage and price controls. These were the first peacetime, economy-wide socialist measures in the history of the Republic. It took more than a decade for the economy to begin to recover from that Stalinist-style blunder. It also taught Buchanan a lesson.

Nixon was not your "One Bad Idea" president. Pat Buchanan's first White House boss also decided to turn his back on a loyal ally, the Republic of China on the island of Taiwan, and to recognize one of the most brutally repressive and backward governments in modern history, Red China. From that day forth, all Americans have been required to refer to that country officially as the People's Republic of China. Buchanan vowed to himself that it would be a cold day in hell before *he* would sell out an ally to please a powerful enemy.

Buchanan next served President Gerald R. Ford and Vice President Nelson A. Rockefeller. They never managed to equal the enormity of Nixon's wage-price controls or of kow-towing to Red China, but they did come up with something called the Nixon-Ford Hundred Billion Dollar Energy Independence Agency. This little sucker would have had bureaucrats in Washington pick and spend billions of dollars on the "winning" technologies to free America from "dependence" on fossil fuels (oil and natural gas) produced by, ugh, foreigners. Buchanan learned another lesson and came out of the Ford White House with the credentials to launch a syndicated column, which was noteworthy because it was not liberal like most columns of the day.

But he then suspended his column to join the Reagan White House, this time in the exalted post of communications director (chief speech-writer).

There he served a president who would prove closest to Buchanan's emerging brand of conservatism in most, but clearly not all, ways. Reagan believed in free trade with a religious fervor. Buchanan thought certain trade rivals of America were using our free-trade principles to take advantage of us. Reagan practically moved the capital of the United States to Tel Aviv when it came to siding with the economic socialist government in Israel. Buchanan saw more risk and less utility in that intervention in the Middle East than most Reaganauts did. But then Reagan espoused the active export of democracy around the world, and intervention — military if necessary — on behalf of Western ideals and values. Buchanan was of the school that looked at history and concluded that no good deed by the United States ever goes unpunished.

So, in spite of — and in a real sense, because of — his Nixon-Ford-Reagan service, Buchanan emerged as his own man, as author and exponent of a new foreign policy for a new time: the post Cold War era. It was simple, straightforward, and logical. It said that with the threat of global Communist hegemony gone, America henceforth should mess around in other countries' conflict and problems, militarily or otherwise, only when her vital interests are seriously and imminently threatened. He said the forced export of democracy and American values abroad was "globe-baloney," meaning an excuse to move toward world government and a surrender of American sovereignty, and an invitation to break our back and our bank, minding everyone else's business but our own.

Buchanan suggested that some who advocated this role for America as policeman and social worker to the world, actually wanted a rationale for American boys spilling their blood to defend Israel, if the need ever arose. Others in his party and in the foreign policy establishment hissed, booed, and laughed. They called him a heretic. An isolationist. Instead of flinching, he turned around and said their New World Order was just more "globe-baloney."

He really started getting into trouble with the establishment when he pugnaciously defended Carmelite nuns who had a convent at the former Auschwitz concentration camp. Some Jews said Auschwitz was their memorial and the Catholic Church had not been without blemish during Hitler's era of ethno-religious cleansing.

To get himself further into trouble, Buchanan seemed to go out of his way to appeal to a so-called populist strain in American politics, to working-class white Christians with ethnic surnames and to black Americans. He claimed they would be fighting and dying in Desert Storm because they tend to do the fighting when the United States gets involved in a military action, while young Americans with Jewish surnames tend not to be in harm's way. The implication: Jews are too rich, too smart, or insufficiently patriotic to don uniforms of the armed services of the United States and do battle for the Stars and Stripes.

Buchanan was not shocked that many Jewish-Americans took umbrage. But he was a bit stunned that so many serious commentators started debating whether he was anti-Semitic. Some Jewish pundits, such as Robert Novak, asserted Buchanan was not even remotely anti-Semitic, but the issue was out there, and Buchanan had put it there. He was genuinely shocked when William Bennett made his 1992 and 1995 comments about Buchanan's flirting with Naziism.

For four years, he fought virtually alone for an America-first foreign policy, and when George Bush sought reelection, Buchanan quit his lucrative TV slots on the *McLaughlin Group, Crossfire* (his radio show), his syndicated column, and his newsletter, then challenged a sitting president of his own party for the nomination. He gave George Bush the scare of his life in New Hampshire and almost woke the man up to his ideological and policy shortcomings.

By the second year of the Clinton administration, virtually every Republican officeholder was spouting the Buchanan line — and never giving him credit — that America should not be policeman to the world and should intervene only to defend her vital national interests. Buchanan had warned against intervention in Somalia, and that intervention turned out to be a disaster under two presidents. He warned against intervening, under the blue flag of the United Nations, in the Bosnian civil war, which turned into a disaster. Even the Democratic president, Bill Clinton, sounded at times like Pat Buchanan of previous years explaining why America can't get involved everywhere.

Buchanan had been railing against too many immigrants coming from cultures that were hostile to the Western European foundations of the United States. Foundations like equality of opportunity, the concept of majority rule, minority rights, to church-state separation, private property, scientific epistemology, to individual responsibility, the work ethic, and limited government.

Buchanan said the striving of newcomers to assimilate into the American culture and to learn the American language, history, and traditions that characterized previous waves of immigration was often absent now. Demagogic ethnic leaders with socialist mind-sets were forming newcomers into special-interest blocs that claimed welfare and social security benefits, special civil rights, victimhood, ballots, and classrooms in their native languages. These same ethnic leaders claimed newcomers have the right to belittle Western values and American history. Buchanan's point: While these newcomers have free speech, America has free will, and doesn't have to open its borders to persons intent on destroying America's culture and history, while draining its treasury dry.

Buchanan saw Christianity under attack. American culture under siege. Hoodlums had taken over the streets of American cities. America was in the midst of cultural wars. In his mind, purveyors of popular culture had become purveyors of filth and violence, of sexual immorality and moral relativism in virtually all other matters. Buchanan wanted back the America of his youth, and offered to lead like-minded Americans in that cause.

Democrats and particularly liberals hooted at Buchanan, called him a mean-spirited Neanderthal. Xenophobe. Nativist. Isolationist. Republicans were either embarrassed, or nearly as hostile.

By 1995, leading Democrats, including Clinton, were borrowing elements — in disguised form for their own use — from Buchanan's 1992 Houston Republican National Convention speech that the liberal press had reviled. And virtually every Republican candidate had adopted virtually every one of Buchanan's major policy stands, from opposing racial and sexual quotas, to reducing legal immigration,

****

walling off America's southern border against illegal immigrants, ending affirmative action, wider use and quicker implementation of the death penalty, disallowing U.S. troops from being put under foreign UN commanders, denying welfare and other benefits to noncitizens, to name a few.

None saw fit to acknowledge Buchanan as a prophet, as having had the courage and insight to identify problems and publicly offer solutions that would take time to find public, or media, or establishment acceptance. Buchanan simply had crossed the line of acceptability too many times.

How, then, did Buchanan manage to come so far as a candidate, on so little money and with so much ideological baggage? All the while he was out of government and then challenging George Bush, Buchanan had been building up to the kind of coalition that he finally laid out on the table for his 1996 nomination campaign.

At the outset, he said he intended to construct a campaign that "uses all the coalitions which have the fire and energy in the 1990s." His would be, furthermore, "an issues campaign different from the others — we have a lock on the moral and cultural issues."

The coalition Buchanan was constructing includes abortion foes, which is, of course, the same group every serious Republican nomination dreamer also targets, with the exception of Governor Pete Wilson of California. (Wilson had staked out enough conservative positions, and could raise enough money and field enough cadres, to be taken seriously, in spite of his pro-choice views.)

What's a coalition without regular churchgoers who find it in their hearts to praise you as well as the Lord? And who ring doorbells, pass out leaflets, and hold meet-the-candidate nights in their living rooms? Buchanan has his welcoming arms out to them all: traditional Catholics, Protestants, and Jews. *Jews?* Yes, Buchanan has some Orthodox Jewish rabbis who come to speak at his American Cause Foundation seminars, and think Buchanan is the cat's pajamas. Besides, Buchanan's pollster in his 1992 primary challenge of George Bush was Frank Luntz, a Jewish American who had just done polling for the Israeli government before seeking and landing a job with the Buchanan campaign.

In particular, Buchanan wants as many state organizers and local members of Pat Robertson's Christian Coalition as he can attract. The Christian Coalition is not only one of the most politically organized and aware religious groups on the Right, it also has high media visibility.

If Buchanan's reach for the moral-values groups does not turn out to exceed his grasp, he could achieve some startling things. Professional vote counters estimate that half of the national Republican vote is driven by values.

Two out of three Republican primary and caucus voters turn out because of their conservative positions on moral-values issues. There may be considerable overlap, with the same voters also concerned about economic issues. Two-thirds of that two-thirds, in turn, are highly motivated religiously.

A second constituency Buchanan wants for his coalition is composed of gun patriots and Second Amendment worshipers. The hunters and target shooters, who don't want anybody messing with their right to own and use guns, are not a guaranteed constituency of Buchanan's, since hunters and plunkers aren't necessarily America-firsters, or cultural warriors or flat taxers. But most of the gun lovers fit into one or more of these categories. The problem for Buchanan is that they also know who Phil Gramm is, and that nobody else in Congress can claim to have taken a more forceful and visible role in defending the Second Amendment than Gramm, himself an avid duck hunter and believer in guns for self-protection. His eighty-plus mother has a gun just for that purpose.

Gramm has an advantage over Buchanan on this score because, although Buchanan has written newspaper columns in defense of gun ownership, Gramm actually wrote laws guaranteed to ruin the day of violent criminals and the welfare-mothers' lobby.

Indeed, the pro-gun coalition is also made up of a growing number of persons who own guns solely to protect themselves in an America where the local police do not, and perhaps cannot, handle the job any longer. This crowd's front-gate sign of choice advises any who approach (and can read) to "forget the dog, beware of the owner." For such self-defenders, there is a certain resonance in Buchanan's ringing demand that "we take our streets back." Buchanan doesn't always say from whom, but everybody knows he means the murderers, rapists, druggies, and testosterone-crazed illegitimate sons of teenage welfare mothers who live in a values-free amorality that the bleeding hearts and drooling practitioners of infantile liberalism have created.

Another potentially huge segment of the total population that Buchanan set out to attract to his coalition is made up of the hundreds of millions of Americans who have strong feelings about the Internal Revenue Service, a quaint, eighteenth-century term for a hated and hateful bureaucracy. Untold Americans secretly fantasize about having IRS leaders and employees rounded up and placed on a remote island with the only communication available being radios permanently tuned to G. Gordon Liddy, Patrick J. Buchanan, and Rush Limbaugh.

Buchanan understood the smoldering hostility of Americans toward the IRS as the symbol of the government being right all the time, and the citizen being wrong all the time. The history of the American judicial system is that the individual is presumed not guilty, until proven guilty. Poll after poll shows that Americans today don't trust their government because they believe it has come to represent the policy that the IRS is spreading. It is the policy of all dictatorships: the citizen is guilty until he proves himself otherwise. And good luck on that score.

Buchanan was the first major GOP nomination candidate to propose abolition of the IRS by substituting a national sales tax to replace the federal income tax. But by midsummer 1995, Buchanan had dropped the national sales tax idea in favor of a tax he had always had a hankering for, the flat or single tax rate that would exclude the first $25,000 of income for a family of four. Neat. And get this: All mortgage interest and charitable contributions would be excluded.

The Buchanan tax reform had some elements no GOP rival would dare offer. Make him president, and he'll eliminate income taxes for every small business in America, he said. Depending on how you define "small business," that could mean anywhere from 12 million to 21 million tax returns that would no longer have to be filed. That's a lot of deliriously happy, potentially ex-taxpayers, who just might want to vote in Republican primaries for their man Pat.

****

To offset the lost revenue from no longer taxing small business income, Buchanan promised a 10 percent across-the-board tariff on Japanese imports. It doesn't take a Tokyo University rocket scientist to figure out that appeals to former Perot voters, trade unionists, businessmen and leaders of corporations hurt by Japanese imports — not to mention your run-of-the-mill xenophobe and Jap-basher. (Those carried away with the potential for humor here might imagine, though incorrectly, Buchanan's saying, So what if Pearl Harbor was a long time ago? I remember the *Maine*, and it *still* has me fuming.)

He also appeals to small business people and family farmers by proposing to abolish the inheritance tax on family farms and small businesses. The cost to the Treasury in lost tax revenue would be offset with a 20 percent tariff on all Chinese imports. None of this sits well with free-trade fans, who happen to make up the bulk of the Republican membership in both Houses of Congress.

Buchanan also targets for his coalition folks who want to make English the official language of the United States. The chief organization, English Only, has a half-million donors, who range from small business persons to conservative activists, legal immigrants and labor union members — substantially more in total number than most national conservative or liberal organizations claim. English Only supporters are generally the same persons who are freaking out over the unprecedented flood of immigrants, legal and illegal. Their big concern is that the latest wave includes far more persons than ever before who come from cultures that wouldn't know the Magna Carta from Adam. Who, once in the United States, are actually encouraged to use ballots printed in their native tongues, and to learn algebra in an American public-school classroom, in which both the teacher and the students never use that imperialist invention of Western oppression: English.

Speaking of coalitions, to be considered a serious candidate capable of winning the nomination and defeating Clinton in 1996, Buchanan has to somehow unite behind him two of the groups he is targeting: (1) the Perot voters who tend to be pro-choice Republicans, and (2) traditional pro-life Republicans who tend to be free traders.

Asked how he could pull this off, Buchanan said, "The folks who

****

care most about life understand my argument on NAFTA and GATT, and the people who care most about sovereignty know I have been with them all the way. And they don't hold it against me that I am pro-life and I tell them I am going to be faithful to all our constituencies." All his constituencies? Neat trick. Reagan, more or less, pulled it off. Buchanan has never had an elected term at anything.

Although Buchanan may never cement the coalition he envisions, he already succeeded in showing strength where no one, not even he, expected it. He trounced Dole, Gramm, and the rest of the GOP presidential nomination field in a Virginia Republican party convention straw poll, the summer of 1995. "It shows Pat Buchanan has considerable organizational strength," said Virginia GOP chairman Pat McSweeney. "These are pretty substantial numbers for a straw poll. I thought it would be closer."

By the summer of 1995, Buchanan's outpolling Senator Gramm, and Senator Dole by 59–7 and 59–8 respectively, was particularly interesting to veteran campaign professionals because Buchanan, in his 1992 challenge of George Bush, showed far more talent and interest in ideas, rather than organization. "It showed formidable organizing skills on Buchanan's part," said Republican campaign consultant Eddie Mahe, who is not working for any of the GOP nomination candidates. "You don't make this strong of a showing without intense and effective organizational activities. You have to give that to Buchanan, and I am not a fan of his because of his position on trade."

Well, yes, you have to give Buchanan credit for having the appearance of organization, and for getting the job done as if he had a full-scale, top-of-the-line presidential campaign organization in place. He doesn't. It is an organization of mostly volunteers. It operates on a shoestring budget and does everything as cheap as possible, but with surprising skill and dedication.

What the Buchanan organization seems to have that is most important is a message and a believable messenger. In launching his 1995 campaign, he didn't exactly mince words, pledging to "chase the purveyors of sex and violence back beneath the rocks from whence they came."

"I will use the bully pulpit of the presidency, to the full extent of my

****

powers and ability, to defend American traditions and the values of faith, family and country from any and all directions."

"When I am elected president, there will be no more NAFTA sell-out of American workers, no more GATT deals done for the benefit of Wall Street bankers, and no more $50 billion bailouts of Third World socialists — whether in Moscow or Mexico City."

What unsettles some folks in his party, and in a variety of interest groups, is that neither they, nor the press, listened to him and said, "Not to worry, this guy'll say anything to get the nomination." Rather, what consoled his critics is that the smart money was betting from the beginning that he has, in their view, only two chances of actually becoming the nominee: fat and slim.

Maybe. But although he wants to be the nominee and will fight to the end, as he did in 1992, he had already won a major goal a few months into his campaign. From affirmative action and fighting the cultural wars, to immigration reform, welfare, and an America-first foreign policy, he has already set the agenda for 1996 and beyond.

When Pat Buchanan ran against George Bush in 1992, and stayed in through the Republican National Convention in Houston, most pundits felt he had been fighting a losing cause. The truth is that he won in 1992 in the same sense that Barry Goldwater won in 1964. History will judge that it was Buchanan's values, his programs, and his dreams for the future of America that have set the agenda for the 1996 election. Not only has the Buchanan agenda been adopted by every serious Republican candidate, but much of his vision has been adopted by Bill Clinton and his sometimes political guru, sometimes — Republican Dick Morris.

No matter who gets the Republican nomination in 1996, he'll be running on Pat Buchanan's 1992 program.

★ ★ ★ ★ ★ ★ ★ ★ ★
MARIO M. CUOMO
The Future Lies Ahead

MARIO M. CUOMO IS AN ADMIRABLE DEMOCRAT and an admirable human being, in many ways. But, then again, in many ways, he's not. Even those who don't like him find something to like about him.

Cuomo graduated from St. John's University law school at the top of his class. No Wall Street law firm would grant him a job interview. Too many vowels ending his first and last names. One reason he carries a chip on his shoulder, he refuses to acknowledge he can be bettered and thinks he's the smartest and classiest guy in the room.

He quit presidential politics the way he quit minor league baseball: before anyone could find out if he could play or before he got hurt again. He once got beaned playing for a Pittsburgh Pirates' Georgia farm team and decided there was a message in that. What message? Go home. He did. Mario listens a lot for messages from somewhere.

One message he got while teaching law at St. John's University School of Law was: "*Psst*, go into government. It's better than plastics." It was. He enjoyed government so much he let New York State taxpayers employ him from the time he first got into government work as secretary of state in 1975 until the voters finally told him to take a hike in 1994.

At the tender age of sixty-three, he got himself a job on talk radio instead. He was offered television, but had an excuse for turning it down. The excuse didn't ring right, any more than this excuse he gave as New York governor, for not running for president in 1988 or 1992. He picked a relaxed radio slot because, he said, he wanted a forum that would allow him to be intelligent, to follow up a brilliant premise with an appropriate elaboration, and not be forced into a rush-rush, keep-them-entertained medium. Now that's a nice thought. A likable thought from a likable man. All it takes is a willing suspension of disbelief. And for you Mario, *any*thing.

Cuomo's political history is not without its down side. During his twelve year gubernatorial reign, New York taxed its citizens more than almost any other state and spent more per capita. You'd have thought spending all that money and collecting all those taxes would be *fun*. But, no. Mario being Mario spent much of his time brooding and thinking *heavy* thoughts. The more he brooded, the more the popular press wanted him to please be the Nation's chief brooder and live at 1600 Pennsylvania Avenue where he could watch over all of America. Oh boy.

Prior to the 1988 elections, Cuomo raised New York's educational spending by 60 percent. Nothing changed. Student illiteracy and performance records remained about the same as before. As the nation headed into 1992, the once proud New York university system was in decline. The state's bridges were substandard. Crime was out of control. Mario brooded and passed the blame, alluding to those damned Republicans in the White House. First Reagan, then Bush. Give an Italian-American Catholic boy born and raised in Queens and still living there a *break* for God's sake.

Every presidential election cycle, Mario Cuomo's name pops up. Why not, after that dazzling keynote speech at the 1984 Democratic National Convention, with the patriotic bunting, remember? Mario suddenly was and is the fantasy candidate of liberal Democrats nearly everywhere. So why didn't *he* go for it? Until his timely political demise at the hands of George Pataki, Mario, or his son and chief surrogate, Andrew, had the same response: not now. But, sounded the Democratic chorus, if not now, when. If not you, who? Bill Clinton, as it turned out.

All those years, meanwhile, in Cuomo's favorite metaphor, Mario was waiting for *his* pitch. He waited in 1988. He waited in 1992. He waited out 1996 too. But, hey, 2000 is just around the corner. Gives a man time to *think*.

Some politicians liked to quote Churchill, others Roosevelt, still other Tocqueville. Cuomo's favorite personage when it came to quotes was Cuomo. He quoted himself right up to the end, saying years before that liberals are digging their own political graves, moralizing about things people don't want to hear, and being intolerant of those who don't agree with the liberal moralizing. Whom was he talking about? Who were these intolerant, arrogant liberals? It was, and he meant it to be in his own curious way, all those Cuomos who called up reporters before dawn to chew their behinds off for having written or said something critical of the Cuomo of 1983 or '87 or '89 or '91.

Cuomo is, or was when he was in government, the Jesse Jackson of his race of Democrats. Cuomo talked the talk but was elsewhere when follow through was required. The legislators and lobbyists who knew him best confided to others that he was all words and no action. He was interesting — the press called him eloquent — when he introduced something new to the legislature in Albany. But he seemed unwilling or unable to roll up his sleeves and do the work it takes to get a legislative initiative enacted.

You know what that's all about, that grimy stuff that plebeian lawmakers have to do. Like actually talking with each other, seeing who wants what and what can be traded and whose toes might be stepped on if these words as opposed to those words are used in this section of a bill or in this afternoon's press conference. This would be dealing with individual persons in the flesh. Cuomo was enthralled with the bleeding masses whom he could discuss in the vacuum of a news briefing, just he and the inanimate microphones, with the press on the other side of his personal space.

He preferred to say little to his closet associates in person but instead to get business done in long conversations on the telephone. Nice sanitary separation from the warm bodies of real people, thanks to Mr. Bell's invention. A real godsend to Cuomo.

Cuomo's little secret, the reason he never ran for president, and was upset in his last reelection bid for governor by that unheard-of Republican named George Pataki, was not just that he was a liberal's liberal at a time when even the most distracted voters were fed up with liberalism. Cuomo's secret was he was an indifferent politician.

✯✯

He not only didn't have a clue as to where in the world the electorate was heading over the past two decades, despite speeches that
asserted he knew where, while the Democratic Party leadership did
not. Yeah, but still, he didn't like doing what politicians who want to
rise above the rank and file and leave a mark or go for the top have to
do. If Cuomo didn't like it, he didn't do it. You got a problem with
that?

He didn't do it even for the things he really liked. He might go the
whole eight yards, but not the ninth. He proposed having the state
take over Medicaid. It never happened. He proposed public financing
of campaigns. It never happened. Except for more prisons. His tenure
saw more prisons built than ever before. They were needed. He
opposed capital punishment. He even opposed incarceration. It didn't
change criminals or stop crime. To say he didn't get it is to say the
obvious.

What he did propose or support and see through to the end was
destructive to the state and to those of its citizens vulnerable to being
made dependent on government. He expanded and extended welfare.
But mostly, if he didn't like doing it, it didn't get done.

He had a problem with that. Cuomo did not leave a mark on New
York State politics or government. Nothing major bears his logo. He
proposed some grand schemes but, like Jesse Jackson, he didn't stay
with them to guide and prod them into reality. He was off on to something else, and something else after that.

That brooding indecision, as charming and even romantic as it was,
wasn't the tragically ineluctable product of the conflicted intellectual
who sees too many sides of life's complexities to act decisively. It was a
man who was constitutionally incapable of connecting words to deeds.
He was a liberal who came not to believe in liberalism but remained a
despise of conservatism and a man who didn't have a terribly good
handle on either.

He was constitutionally unable to identify and carry out priorities.
Everything mattered equally, never mind that more and more voters
were thinking, hey, the money's not there and, even if it is, government had no business doing it.

He talked, and did *that* so well and so often and so much in lieu of action that his state of the state addresses grew to near Castro lengths.

When he talked about abortion, he said that he personally opposed it but wouldn't inflict his morality on the people of New York. When he talked about capital punishment, he said never mind the polls that kept showing that the people of his state wanted to see the death penalty imposed. The New York legislature kept pushing it and he kept rejecting it, saying at one point that he was ready to commute every death sentence handed down. Opposition to the death penalty was something Cuomo truly did believe in. When it came to capital punishment, it turns out he was willing to impose his morality on the people of New York.

Mario really gave it away for the attentive Cuomo watchers when he complained that his 1984 keynote address at the Democratic Convention got rave reviews and made him a national figure. Now, Mario, why was that bad? Because people assumed anybody who could speak that well couldn't possibly govern his way out of a paper bag. In other words, he believed, or wanted you to believe, that people thought he was a lousy governor, or couldn't handle running the White House if he ever got the job, because he spoke too *well*. I think they call that rationalizing your problems.

It's a trait liberals and conservatives often share. It's found among Republicans and Democrats. None bears his so charmingly as Mario Cuomo. See you in 2000, Mario?

☆ ☆ ☆ ☆ ☆ ☆ ☆ ☆ ☆

BOB DOLE
Born Again

NEWT GINGRICH AND THE SUPPLY-SIDE GANG in the House once called Robert J. Dole the tax collector for the welfare state. But Bob Dole has been born again. Now he is running as a Jack Kemp–Newt Gingrich–Ronald Reagan conservative, in what amounts to an old war hero's last electoral hurrah.

Dole, the Senate Majority Leader and World War II hero, formally launched his campaign for the Republican Presidential nomination on April 10, 1995, in Topeka, Kansas. Why not in his hometown of Russell? Because he is not the same Bob Dole who lost the Republican nomination to Ronald Reagan in 1980, and then to George Bush in 1988. Nor is he the same Bob Dole who was the designated Democrat-basher and the media-tagged SOB *extraordinaire* on the losing Gerald Ford ticket in 1976.

Media gave him that title during the 1976 presidential elections, when the Democrats maneuvered him into debating dull-as-paint Walter Mondale in a TV studio without an audience present. The Democrats knew that Dole's humor would sound mean and even cruel without the laughter of a live audience. Thus the image was created and the press picked up on it.

The old Bob Dole used to begin his presidential campaigns in Russell. The new Bob Dole begins his speeches by pulling out a copy of the Tenth Amendment of the Constitution — the states-rights, power-to-the-people amendment. And Topeka is the capital of Kansas. A *state* capital, if you catch the drift here.

The new Bob Dole, like the New Republican Party, wants power to

****

evolve to the Topekas of America. Better still, he wants power to bypass government altogether and go straight to the people. "Reigning in government, reigning in government," he repeats. "It resonates with people out there. I don't care what their party is."

Bob Dole didn't just come to this love, respect, and admiration for the Tenth Amendment.* He studied its fine wording. Even researched the Founding Fathers' reasons for choosing those words. He practically memorized its meaning: that the Constitution enumerates precious few powers as belonging to the feds, that every other power imaginable, and not yet imagined shall reside only with the states and the people. He studied the words long and hard — on a TelePrompTer. And after a few stumbles before early audiences, he got them right, almost every time.

These words have now become Bob Dole's heart, and it may be the heart of a conservative. But his heart has a mortal enemy, and that enemy is his mind. It has the incredible ability to find the logical middle ground and feels compelled to offer that as the solution. But battles are not won by finding the logical middle ground. They are won by people who have total conviction about their cause, and a willingness to fight a battle when outnumbered or with no apparent chance of winning. In offering middle-ground solutions, he relinquishes to the opposition, positions they don't have to fight for. To conservatives who know him well, when Dole's heart is in control of his mind, he is a winner.

You could not have gotten the old Bob Dole to yank from the inside breast pocket of his suit jacket a laminated copy of the Tenth Amendment and wave it before audiences. Why, the whole exercise would have smacked of *vision*, as in his seeing an America under his leadership, returning to the Founding Fathers' vision of limited government. "Academic claptrap. Show me a bill. Let's make a deal." That was the old Bob Dole's persona.

---

*Talk about conciseness. Here are the twenty-eight words making up the whole of the Tenth Amendment: "The powers not delegated to the United States by the Constitution, nor prohibited by it to the states, are reserved to the states respectively, or to the people." And, hey, the Ninth Amendment ain't bad, either: "The enumeration in the Constitution, of certain rights, shall not be construed to deny or disparage others retained by the people."

Bob Dole began his third grab for the brass ball (rings just aren't Bob Dole, not even the new version) by saying the new him is more relaxed. Skeptics immediately wanted to know if that meant he would be more ideologically predictable.

Put former education secretary William Bennett down as a skeptic. Bennett likes Dole "enormously" but doesn't "understand his political persona. Where are his 'can't helps,' as Justice Oliver Wendell Holmes used to call them? His political convictions that aren't subject to negotiations?" In short, is Dole talking like a conservative out of conviction, or because that's where his Party's primary electors live? Fair question, even to the new Bob Dole, who allows you to ask the question without biting your head off, or putting out the political equivalent of a contract on your life.

"Dole is definitely conservative, and he defines how far the Republican Party has shifted in the last twenty years that people have to ask that question," says Vin Weber, a Republican consultant who represented Minnesota when he was a member of the U.S. House of Representatives. Such definitive ratification is a surprise coming from Weber, who was not only a Jack Kemp conservative but was Gingrich's closest friend and intellectual adviser in the House. Still, can Dole be trusted to pursue in the White House the conservative line he is dishing out in the campaign? The answer is yes, says Weber. "Dole's leadership role for the last fifteen years has often put him at loggerheads with the ideological true believers. He has the skills required to negotiate with Democrats. But you shouldn't confuse that with a lack of genuine commitment to the cause. Ronald Reagan made lots of compromises when he was president, and nobody said he wasn't a true conservative."

The Reagan analogy may be a stretch for some hard-core skeptics, but there is evidence of change. The old Bob Dole supported affirmative action, hand-gun registration, tax increases, and freezes on Social Security cost-of-living adjustments in order to keep deficits from growing wild. "That was principled fiscal conservatism. He is a Midwestern, old-style Republican conservative who got caught in the philosophical divide that hit the party with the popularity of supply-side economics," says longtime Dole friend David A. Keene, who is chairman of the American Conservative Union. "That's not an example of slipperiness and opportunism, but showed he had a set of beliefs and was not willing to change because styles had changed."

The new Bob Dole began to emerge in 1993, when he led his Senate Republicans into victory against President Clinton's stimulus package and then kept them united against the Clinton budget, although at the time, he gave fellow Republicans heart palpitations over fear he would cut a deal for new taxes.

The new Bob Dole was the first in the field of 1996 Republican nomination contenders to strike out against affirmative action. And he is a Second Amendment stalwart when it comes to reversing the assault weapons ban in the 1994 crime law. In fact, Dole hits home runs on virtually every item on the conservatives' list of hot issues.

Another example of the new Bob Dole: instead of hiring an old crony, he hired a tough young operative, Scott Reed, as campaign manager. Already, Reed had grabbed himself an invaluable commodity: fifty-state national campaign experience as executive director of the Republican National Committee under Chairman Haley Barbour, the Chubby Checker of Republican operatives. Barbour and Reed helped Republicans thunder to victory in the historic 1994 elections, that brought Republicans into control of both houses of Congress for the first time in forty years. It gave them thirty of fifty governorships, plus major gains in state legislatures and local governments across the country.

But the new Dole still needs the security of the 'teddy bears' the old Dole had. He still needs a man like William Lacy around as a reassuring presence from the old days. Lacy has a cautious, experienced policy hand who has been with Dole on and off for more than a dozen years. Dole trusts him.

The new Dole is still the old Dole when it comes to having another teddy bear from his "youth," his closest political adviser, Jo-Anne Coe. She has been around twice as long as Lacy. Coe headed Dole's multi-candidate political action committee, Campaign America, then became the Dole-for-President finance director. He calls her every night around 9:30 or 10:00, touching base. Stars where they should be in the firmament? They were, thanks in large part to her: Coe raised

★★

an unheard of 9 million dollars in a single three-month period, during the second quarter of 1995, for the Dole campaign. Talk about bringing home the bacon. *You'd* call her every night, too.

The new Dole still needs focusing at times, and no one can do it like another teddy bear from the past, Mari Maseng, who wrote speeches and directed communication for Dole's last campaign. Mari Maseng is brought in whenever it is felt that the old Bob Dole is emerging and needs his attention refocused on some particular subject or project.

Another female teddy bear the new Dole relies on as much as the old Dole is his campaign's political director, Jill Hansen, who knows her stuff. She knows how to make progress "on the ground." The tangible gains Dole likes to see — endorsements from state politicos, the hiring of someone else's key staffer. Hansen is focused and effective, with a strong base in the Great Lakes states, and with all of the GOP governors.

But it is to Scott Reed, the freshest face of the teddy bears, that he places a telephone call first thing in the morning, like clockwork. That's the all-new Bob Dole at work, getting his daily progress reports and plan of action from a young man who can make snap judgments, explode into action when necessary, take risks when necessary, and still be the total planner. On January 27, 1995, Reed started lining up his ducks so that by March 15 Dole could count on getting virtually every elected Republican in New York to announce for Dole on March 15. He got all the Republican members of the state Senate, all Republican assemblymen, and all 62 Republican county chairmen. Talk about delivering. *You'd* call Reed every morning, too.

But only the new Bob Dole would understand the importance of having a young dynamo such as Reed, who had accumulated access to Haley Barbour, who doled out money to candidates all over the country in the last election, such as $1.5 million for George Pataki for governor of New York. Pataki was one of those endorsers from the Empire State, who lined up behind Dole in March.

The old Bob Dole was content to get bad advice in 1988 and to follow it. The good advice from two friends and consultants, Keene and Don Devine, went nowhere. The old Bob Dole let his top bad advice-giver, Campaign Chairman and Dole contemporary William Brock, unceremoniously kick Keene and Devine off Dole's campaign plane, which by then the press was unaffectionately calling the "plane from Hell." The old Bob Dole and his Campaign Chairman Brock, instituted a reign of terror over the campaign staff, so that even relatively senior advisers that survived would rather be caught dead than be seen talking *at any time* with any member of the traveling press corps. Everyone in the Dole-Brock world was the enemy, no one was to be trusted. For good reason the Dole 1988 effort itself, came to be known as the "campaign from Hell."

Finally, the old Bob Dole began, but didn't stay "on message," that is, pick a winning issue and stay with it, rather than flittering all over the issues menu. However, he did try to run the campaign himself, and he did blow up in a snarling fit of anger on camera, establishing himself as one of the great sore losers of all time. The old Bob Dole was himself the "candidate from Hell."

What a difference eight years seemed to make — and an understanding that this is the last shot — makes. As a result, it's the new Bob Dole, the candidate from heaven, who has emerged. It was the new Bob Dole who deliberately chose Reed, an ambitious man with no other concerns, business or otherwise, to distract him from devoting every long waking hour to the single task of getting Dole nominated, and then-elected president. And Devine and Keene were back with their good advice. That is not only a new Bob Dole at work, but a very smart new Bob Dole.

The question on everybody's mind, including Dole's, however, is whether his newness extends to his mouth, noted for emitting the most savage humor this side of Don Rickles. In February 1995, only two months before he launched his 1996 nomination campaign, the new Dole sounded for a moment like the old Dole, as if he were saying, Hey, didn't you know you can't teach an old dog not to bite the mailman? Dole's equivalent of biting the mailman was to repeat a joke he has been chuckling over since Ronald Reagan's administration. At the time, Dole had skillfully gotten Reagan on board and had managed to stitch together a deficit-reduction package that would have saved hundreds of billions of dollars, in part through a modest one-time partial freeze on Social Security cost-of-living adjustments. At the last minute, Kemp and his supply-side gang got Reagan's ear, turned his head, lined up Democrats and pulled the rug out from under Dole. The Kempians argued that touching even a hair on Social Security's old gray head would represent a return to "green eyeshade, country club" Republicanism. It would show insufficient compassion for the old, the lame, the halt, the sick and all the other groups Kempians think they can persuade to vote Republican if only... Anyhow, here it was, February 1995, and Dole tells his joke: "A bus full of supply-siders went over a cliff. That's the good news. The bad news: There were three empty seats." Weeks after telling the joke, there was Dole calling a press conference with Newt Gingrich, so the two of them could throw their arms around the shoulders of their good friend, Jack Kemp, a tenured professor in the Supply-Side, Tax-Cutting, Deficits-Be-Damned School of Economics. Kemp, before becoming President Bush's one and only secretary of Housing and Urban Development, was a New York congressman who sold President Reagan on the idea of a 30 percent reduction in the growth of personal and corporate income tax rates over three years (it got through the Congress as a 25 percent cut over three years).

In *April*, Dole and Gingrich named Kemp to head a commission to study, of all things, "pro-growth tax ideas." Strange. It wasn't so long ago that to Dole's ears it was like chalk scraping a blackboard when committed supply-siders like Kemp would utter the expression "pro-growth tax cuts" with the same reverence and frequency that serious followers of Islam repeat the words "Allah O Akbar" (God is great).

It should be explained here, for those who came in late, that there are two kinds of Republicans who have a major hankering for tax cuts. One kind wants them because they leave more money in the pocket of taxpayer-consumers and the bank accounts of businesses and corporations for savings, investment, and job-creating economic growth. But what is really meant is that if you give the government less in tax revenue, and even if it's a deficits-be-damned government, it will have less to spend on government programs. It's called a "starve the beast" strategy for shrinking government. Gramm clearly fits this category. Alexander's campaign rhetoric makes him sound as if he too fits in the shrink-the-beast category. Buchanan might fit but for his "populist" pitch.

The other kind of Republican also says he wants tax cuts for economic growth but, regardless of his antispending rhetoric, economic growth is *all* he wants, not spending cuts. He believes cutting tax-rates produces economic growth. This then will make up for the tax-rate cuts, and then some, leaving the government even more money to spend on things that make this kind of Republican feel all warm and fuzzy inside: Head Start, WIC (Women, Infants, and Children nutritional programs), subsidized housing for the "poor," and, of course, public education — never mind that there has been an indisputable, growing *inverse* relationship between the amount of money government spends on education, and the quality of education that has resulted.

This kind of Republican probably can think of dozens, maybe billions, of other do-good programs on which to spend the money you earn, programs that don't necessarily infringe on the private sector but sure fatten the public sector. And if the tax-rate cuts don't produce the growth that produces the increased revenues this kind of Republican expected, does it mean cutting back on government itself? Not to worry. Increase Head Start. Grow the Education Department. Deficits are overrated as a problem, and people are more important than balance sheets, aren't they? This is where Jack is and always was. Dole was in neither the starve-the-beast nor the deficits-be-damned faction. He was a traditional conservative who worried about balancing the national checkbook, and was willing to raise taxes to pay for the pork-barrel spending to which he and his colleagues were addicted, so long as you balance the books, for gosh sakes.

So what was going on with these oil (Dole) and water (Kemp) Republicans chumming it up? Symbiosis. Kemp needed Dole's power if he was to have any influence in the next Republican administration and Congress. Dole hungered after the bloc of votes of progressive-conservative loyalists around the country who had made Kemp the leader in the polls for the GOP Presidential nomination (until he dithered around about running and finally ruled it out).

What, if anything, does the Kemp-Dole entente predict about how

✶✶

Dole would act if he wins the nomination and the general election? Would he act like a gung-ho Tenth Amendment government shrinker or a "big government conservative" la Kemp? "The appointment of Jack is no small matter," said Weber, who is a Dole campaign cochairman. "It signals that Dole understands the importance of the growth issue, the tax issue and the recapturing of those issues for the Party, to the extent they have been lost." Uh-oh. Sounds ominous for the small government conservatives, doesn't it?

Not necessarily. The Dole-Kemp entente also signaled that Weber and Kemp understood that unless they hitched their wagons to the star of Bob Dole, who appeared at least as likely as any other Republican — and more likely than most — to be the next president, they could sit out the rest of the twentieth century in lonely isolation, devoid of significant influence with the new administration, and therefore less well equipped to earn a living doing what folks do for a living in Washington: trading on influence and connections. Or getting appointed treasury secretary or maybe secretary of state?

Phil Gramm was an unlikely alternative for Kemp and Weber, since Gramm can't keep a straight face when someone has the bad judgment to mention one of the "Kempian bleeding-heart progressive conservative" schemes in his presence.

Any influence Kemp may have on a Dole administration, meanwhile, is likely to be at the margins. There will be too many other far more powerful forces at play. If Dole wins the White House, Gramm and his conservative allies will still be in the Senate (Texas law permits him to run for the presidency and for Senate reelection). The most conservative House of Representatives in modern history is likely to remain in place, and even have its conservative ranks reinforced. And Dole would have a lot of markers out to conservatives, without whose active help he couldn't possibly win. In other words, the new Bob Dole, who talks far more conservatively than the old Bob Dole on social issues, is likely to remain the new Bob Dole when it comes to budget balancing, and a Republican Congress has shown it can wield a pretty big, sharp, pork-cutting knife.

But Dole has to get there first, and a potential obstacle always has been that Dole's principled side can show itself as self-defeating stubbornness, as when he refused to sign the no-tax pledge before the 1988 New Hampshire primary. It may have been politically stupid but certainly was not a sign of being unprincipled, according to Keene.

The new Bob Dole took care of that on day one. At a campaign stop on Monday, April 10, in Exeter, New Hampshire, hours after his Topeka kickoff speech, he made news not for what he told several thousand persons in the town square, but what he didn't tell them: in his Senate office three days before, he had signed an updated version of the Americans for Tax Reform "Taxpayer Protection Pledge" that he had refused to sign at the time of the 1988 New Hampshire primary.

Only a candidate from heaven could put together a campaign team that planned and executed this event so flawlessly, with the candidate himself taking directions as if he had been reborn as experienced actor Ronald Reagan, playing the presidential candidate. Reporters traveling with the Dole campaign learned about the signed pledge only at the precise time Dole strategists wanted them to. Dole aides passed out copies of the signed pledge to the press as Mr. Dole was delivering the same speech he had given in Topeka hours earlier. Dole Campaign Manager Scott Reed then "candidly" explained that the difference between 1988 and now is that in 1988, the Democrats controlled Congress. Dole could not count on spending cuts being enacted in order to head off massive deficits then, don't you see? But now that his party controls Congress, it's not a problem.

In another master stroke that contrasted the old candidate from Hell with the new candidate from heaven, Dole never once had to stand up and tell an audience that he had signed the pledge he had not signed eight years before, which would have left hanging in the air the implication that he was doing it now for opportunistic reasons. Instead, Reed told reporters Dole did not mention the pledge in his speeches in Topeka or Exeter "because there was no need to." Sure, the way Reed planned it, there wasn't. Dole proceeded to stay "on message," never allowing extraneous items like the pledge to creep into his carefully crafted speech.

Meanwhile, the campaign from heaven was working another minor miracle. It made Newt Gingrich associate — Grover Norquist, who

★★★

heads Americans for Tax Reform, and who actually crafted the language in the no-tax pledge, appear out of nowhere, on that day, in the Dole motorcade and in that town square in Exeter, New Hampshire. There was the earnest young Norquist with the totally focused young Scott Reed, ready to field press questions about Dole's having signed the pledge. In fact, Reed had the Washington-based Norquist picked up in Boston, so Norquist could meet Dole's arriving campaign jet at Pease Air Force Base and ride in the ten-car Dole motorcade into Exeter. It was important symbolically that he was seen as part of the campaign entourage.

Every one of Dole's rivals for the nomination was counting on Dole eventually reverting to his old self at some future point in the campaign. Surely, the SOB in him would claw its way out. Inside this new relaxed, mellow Dole was a voice waiting to scream, "I don't have to stay on message and take stupid advice from people who never got to be the majority leader of the United States Senate. Out of my way, you idiots. This is *my* campaign, and I'm taking over this show."

Instead, he bowled all of them over on the second day of his kickoff tour, launching into an attack on the entertainment industry for *its* assault on traditional values, and the basic morality that keeps a culture intact and healthy.

Every parent knows the way the popular culture ridicules family values, he said in Columbus, Ohio, and later that day in Des Moines, Iowa. "Our music, movies, and advertising regularly push the limits of decency, bombarding our children with destructive messages of casual violence and even more casual sex."

The old Bob Dole would not have borrowed a concept — "shame" — that his chief rival for public attention, the new House Speaker Newt Gingrich, had extolled only days before as an age-old tool for instilling and enforcing moral standards. The old Dole would have said, "Naw. Gingrich used it? What's it supposed to mean? Doesn't he know what century this is?"

The new Bob Dole said, "Shame is a powerful tool. We should use it against the entertainment industry, which poisons the minds of our young people. We must hold Hollywood accountable for putting profits ahead of common decency."

****

Profits ahead of decency? This was not the Bob Dole that has been running for president or vice president longer than most college freshmen have been alive. That Dole, like his chief Senate rival for the GOP nomination, Senator Phil Gramm of Texas, is not remembered for having complained about raw gratuitous sex and violence on television, either in his public speeches in the Senate or in conversation with his colleagues.

The old Bob Dole, when challenged on the genuineness of this sudden awakening to the insidious nature of popular culture, would have sprayed the air, like an assault weapon set on fully automatic, with cutting wisecracks and stinging one-liners. Such a natural reaction on Dole's part would have succeeded in distracting attention from the question, but also would have reminded everyone that beneath his tall good looks, there was a man.

Not the new Bob Dole. He was ready. In his informal chat with reporters in the aft section of his campaign plane after his moral-values speech, he was asked if he personally watches enough television to be offended by the sex and violence in shows and advertisements — or reads the type of popular magazines that run such ads. The new Bob Dole still speaks in thought fragments, as if the sound chip in his mental processor skips randomly over some bites. But what he says, he says calmly, without a trace of an about-to-erupt volcanic anger. "Pick up your mailbag every morning and find people concerned about violence on TV," he said, meaning citizens register their complaints in letters they send him. He even added that he happened to be carrying with him on the plane that very moment an example of a sexually tasteless popular-magazine advertisement that a constituent had sent him.

The campaign from heaven had been smart enough to have quietly commissioned a national poll to find out what Americans really hated, and Hollywood producers, directors, and scriptwriters soared off the charts in that poll. But the old Bob Dole would have dismissed the poll findings as having nothing to do with him. "Preaching moral values isn't my thing. Bring me a bill. Let's make a deal."

The new Bob Dole said if that's what it takes to win, then so be it. "It's a deal. Bring me a speech. I'm going to preach."

✴✴

The Hollywood speech originally was planned for delivery in Ohio on April 11, the second day of the Dole announcement tour. But the moral-values preachments went over so well nationally that Reed and Lacy later decided to have Dole go on the last day of May to the lion's den and deliver an expanded version in Los Angeles, on Hollywood's doorstep. The new Bob Dole was all too eager to cooperate.

The site Reed chose was a GOP fund raiser, perhaps not the perfect forum for a ringing moral-values speech, but one Reed and Lacy could totally control. It wasn't a speech at, say, a Rotary Club that was open to outsiders inadvertently screwing it up.

Reed and company left nothing to chance. They had a TelePrompTer in place. They worked three weeks to get national media attention and presence. The speech was scheduled for, and delivered during, the slow news days of the Memorial Day recess of Congress.

Finally, and probably key to the spectacular success the speech had in national exposure and comment, at 9:00 A.M. Reed leaked the speech to selected outlets, including the *Washington Times*, and to John King, the ace national political reporter for the Associated Press, who had it on the AP wire by 4:00 P.M., with a 7:00 P.M. Pacific time embargo. That allowed editors plenty of time to see and assess the importance of a speech that had yet to be given. Then to make, to the Dole campaign's delight but not surprise, page one of the next day's issue of the *New York Times*, not normally a ready platform for conservative social ideas, especially not conservative Republican social ideas. The new Bob Dole had practiced hard and dazzled his audience and press, and his campaign generals had manipulated the environment the way the old Bob Dole had only hoped for, but rarely saw materialize in his past campaigns.

Something else the new Dole did was *let* his campaign perform like the White House Liaison Office, reaching out to social conservatives to get them on board *before* the speech. Reed and Lacy sent drafts of the speech, with invitations to comment and make suggestions, to such opinion leaders as Ralph Reed, executive director of the Christian Coalition, to Gary Bauer, head of the Family Research Council, and to Vin Weber, a close Newt Gingrich associate and former congressman from Minnesota. So, when reporters called their usual sources for comments on the Dole Hollywood speech, those sources felt almost a pride of authorship, and their responses were generally glowing. Pat Buchanan called it one of the best speeches Dole ever gave. Dole made the cover of *Time* magazine with a speech that stood up for morality and bashed Hollywood, not his fellow Republicans.

Nowhere did Dole spell out his born-again willingness to do what it takes to win more explicitly than at an August 1995 appearance at the Republican National Committee's annual summer meeting in Philadelphia, where he said he would do whatever it takes. "You want me to be Ronald Reagan? I'll be Ronald Reagan." Norquist, in a momentary lapse from self-containment, remarked moments later that Dole was ready, willing, and eager to be all things to all people and that Dole was saying, "You want me to be a clown, I'll be a clown, if that's what it takes to win."

Not quite. There are some principles Dole simply can't bring himself to compromise. On that stage in the square in Exeter, he did not mention his having been severely wounded in the Po Valley of Italy in World War II. He never does. But he simply recalled that he revisited battle sites for the fiftieth anniversary of D-day last summer, including those in Northern Italy, "where I served in the 10th Mountain Division." The one concession he made to theatricality was the presence, on stage with him in Exeter, of several other survivors of the 10th Mountain Division. Still, he couldn't bring himself to exploit the opportunity to the hilt. He was awkward and brief, almost shy, in alluding to the presence of these men who, like him, had fought their country's battles in an era when nobody, but *nobody*, even privately, sniggled at the concepts of duty and honor. Dole, permanently crippled right arm and all, doesn't need to be reborn into a more likeable, laid-back politician to convey the image of an old soldier who tried to do his duty as God gave him the light to see that duty. But Dole does not see himself as an old soldier about to fade away. And unlike the late General Douglas MacArthur, who once used those words to wow a joint session of Congress, Dole did not mount the national podium in 1995 to say goodbye.

No way. For the new Bob Dole, it's more like "hello" to the cutting edge of his party's conservative ideas. The new Dole calls for dismantling major departments of the federal government, from Education and Energy, to Housing and Urban Development. The old Dole, like so many of his Republican colleagues in the Senate, bought into the hysteria over a supposed health-care crisis that President Clinton and the Democrats were selling. The old Bob Dole initially had his name as cosponsor on just about every Republican bill that would get the government deeper into the health-insurance business. Eventually, he saw the light and helped stop the health-care hysteria cold. But he wasn't exactly at the cutting edge of that debate. In fact, about the only cutting edge the old Bob Dole had was his tongue.

By June 1995, however, the old Bob Dole and the tongue that gets him in trouble began to make sporadic reappearances. Nothing fatal, or even crushing. But enough to make his own people a bit edgy at times. He said to attendees of the Republican National Committee's summer meeting in Philadelphia, "I'm willing to be another Ronald Reagan if that's what you want. I'll be another Ronald Reagan. I'll do the best I can to rein in the federal government, to reconnect the government with the values of America, to reassert our nation's prestige around the world wherever and whenever challenged." That elicited this crack from Grover Norquist, who had gotten Dole to sign the no-tax pledge in April: "Dole seems ready to tell Republicans he'll put on a clown suit if that's want they want." The Dole remarks in Philadelphia seemed to play into the idea behind the nickname some in the press had already given him: "pander bear." In midsummer, Dole gave a few interviews including one to the *New York Times*, that suggested that Gramm and the other candidates competing for the Reagan mantle were too far out in right field, and only Dole was fully appreciative of the *good* government can do. Dole then flabbergasted his strategists by going off message big time in a nationally televised speech before an August meeting of Ross Perot's United We Stand America. Again, he suggested that some of his rivals for the nomination were too far to the right, and failed to appreciate the good government does. Then came the Iowa straw poll on August 19, 1995. Dole addressed the more than 10,500 attendees with a well-crafted speech that was conservative to the core, and that kept him "on message" the way the new

****

Bob Dole was supposed to be. But the members of that audience were also voting in the straw poll, and their vote revealed that Dole and his campaign organization in Iowa were caught asleep at the switch, as they had been in 1987, when Pat Robertson scored a stunning upset of Dole in the same straw poll. This time it was Gramm who tied Dole for first place, with each getting exactly 2,582 votes in the poll in his own backyard. Pat Buchanan was close on their heels, with 1,922 votes.

The embarrassment for the Senate majority leader was significant. For years, folks in Iowa have regarded Dole, their Kansas neighbor, as Iowa's third senator. But in August 1995, the campaign organization of Phil Gramm, the Georgia-born senator from Texas, showed superior organizational skills and more local savvy than Dole's did in Iowa. So did Pat Buchanan's underfinanced organization, which managed to bring him in just behind Gramm and Dole in the race to see which of the ten declared candidates for the GOP nomination could buy larger blocs of twenty-five dollar tickets to the event, hire more buses and planes to bring folks in from around Iowa and from other states to vote. The Iowa Republican Party straw poll is a party fund-raiser first and foremost, and Iowa Republicans don't care how you get people there to contribute to the party, so long as you get them there in large numbers. So they have what is the biggest rigged "election" in the Western World, but it is open rigging, equal opportunity rigging, free to all comers to test their organizational skills and their ability to use effectively the money they've raised. "We got our butts kicked," Reed, the Dole national campaign manager, commented afterward.

Next, Dole walked into a trap at the beginning of September when he let Gramm do to him on abortion, what Bush and the other GOP nomination contenders had done to him in the 1988 presidential nomination campaign in New Hampshire on the no-tax pledge. At a two-day Christian Coalition convention in Washington, D.C., Gramm spoke on the morning of the first day, and challenged Dole to sign a pledge to keep in the 1996 GOP platform the strong pro-life plank that had been in every GOP platform since 1984. When Dole appeared a few hours later to address the same Christian Coalition audience, he was greeted with chants of "Sign the pledge, sign the pledge." Instead of doing just that, he dismissed the importance of such "rhetoric" and said his record in the Senate on defending the right to life was enough. But some political observers saw it as a repeat of the 1988 refusal to sign the no-tax pledge. The old Bob Dole was back, still running behind the learning curve. But Dole got back on message again, and the new Bob Dole got some warm praise from Pat Robertson, founder of the Christian Coalition. During the Christian Coalition convention, he told a *New York Times* interviewer that Dole is not an ideological "chameleon" as some detractors have claimed, but rather a "life long conservative." If he is "somewhat of a compromiser," Robertson said, hey, that's part of the job of being majority leader.

Indeed, it may be that sometimes. But, will there come a time when the old Bob Dole accuses the new Bob Dole of lying about the old Bob Dole's record? Maybe it will. Maybe it won't. You never know with the Doles.

★ ★ ★ ★ ★ ★ ★ ★ ★

BOB DORNAN
This One's for Him

BOB DORNAN, the Orange County, California Republican congressman with red hair, sometimes red beard and mustache, and a worldview that is always red, white, and blue, is like a fine wine whose time has come. He's worked for everybody else's nomination and election as president. Back in 1986, he was among the first Republicans in the House to get behind then-Vice President George Bush's upcoming 1988 presidential bid. "Now it's *my* turn," he confided on the telephone one morning before announcing that he was thinking of declaring for the 1996 GOP presidential nomination. "My *wife* says it's my turn. *I* say it's my turn."

Okay, Bob, it's your turn. It's about time the GOP nominated for president a Catholic of Irish descent who was born on April 3, 1933, the same calendar date as the crucifixion of Jesus Christ, only a couple of thousand years ago, as Bob likes to point out. Now, there is also this fellow Pat Buchanan, who is Irish Catholic and who would be president. But *he* wasn't born on April 3, 1933. So there it is, Bob, the field's clear in that regard.

It's also about time the Republicans took off their green eyeshades, left their country clubs, rolled up their Pima cotton sleeves, and got behind a man like Bob, whose working-class district includes Disneyland and boasts a large number of Hispanic residents. Go for it, Bob.

It's also about time the GOP nominated someone whose legislative voting record is nearly perfect according to just about every rating group on the Right and beyond atrocious according to every rater on the Left.

Would you believe Dornan earned 100 percent ratings for his votes in 1993 and 1994 from the National Right to Life Committee? And from the National Abortion Reproductive Rights Action League? And from Pat Robertson's Christian Coalition? And from the American Conservative Union, American Security Council, and the National Rifle Association?

But, alas, true perfection eluded Dornan. The U.S. Chamber of Commerce gave him only a 91 percent and the American Farm Bureau Federation a mere 86 percent. The National Taxpayers Union, a tough rating outfit if there ever was one, gave Dornan only 77 percent, but then other lawmaker–presidential aspirants on Dornan's side of the aisle didn't do all that hot either with NAT. Senator Phil Gramm of Texas got only 79 percent, followed by Senator Richard Lugar of Indiana with 76 percent, Senate Majority Leader Bob Dole with 74 percent, and Senator Arlen Specter of Pennsylvania with 57 percent.

On the Left, Dornan tasted as bad as a conservative should. The AFL-CIO allowed him a 33 percent, the National Council of Senior Citizens a 20 percent, and the Leadership Conference on Civil Rights a 14 percent (never mind that Dornan is militantly antiracist). Hillary Rodham Clinton's favorite, the Children's Defense Fund, was able to spare only 11 percent for Bob, one percentage point more, however, than the Consumer Federation of America gave him. Finally, the League of Conservation Voters barely found him worthy of inhabiting the planet. The League gave him 4 percent.

Is this guy good or *what*? He once called himself a "flaming liberal." Come again? Dornan, the guy who almost single-handedly created the national antiabortion movement?

Well, turns out he's a closet PETA-ist. Yes, B-1 Bob, ex-fighter-pilot Bob, that same Bob got named the 1989 Legislator of the Year by that animal separatist outfit called People for the Ethical Treatment of Animals, or PETA, to its human friends. Actually, Dornan had to share the award that year with another Bob, who was also a Republican and a right-winger, then Congressman (now Senator) Bob Smith of New Hampshire.

Dornan and Smith, as you no doubt have forgotten or would have forgotten if you had ever known it in the first place, championed PETA's efforts on behalf of the notorious "Silver Spring" monkeys. PETA made millions and built its national reputation on its campaign to free the Maryland research animals now residing in New Orleans. PETA cofounder Alex Pacheco introduced the American press to the animal separatist movement when he claimed biomedical researcher Dr. Edward Taub was torturing his monkeys. People with warped minds who thought he was accused of torturing his "monkey" (singular) took it as a joke. You know who you are.

Anyhow, Dr. Taub was working on the still-elusive, but vital area of nerve cell regeneration and the possibility of retraining the body — NOW STAY WITH US — THIS PART WILL BE OVER IN A COUPLE MORE SECONDS — and brain to use limbs after severe nerve trauma — an area critical to stroke and spinal cord injury patients.

Okay, so the point is: PETA never mentioned that to Dornan or Smith. So what happened to their intellectual curiosity that they didn't inquire, you ask? Don't ask.

Dornan sees his effort on PETA's behalf as constituent service. His daughter, a Hollywood PETA-phile, begged him to intervene. He also sees it as a continuation of his life's quest to liberate the oppressed. That's why he went to Vietnam. That's why he marched with Dr. Martin Luther King, Jr., when the civil rights leader was alive and leading that revolution.

Dornan also subscribes to PETA's antifur obsession. During the Bush inaugural ball, he fumed over a "fat cat" Republican's wife decked out in a leopard coat. The object of his derision was the dethroned former Democrat Speaker Jim Wright's spouse. The woman, not the coat, if you follow?

You could argue there's another closet-liberal aspect to Dornan. He *loves* Hollywood. Back in the 1920s, his mom was a vaudeville trouper. His uncle, Jack Haley, was a minor Hollywood legend for his role as Judy Garland's Tin Man costar in the original *Wizard of Oz*. Dornan's daughter, Kathleen, is an actress. His father was in show business, kinda. He was an Olympic boxing coach (which explains the good congressman's pugnacity).

****

Now, truly demented right wingers would argue that Dornan has another liberal trait, the tendency to argue *ad hominem*. Which is to say, Bob Dornan loves to turn every political debate into a personal attack on his opponent. True, a lot of your better known Democrats and liberals do it. Mario Cuomo and Ann Richards come to mind. And Bill Clinton does it. His 1992 campaign strategists James Carville and Paul Begala do it. Jesse Jackson does it. Virtually every liberal Democrat from New York City does it. Former Senator Howard Metzenbaum took it to an art form. Lacking substantive arguments to defend their positions on issues, liberals level vitriolic personal attacks on their opposition. But then Republicans aren't immune to dabbling in such things. Remember Bob Dole snarling at Dan Rather regarding George Bush? "Tell him to stop lying about my record!"

But when Dornan does *ad hominem*, he does *ad hominem* better than anyone else does *ad hominem*. Remember "coke-snorting, wife-swapping, baby-born-out-of-wedlock, radical Hollywood Left?" His words for California Senator Barbara Boxer's constituents. How about "triple draft-dodging adulterer?" His words for Bill Clinton. Or "sick, pompous little ass"? Can you guess who? Stop trying. They were his words for almost any of his Democratic colleagues momentarily in his extreme disfavor.

Dornan is as comfortable on television and radio as was that old baseball announcer, Ronald Reagan. Dornan has been all over C-Span and has brought his mile-a-minute mouth and charming bombast to guest spots and stints as substitute host for the Rush Limbaugh show.

You can understand why he talks faster than he thinks if you know the real truth about his birth: he made his natal debut in New York City, then moved at a tender age to Southern California, where thinking before you talk, or at all, is reputed to be a misdemeanor, at least for first offenders. Dornan attended a good Catholic school, Loyola University, before enlisting in the Air Force after the Korean War.

All that turned him into a bit of an Irish poet, playwright, and Druid priest. He can enflame his audience in the tradition of Synge and Yeats, when theatergoers erupted into riots and poets led rebels against Black and Tan oppressors. His knack for keeping an audience of young and old spellbound throughout a forty-five minute speech on the moral objections to abortion is legendary, not to mention well known. His more frequent tendency to wander off to all four points of the compass in a major speech or a private discourse is equally legendary. Of course, his choice of venues has a great deal to do with audience response. At the annual Conservative Political Action Convention in Washington, the applause was thunderous and he was mobbed by moved admirers. The same speech before the National Organization of Women would also get its listeners to their feet, but their aim would be to wrap their hands around his throat, not pat him on the back.

With the abandon of the jet jock he once was, Bob Dornan lives for a good public political brawl. Something that is also quite in keeping with liberal Irish politicians, whether born in America or Ireland. Ask any of the Kennedys or their cousins, the Smiths. Also faithful to his ethnic heritage, Dornan says people who are disturbed by his "firebrand" style are simply mistaking temper for passion.

His rhetorical "passion" does have its downside. Dornan was banished from the House floor for twenty-four hours because of his "poetic" use of language in calling Bill Clinton's college antics a source of "aid and comfort to the enemy." His temporary exile was punishment, not because he was wrong, but because it violated House etiquette. It's just not polite to be so openly accurate about a sitting or jogging president.

Not surprisingly, young folk, particularly young folk who fancy themselves conservative, are enthralled with Dornan, the same way liberal kids flock to the best of the liberal politicos. Part of the attraction in Dornan's case is his penchant for voicing his opinion in unvarnished, in-your-face language that kids interpret as refreshingly straight from the shoulder. Critics would ascribe the point of origin to another part of the anatomy.

Anyhow, here's an example of Dornan's attraction for young people and Dornan's honesty. In 1992, while stumping in New Hampshire for George Bush, a dozen young Buchanan Brigade volunteers cornered Dornan in his hotel lobby. Their admiration for the Californian was genuine and boundless, even if they didn't much care for the man for whom he was playing surrogate. After a long evening trading stories, he bade them good night and said, "When I get back to Washington, I'm going to tell the president that I have met the brightest and best young conservatives our party has. And I have to tell you, Mr. President, they're not with us. They're with Pat Buchanan."

Dornan, however, likes to go with winners more than he likes to stand with ideological soul mates who don't look like sure winners. He claims it's his love of the American military's role in defending America and its values that make him inclined to campaign for Bob Dole if Dornan's own campaign runs out of money and steam. He considers Dole a true "war hero," and for that reason is willing to overlook some of Dole's past "mushiness" on traditional conservative issues.

So what about Mr. Family Values's own family? His wife, Sally Dornan, and their five grown children were on board for his 1986 try for the GOP presidential nomination. This was a sacrifice on Sally's part. His long absences from home while he went gallivanting around the world on foreign policy trips as a congressman nearly wrecked their marriage more than once.

Dornan's campaign motto for 1986 was "Faith, Family, Freedom." And he launched his campaign in April 1995 sounding just like, well, Bob Dornan, spouting bravado, hubris, humility, pugnacity, discernment — and that was just in the first sentence.

"Here's one congressman that has never yelled at his staff; that has tried to motivate my children by example, not by harshness; that has never in subcommittee or committee or at a press conference ever showed anything but passion. On the floor of the House, yes, I've been tough. [But] I apologize for nothing."

When he got to the moral-values stuff, you knew why he was reelected every term since his first election to the House in 1976. He said, "I will tell you that if...somebody is not publicly indignant and saying, 'stop this,' with our cultural meltdown and moral decline, then I'll show you somebody who doesn't understand the facts. I'll show you somebody who's a bystander watching the destruction of our country."

See? Bob Dornan *can*, at times, think and talk.

⭑ ⭑ ⭑ ⭑ ⭑ ⭑ ⭑ ⭑ ⭑

STEVE FORBES

Funny, He Doesn't Look *Like Jack Kemp*

IT WAS A QUIET FRIDAY in the third week of September, 1995, when magazine mogul Malcolm S. "Steve" Forbes, Jr. fired a shot heard 'round the National Press Club. The world also took note; whether it will long remember is another matter.

There he was in a room on the 13th floor, pudgy faced, with eyeglass lenses like the bottoms of Coke bottles, telling a small audience of supporters and reporters that he was officially seeking the 1996 Republican presidential nomination. The event was cleverly timed to make the Friday night evening television news watched by those Republican voters who have nothing better to do on Friday night and to make the next morning's editions of newspapers read by voters who have no Saturday chores and no parties to go to.

With that in mind, Forbes solemnly pledged his sacred honor to make America safe once again for the gold standard and 4.5 percent mortgages. His supporters applauded. Some reporters suppressed a giggle, the way they used to when Jack Kemp would rhapsodize on the advantages of tying the dollar to the value of gold.

Forbes, the new darling of the supply-side, anti-tax, pro-growth lobby, wants to stand right up and address issues that the other candidates hadn't dared touch on — mostly because they thought it would be stupid or boring, or both, to talk about those issues while trying to get elected. Nonetheless, Forbes thinks real men talk about moderating the rate of growth for benefits to retirees and restoring integrity to

THOSE WHO THINK THEY SHOULD BE PRESIDENT. . .

****

the dollar through fixing the dollar's value to the price of gold or some other "anchor."

But, hey, he said economic growth is what brought him into the race in the first place. The other candidates weren't talking about it. And why weren't they, Steve? Did Phil Gramm, Bob Dole and Pat Buchanan hate seeing growth in the economy? Hate seeing the jobs growth produces? Or want slow growth? No, not exactly, Forbes says. He understands that the other GOP nomination candidates were not opposed to economic growth, but the "difference is that virtually all of them are political insiders who, if they had the answer, would have implemented them by now."

He acknowledges good-naturedly that his looks leave something to be desired as a presidential candidate, at least by "Hollywood's Central Casting standards. But most great presidents and great leaders would not have come out of Central Casting."

Like his good friend Kemp, Forbes is fascinated by the things that put the rest of the Western world to sleep: economics, monetary policy, the Federal Reserve Board, foreign exchange rates, and international lending institutions. And Forbes wants to *do* something about *all* of them, which is fine since his ideas are good. Just so he doesn't *talk* about them. At least not *too* much.

Actually, he can talk about them more substantively than Kemp because Forbes has a more intimate grasp of them. He *is* the kind of entrepreneurial capitalist about whom Kemp, in his 1988 GOP presidential nomination campaign, talked. And talked. And talked. And about whom he continued to talk and talk and talk afterward.

Like Lamar Alexander, Alan Keyes, and a number of other GOP presidential hopefuls, Forbes is running as — *surprise!* — an outsider. A man not of Washington. *Heavy.*

"I will tell you, frankly, that any one of the Republican candidates would be a vast improvement over the incumbent," he said. "But I believe their vision of what we can do is narrow, cramped and constricted. They have been in Washington or in politics, or both, all of their adult lives. They haven't been at the center of the entrepreneurial economy. I have..." *Ouch.* That man knows how to hurt, doesn't he?

What Forbes, who will be forty-nine on Inauguration Day, 1997,

✳✳✳

has going for him is not that he is your basically homely but business-wiser version of the handsome former quarterback, Jack Kemp. No, it's something more basic. Forbes is filthy rich. As president and chief executive officer of Forbes Inc., he was the only guy in the GOP field who said he would, and who *could*, write out a personal check for twenty-five million dollars, or more if necessary. That was what it would probably take to get his name recognition up high and keep it there in the dozens of expensive media markets he would have to compete on March 26, 1996. That's when the California and Connecticut primaries would cap the most compressed string of primaries and caucuses in U.S. history, probably deciding the nomination by then.

Does Forbes need that kind of money for name recognition? Who *doesn't* know the man who heads a sprawling media empire, who is the billionaire editor of *Forbes Magazine* and the son of the late, illustrious Malcolm S. Forbes, Sr., who used to throw birthday parties for himself that made the late Shah of Iran look like a piker?

Steve Forbes is the son of the man who played with, and had magazine photographers photograph him playing with hot air balloons and motorcycles, and Elizabeth Taylor and horses, and yachts and anything else that would raise the visibility of his name and therefore of his media empire.

Who doesn't know Steve Forbes?

Pete Hallgren, a lawyer and chairman of the Republican Party in Alaska, isn't sure he knows him, and is sure virtually nobody else whom he knows knows Forbes. "I'm just guessing, but I think he's in the magazine business. I don't think I've heard anyone in my whole state mention his name," Hallgren said a few days before the announcement.

"How do you spell his last name?" said David Opitz, chairman of the Wisconsin Republican Party, who actually does know how to spell Forbes but not much else about the man. "I don't know anything about what Forbes' positions are. I suppose he is generally conservative and business-driven," Opitz said about the time Forbes announced.

Bob Bennett, Ohio Republican Party chairman, had little to say that was encouraging for Forbes just before the media magnate announced. Bennett figured that if he surveyed his 13,000 committeemen across the state, "probably no more than about 5 percent would know who this guy is."

If only business magazine readers and a few other politically aware Americans knew who Forbes was so late in the game, why was anyone taking him seriously enough to write about his candidacy? "Anyone who can write a personal check for $20 million or $30 million in the primary has got to be taken seriously," said a top aide to one of the leading GOP nomination contenders. "He can't win the nomination, but he has taken a lot of attention away from the rest of us."

But if he couldn't win the nomination, or wasn't likely to, why was he willing to throw away that much of his personal fortune? Three reasons. One, he's human, which means he has an ego. Nothing is more ego-gratifying than running around the country telling Americans you want to be their president, having people turn out to hear you say that, and having the national press corps and the local press run after you, shoving microphones in your face, jotting down your every word, seeing yourself on network television news, on the cover of news magazines, and on and on. If you have Forbes' money, you make it happen.

Two, his sainted father showed that having a good time at great expense is a good business investment. The millions of dollars he threw away on lavish parties and adult toys raised his name recognition and that of his magazines. It was adverting of the best kind, because it appeared in the news columns. *Forbes* magazine, known to a few hundred thousand Americans, would become a household word before the 1996 GOP presidential primary was history.

Reason three. Steve Forbes, a Princeton graduate, is every bit the socialliberal and anti-tax conservative that Kemp is. This means he feels you need to have tax cuts without taking away "nice" things the government does *for* people, such as the multi-billion-dollar Head Start program, which even supporters say hasn't worked because taxpayers haven't spent *enough* on it. And the Women, Infants, and Children program. And Social Security. And the social safety net. The only way you can have tax cuts and not take these things away is by making the economy grow so *fast* that you produce enough tax revenue, even with lower tax rates, to pay for the social spending that *cares* for people and shows you care for people.

Forbes, who sees eye to eye with Kemp on issue after issue, headed and helped finance a sort of think tank and advocacy outfit called Empower America, which Kemp helped found. They talked all the time. Forbes didn't like the GOP's position on immigration. Kemp didn't like it either.

Never mind that middle-class, first-generation Hispanics and immigrants from all over, who were aspiring to the middle class or had made it, were saying immigration in the United States was out of control. Too many legal and illegal immigrants from disparate cultures speaking too many different languages were flocking here too fast in too great of numbers for the kind of successful assimilation that historically made America the biggest cultural-economic success in the history of the world. Even the black head of a commission which President Clinton appointed to study the matter, concluded as much.

Yet, Steve Forbes, whose grandfather was an immigrant from Scotland, took to lecturing persons whose parents were immigrants and were married to immigrants. He took to lecturing them about the joys of immigration on a more-the-merrier basis that harkened back to the 1950s, but showed no hint of an awareness of the seriousness of current problems.

"I oppose illegal immigration, but my grandfather was an immigrant; and the problem we have is not with legal immigration," he said in an interview in September, 1995. " We are not kept together by a common religion or race or ancestry, but by a common set of values and beliefs; and if we don't impart that to newcomers, it is our fault."

His friend Kemp, at the urging of Forbes, had come out on the eve of the crucial California gubernatorial election in 1994 and opposed Proposition 187, which denied social and education benefits to children of illegal immigrants. Pete Wilson, the incumbent Republican governor, was backing the ballot initiative and counting on it to help him get reelected. What Forbes and Kemp did could have cost Republicans a crucial governorship. But the initiative passed overwhelmingly anyway, and Wilson was reelected. But the incident presages the kind of social policy a Forbes presidency would bring.

Forbes, like Kemp, was reluctant to take on illegitimacy teenage pregnancy, and welfare dependency if it meant seeming to show insufficient compassion for the "poor."

"I reject the grim notion of the Washington politicians that America must learn to make do with less," Mr. Forbes, joined by his wife, Sabina, and their five daughters, his three brothers and his sister, said in his announcement speech.

Sounding the upbeat, anti-tax, but not stridently anti-spend, "progressive conservative" theme of Kemp, Forbes said he rejects the idea "that the American people have spent too much, and now the American people must pay."

In a swipe at Senator Gramm who says he wants the kind of welfare reform that will have persons riding in the wagon get out and help the "rest of us pull the wagon," Mr. Forbes, sneered at the idea "that the wagon is heavy and crowded, and now is the time to start throwing people off."

"I reject the equally grim notion that the American people must constantly pay in taxes for the mistakes the politicians make in Washington, such as a deficit which, despite years of bluster and two of the largest tax increases in history, continues to grow," he said. What he did not say was that one of the two largest tax increases in inflation-corrected dollars was signed into law by President Reagan in 1982, and the other was signed by President Clinton in 1993.

Forbes, like Kemp, has argued that sustained high rates of job growth and income growth with low interest rates and virtually no inflation took place when the United States tied its currency to the value of gold.

Forbes also vowed to return the nation to the gold standard, one of his more sound ideas that has nothing to do with social liberalism. "We must take our money out of the hands of the politicians," he said. "We can bring back 4.5 percent mortgages, lower interest rates, and give the economy a boost. As we did throughout our nation's history until the late 1960s, we must tie the value of the dollar to a fixed measure such as gold, so that a dollar today will be worth a dollar tomorrow."

Forbes opened his campaign with a surprising number of concrete proposals for change. Unlike some other GOP candidates who had vaguely endorsed "flatter" or "fairer" taxes, Mr. Forbes said he would replace the tax codes with a single 17 percent tax rate that would apply only to incomes in excess of $36,000 a year. Anything less than that would not be taxed at all." On a $50,000-a-year salary, the actual rate would be only about 2 percent.

"Imagine what that would do for family life," he said. "We would see a renaissance the likes of which has never been seen before. Families could step off the tax treadmill. Wage earners could relax a little — save more easily. Parents would have more time to spend with their children and with each other. They would have more time to devote to where it belongs, to the home and hearth, where all the true value lies."

Earlier he had said he would also tackle reforming Social Security during his nomination campaign. The issue was considered a candidacy killer, and no one was even discussing obliquely the possibility of adjusting retirees' benefits downward in order to keep the system financially sound.

On abortion, he did the usual straddle of Republican politicians who know how to read the polls, and therefore know the American public is of two minds on the issue. Thus, Forbes wants "to create an environment where abortion will disappear." He opposes abortions in late pregnancy barring an emergency, abortions for sex selection, and "mandatory government funding." But he favors parental notification for minors.

Even at his late date of entry into the campaign, Forbes managed to buy some pretty good talent to run his campaign organization. Forbes has hired a young hot shot pollster, John McLaughlin, who is a libertarian-conservative Republican and whose partner, Tony Fabrizio, was hired by Bob Dole's campaign. Hey, but that's Washington.

Forbes has also hired Tom Ellis, who headed the North Carolina Congressional Club and was Senator Jesse Helms' top campaign adviser. Also on board was John Sears, who was briefly Ronald Reagan's campaign manager.

To manage the campaign, Forbes hired long-time Kemp operative and president of Empower America, William Dal Col who, however, does not have 50-state campaign management experience.

✶✶✶

Forbes' political experience is — how to put this? — moderate at best. Ronald Reagan did appoint him to head the commission overseeing Radio Free Europe. That's something. Then, in 1993, Forbes did help draft a plan to cut state income taxes 30 percent for his lifelong friend and next-door neighbor, Christine Todd Whitman, a socially liberal Republican who sought the New Jersey governorship. She made it the centerpiece of her winning campaign and then implemented it, a year ahead of schedule.

When Forbes announced for the nomination, he joined a field that was then made up of nine mostly better-known candidates who had been officially in the race longer, and all of whom had top-notch government experience. The nine were: former Governor Lamar Alexander; the Senate Majority Leader Bob Dole; the United States Senator who coauthored the Gramm-Rudmann Deficit Reduction Act, Phil Gramm of Texas; the best-known conservative pundit in the television business who served as a top aide to three presidents, Pat Buchanan; the governor of the most populous state in the nation, Pete Wilson; a former U.S. ambassador, Alan Keyes; the U.S. senator who grilled Justice Clarence Thomas' tormentor, Anita Hill, Arlen Specter; a veteran California congressman who filled in for Rush Limbaugh, Bob Dornan, and another U.S. senator, Richard Lugar.

Actually, according to the Federal Election commission's official count, Forbes became the seventy-second officially declared candidate for the 1996 GOP nomination, sixty-two of whom were lesser-known or never-heard-of Americans. But, hey, the pool's never crowded when you're having fun. And you can bet Steve Forbes was, is, and will be having what for him is fun. Which, unlike love, is something money *can* buy."

TEN WAYS STEVE FORBES CAN USE HIS FORTUNE TO BECOME PRESIDENT

(1) Change his name to Colin Powell, Sr.
(2) Have his body frozen by cryogenics for 100 years while gradually using his fortune to buy the United States. When he thaws out, he'll already own the country.

(3) Write a book that sells two million copies on a subject he knows something about and that the public is interested in. His challenge: figuring out the subject.

(4) Send a *Forbes* magazine subscription to every poor family in America that is registered to vote.

(5) Arrange for immigrants who don't have U.S. citizenship to vote.

(6) Convince Ross Perot that Forbes regards Perot, not Jack Kemp, as his hero and accept the nomination of the Perot party for president. It would help if Steve changed his wife's name to Evita.

(7) Give Ralph Hallow and Brad O'Leary the $25 million he planned to spend financing his own campaign, and they'll give him a money-back guarantee that if they don't elect him president they will return $12.5 million.

(8) Propose a 17 percent flat tax on personal incomes between $100,000 and $500,000 a year, no tax on incomes under $100,000 and an 83 percent tax on incomes over $500,000.

(9) Come up with the conclusive evidence to prove who *really* killed Nicole Simpson and Ron Goldman, then buy two weeks of network television time to present it to the public.

(10) Hire the nation's best image-maker as his chief political guru and campaign consultant. This is the person who took a boring, unknown, unfocused, dysfunctional politician and turned him into president. This guru would, of course, be Hillary Clinton. With a $1 million salary and Forbes' insider information, she could become richer than she did on pig futures.

✫ ✫ ✫ ✫ ✫ ✫ ✫ ✫ ✫ ✫
ALBERT GORE, JR.
A Tale of Two Als

IT HAS BEEN said that Al Gore doesn't want to be president...Al Gore was born to be president. Ask him and he'll affirm both statements. The two Al Gores. There's the Al that smoked pot and loves outrageous practical jokes. He visibly colors at the thought that power groupies want to drag his hunky body into the shadows to have him punch their Capitol Hill dance cards. He considers abortion the taking of human life, and he is a strong supporter of "abortion rights," as if an abortion has rights. He earned a reputation in the press as an "arms control" guru when he suggested shrinking the size of nuclear-tipped missiles and putting them on railroad cars.

Actually, his rep as a Democratic arms expert is more theoretical than real. He's no Sam Nunn. Somehow, he hit upon a mathematical equation that suggested the rail-based missiles allowed an equally theoretical nuclear stalemate with the then Soviet Union. He didn't have to invoke the traditional Dem Lib strategy of calling for a ban on nuclear weapon buildup, but his idea would have achieved the same effect. New missiles would not have been deployed. A few problems. His idea was rejected by the Pentagon and he missed the real brilliance of railroad missiles. He could have used it as an opportunity to rebuild our aging national rail system and give our economic substructure a boost. The rail-based missiles would have driven Soviet spies crazy as they scurried about the country in ramshackle Russian-built Fiats playing hide-and-seek with moving missiles.

He's the idol of the environmental *Captain Planet* cartoon generation who see him as the embodiment of the animated antipollution crusader. Gore's also the butt of countless monologues by Jay Leno, referring to his zombie-like demeanor. The curious might be tempted to place a mirror beneath his nose to see if he's breathing (not while he's sleeping; while he's giving a speech). Said Leno after reports of woodpeckers pecking holes in the space shuttle's insulation, "Today, NASA brought in a huge wooden decoy: Al Gore." Not to be outdone, David Letterman quipped, "While he was in London commemorating the end of World War II, [Gore] had to wear a sign, 'I'm not the Unknown Soldier.'"

Watch him. One minute he's a polished pol, easily slipping through the halls of power, presiding over gatherings of the nation's and the world's most influential and erudite policy-makers, stirring the faithful with passionate (for him) rhetoric of environmental concern. Next he's Forrest Gump. He's uncomfortable. An outsider. Lost and ill at ease.

Which Al would show up for his first day as guardian of the Oval Office? That's the key question voters must face: Should Bubba Clinton recognize the boat-anchor liability he presents to his party this election go-round and opt for early retirement? Bill Clinton deciding not to run is pure fiction. But if fact did follow fiction, it would set a scenario that would ultimately prove too costly to both the public and Al Gore, no matter what you think of Al or his brand of national politics, and no matter which Al appears to step into the breach.

For better or worse, Al Gore is the archetypal baby boomer. He took his schooling seriously. He's open to approaching issues from untypical perspectives. He respects the hard work his parents' generation put into getting him where he is. He's not into BMWs or faux-alligator-skin tassel loafers. Nor is he concerned with clawing his way to the top, or how much he earned from his last investment venture.

Al Gore knows that he can do any number of things, and do most surprisingly well, but he wonders, sometimes too openly, about what life is all about and where he fits in. And that is precisely the danger the nation faces as long as the two Als remain in politics. Which Al will emerge the winner? Will it be the public Al? Or will it be the private Al?

✷✷

The public Al is a reluctant political prince of privilege, conditioned to react with impeccable proper political decorum, who can do no wrong in Washington, D.C. social circles. Born to the heady world of national politics, Al sees the Oval Office as his destiny.

To his everlasting chagrin, his Washington youth was woefully lacking in basic emotional development. His was a life of emotional abandonment by parents who were too successful and busy to attend to the nurturing side of parenthood. Like his running mate, Bill, Al Gore's childhood was hardly to be envied despite the part-time physical presence of his natural parents. Growing up in Washington's plushest hotel, life had all the impersonal, elitist, and stilted problems of being raised isolated from the "real world" that are associated with life among, say, the Saudi royal family (with none of its innate humanizing advantages). Unlike Arabian princes, young Al had no opportunity to round out his personality by raising unbridled hell and socializing with a horde of cousins and siblings. His play pals were chambermaids and bellhops.

Everything the public Al did, and does, conforms to what is expected of him, not to what he really wants. From his days at the trendy and elitist St. Alban's prep school, to his courtship and marriage to Tipper, to his law degree from his mother's alma mater, Vanderbilt Law School, to his political odyssey in the House of Representatives, the Senate, and the vice president's digs, every act and accomplishment has been dictated by his understanding of what best suits the public Al. Each was chosen at the expense of the private Al.

Private Al was raised by the Thompsons, a Tennessee sharecropper family, every moment that public Al was out of Washington. Some might call it "summer camp" therapy. Some might call it the plight of the spawn of Washington's political elite: eternally campaigning parents who ooze empathy for neglected voters, but have no time for their own neglected offspring.

William Thompson and his wife, Alota, were the devoted and loving parents Al desperately wants to be for his children. His farmstead days in a house with no indoor plumbing, central heat, or air-conditioning remind him of the familial warmth and security that was lacking at the Gore family suite in the Fairfax Hotel.

****

Private Al secretly wants nothing to do with politics. This aspect of his dual personality constantly tugs for his attention. That's why he often seems distracted. Throughout his life, private Al always took a backseat to public Al.

Private Al hated the Vietnam War. Public Al knew he had to enlist in the military to do his part, not for the war effort, but to help his father's reelection bid. (His dad lost and young Al found himself stuck in uniform.) It's the same line he uses when asked about his efforts on behalf of Bill Clinton: "I'll do whatever it takes to make Bill Clinton a successful president." He insists that he volunteered so no one in Carthage would have to serve in his place, a reflection of his desperate desire to be part of the Carthage crowd, a difficult fit for the *petit* prince. Whether he acknowledges it or not, his heart and dreams are still in the Thompsons' home.

Al Gore spent, and spends, his days as an envious Richie Rich, watching a gaggle of neighborhood urchins playing sandlot baseball, and wondering where he belongs, what he wants. His strong sense of inner guilt is based on his private longing for Carthage, and his public rejection of that life for "duty, honor, country, and Tipper." Sure, Al truly loves Tipper and is devoted to his children. Al Gore is a very decent person.

But the private Al loved a young Carthage girl from the moment his hormones hit at age thirteen throughout his high-school years. To his everlasting shame, he kept his two worlds completely apart, and opted to follow his public persona, rejecting his Carthage cutie, Donna Armistead, whom he never once invited to Washington, for the very socially acceptable Tipper.

If you look at his career as reflective of two Als, the flaws and vulnerability of Al Gore become apparent.

The critical moment for any baby boomer is the day he or she confronts the concept of mortality, something never truly part of the generation raised on a steady diet of "unlimited potential" fed by Drs. Benjamin Spock and Timothy Leary.

For Al Gore, his professional epiphany came during his ill-fated and halfhearted 1988 presidential bid when a Manhattanite flipped him a quarter and said, "Here, for your campaign." While a sympathetic but embarrassed press contingent tried not to notice, Gore flubbed the catch. The tinny coin skidded across the filthy New York concrete, and Al's fledgling presidential foray crashed and burned. It was his first professional failure. It was outsider Al having his face rubbed with rejection by the in-crowd, albeit a particularly cynical New York urban in-crowd that warms to only a select and bizarre few: Donald Trump, John Gotti, Howard Stern. Nice guy Al was a lamb among wolves.

On a more visceral and personal level, Al Gore tasted the real stuff of life and death, holding the crumpled and apparently lifeless body of his then six-year-old son, Albert, lying curbside after a Baltimore motorist knocked the boy some fifty feet after a pro-baseball game. Staring helplessly into his son's unfocused, open eyes, the private Al was introduced to what every generation knows, but can't describe to the next, until the newcomers themselves experience the loss, or near-loss, of a child. Fortunately, and thanks to the miracles of modern medicine, young Albert survived. Big Al's private self began to slip from its bonds. His Carthage self muscled aside the Washington Al.

Once his son was on the road to recovery, Al Gore stepped out of the political spotlight to scribble his environmental confessions, *Earth in the Balance*. The best seller is looked upon as public Al struggling to make peace with private Al. Public Al used the book to his advantage. It established him as the hero of the "green" generation and, among the uncritical, is one more example of his intellectual depth and ability to seize upon crucial issues. Students of ecology also see it as a measure of his intellectual depth. He has the words, but his scientific substance is the thickness of newsprint ink, literally. Commented on by a political philosopher specializing in the environment, "Strong on passion, short on science. No, make that no science."

In fact, his whole environmental persona is an intellectual attempt to emulate his surrogate father, William Thompson, and to get back to Carthage, his subliminal home. Public Al's lifeline winds around the Gore family, Washington, D.C., and politics. Private Al's world is made up of the Thompsons, Donna, Carthage, and a farmer's unique relationship to the soil. Private Al wants to be part of that Tennessee dirt. He wants to go home. Public Al translated that longing for a warm, loving hearth and home into "concern" for the more theoretical environment. The environment or, to be totally politically correct, the "ecosystem," is a substitute for "home," just as his liberal parents' concern for the underprivileged was a substitute for concern and love for their children. It's just that real kids sometimes get stinky and dirty, and keep busy parents up at night crying over nightmares, and constituents need tending for a few moments a day, and not only around elections.

What public Al and his horde of ecocrusaders forget is that farm people like the Thompsons, and tribal peoples throughout the world, have a tie with the earth that is quite different from the idealized theories of the so-called environmental movement. The former see value in the land, and the animals in nature. They use the land and wildlife to support and feed their families, and perpetuate their future. If they could make a profit and put a little something away for leaner days, all the better. Public Al and the environmentalists reject human "use" of the earth, or its animals. Instead of seeing man, the land, and critters as players in life's adventure, they hold mankind as nature's great despoiler. The earth and its resources must be kept separate from man, lest they fall victim to his plundering ways.

Given his eternal quest for a substitute family and his choice of "green" issues to let him act out his fantasies, Gore at the White House helm is the great white hope of animal separatist groups like People for the Ethical Treatment of Animals (PETA) to sign the federal decree declaring rats, cats, pigs, primates, and dogs deserving of rights equal to humans.

Al Gore means well. They just can't seem to make up their minds about what path to take, what decisions to make. Deep down, the real Al Gore wants to emerge and throw off the spiritual shackles of public life. He loves public service, but he just can't seem to decide how to be true to himself, and this conflict could be risky for the nation. Imagine, if you will, lying on an operating table awaiting the important event that will directly affect the quality, and the continuance, of your life. Midway through the operation, your surgeon stops. He puts down the scalpel and runs from the hospital. He's just discovered his true calling — to be a honky-tonk piano player in a New Orleans topless bar. Where does that leave you?

★★

What must he do? What does he want? He knows the answer. It is not the White House. That was Al Gore, Sr.'s dream. Al Jr. wants his own dream. What does that mean for voters?

Why would the nation entrust the highest political office in the land, and the fate of our future, to someone struggling with whether or not he will answer his internal call, bid adios to *Air Force One*, hop a train to Tennessee to teach grade chool, and pen insightful articles on public policy as a freelance country wit? If he left, who would finish the job? If he stayed, what kind of job would he do thinking of the life he'd rather lead back in Carthage?

☆ ☆ ☆ ☆ ☆ ☆ ☆ ☆

PHIL GRAMM

Momma's and Daddy's Boy, and Proud of It

TIRED OF PRESIDENTIAL WANNABES with good looks, who get along with the kids on their block? Phil Gramm may be your man. The senior United States senator from Texas wants to be twentieth century's last Republican president, which very possibly makes him the *only* Texan who ever wanted to be last in *anything*.

Tall and stoop-shouldered, with a balding head wreathed in thin white hair, he has a face that in profile bears an uncanny resemblance to a sea turtle. With a complexion so pale you want to send flowers to his next of kin. His blue-gray eyes squint through rimless bifocals that your grandfather stopped wearing before Richard Nixon's first inauguration. The man's countenance can turn charmingly Cheshire when he smiles. It's a somewhat startling event to witness in person, betraying the hint of an inner warmth that eludes the cool eye of the television camera.

On Inauguration Day, in January 1997, he'll be only fifty-four. He looks older. He talks with a Georgia-Texas drawl only a mother could love. His does. She was poor and a widow, but she taught him not to envy the rich — not to get mad *or* to get even, but to get *there*. She taught him that if he studied and worked hard, one day he could be rich, too. Taking all this to heart, Gramm went out and flunked three grades out of twelve. But Momma Gramm remained determined, and prodded him to go all the way to college. He got the hang of it, and finished with a Ph.D. in economics. He then set out to pass on his momma's teachings, first to students, and then to the whole nation (you know, using the bully pulpit and all that stuff). Meanwhile, Phil keeps chugging along, quoting his momma. A lot. Your typical momma's boy. But he also hears someone else's voice in his head, sees another teacher in the memory tunnel of his mind.

Gramm almost never mentioned him in speeches, but his father, a career Army staff sergeant, patiently took this boy, Phil, who would not learn to read, and patiently read *to* him, day after day. It was his father who put the time in with Phil on his homework. It was the old man who passed on to him such quaint concepts as *duty*, *honor* and *country*. His father died when Phil was fourteen. Young Gramm then worked in a peanut warehouse to help supplement his mother's meager income and to put himself through college.

"My interest in ideas and intellectual pursuits came from my father," Gramm says. "He ran away from home at fifteen, and joined the Army. He had no formal education. When I was two years old, he had a massive heart attack and became an invalid. I never knew him when he was well. But he read to me endless hours, kept me inside the house, reading aloud H. G. Wells' *Outline of History*, T. H. White's *Once and Future King*, and Eisenhower's *Crusade in Europe*, and books about the Civil War." Okay, so he's your typical daddy's boy, too.

Anyhow, he says, "To this day, if something is really good or bad, I want it read aloud."

But years later, when he arrived at Texas A&M to teach economics, the local boys' club football team had an unbroken record of defeats and needed a coach. Gramm, the newly minted professor, didn't know football from brain surgery. So he went out and read a lot of *books* about the game. Then he did something you would *not* expect him to do: he led Brian's Boys' Club to two championships out of the three seasons he coached. Sounds a bit much. But, hey, the football thing *is* documented.

So he coached a bunch of kids in the fine art of gridiron warfare for a brief spell? So what's his *real* claim to fame? Well, someone once said, "Phil Gramm is the smartest SOB in the Senate, and meaner than a junkyard dog." It may have been Gramm who said it. He does have the kind of "I don't need notes" intelligence that can rub his Senate playmates the wrong way. That may be putting it too strongly.

Senator John McCain of Arizona suggests that hating his guts may be more accurate. "Phil is smarter than most of his colleagues. Those who are smarter than he is on a controversial issue don't want to be the first to speak out on it. They hate him because he has the guts to speak out where they won't," says McCain. Only if he were national chairman of Gramm's Presidential nomination campaign would McCain get away with saying that. He is.

Actually, Gramm *has* a record of in-your-face legislative leadership to buttress his buddy McCain's claims. In fact, Gramm's combination of megahertz braininess, school learnin', and granite-jawed dismissiveness toward fads made him the first, lonely naysayer at one point during the Clinton administration. There was old stoop-shouldered Phil, seeming to stand athwart history, with palms perpendicular to the onrushing tide of change. He was saying an emphatic *no* to what the Democrats and the media were claiming. To what the pollsters and legislators in both parties were parroting. To their claim that a health-care crisis existed, and the public was demanding a total overhaul of the American health-care insurance system.

The mass hysteria had its origins in the appointment of a socialist-minded professor in Pennsylvania named Harris Wofford by Democratic Governor Bob Casey to finish out the term of the late, slightly less socialist-minded Republican Senator, John Heinz, in 1991. Wofford had to stand for election on his own in 1992, and made health-care reform his big issue. This was on the advice of James Carville, then regarded as a second-rate political consultant, who hadn't won half the races he'd managed. Carville nonetheless made the world believe his advice, that health care was the issue of the century, and taking guns away from Americans was the second issue of the century. Think again, James.

Carville had more than a little help in the way of ground-laying from the other side, from the GOSP (Grand Old Stupid Party). In a move of strategic brilliance matched only by his personal, unilateral choice of Dan Quayle as his running mate in 1988, then-President George Bush forced his liberal attorney general from Pennsylvania, Richard Thornburgh, to step down and run against Wofford. Then, only because Thornburgh, unwilling and unable to conceal his liberal

✶✶✶

inclination, ran one of the worst campaigns in modern history, rivaling in ineptitude George Bush's, and giving Pennsylvania voters no clear conservative-liberal choice, did Wofford win the election. With Clinton also making the "health-care crisis" the centerpiece of his campaign, it was easy and predictable that pack journalists, pack pollsters, and pack lawmakers would conclude, as they did, that Wofford and Clinton won on health care, that the system was in crisis, and that something had to be done. Ergo, the Republicans had better climb aboard or the train to socialized medicine would leave the stations without them.

From Senate Republican Leader Bob Dole to House leaders Bob Michel and Newt Gingrich, every GOP lawmaker was scared silly to appear "insensitive" to the public's supposed unhappiness with health care access and affordability.

Lawmakers in both parties competed with President Clinton to come up with schemes to radically change the system by having the federal government force every American to buy health-care insurance and by having the government play a dominant role in other ways. In a strategy session in the office of Bob Dole, the Senate minority leader, Republican pollsters warned that it would be suicidal for Republicans to oppose Clinton-style health-care reform. Dole, hedging his bets, lent his name to several bills to revamp the health-care insurance and delivery system. Only Phil Gramm, the Senate Republicans' "Mr. Guts," said the whole thing was nonsense, the American health-care system is the world's best, most Americans know that and don't want it turned upside down to resemble socialized health care in other countries. He introduced a plan that was way to the right of the more than half dozen other plans put forward by various Democrats and Republicans. Gramm's plan forced very little on health-care consumers and providers, proposing instead to tamper with the system only at the margins, where there was public consensus that improvements were needed.

When Gramm drawled in that Georgia-Texas accent that Clinton's health-care plan would pass only "over my cold dead political body," he made himself the defender of America's common-sense traditions as well as the hero of common-sense conservatives in his party.

Republican pundits took heart and followed his lead, as did GOP poll-sters. Emboldened by Gramm's stubborn resistance to the latest ideo-logical hysteria, they began pushing the data in their polling that had always showed, on close inspection, that Americans were quite *happy* with their own health insurance, and with the American health-care system period.

His Senate Republican colleagues saw the light and came over to his side. For this, of course, they never forgave him. Nonetheless, Gramm led the way to eventually sinking Clinton's health-care ship with nary a cry of remorse from the electorate that was supposed to love the idea of Clinton-style health-care reform more than life itself, or something like that.

"Even though Gramm did not sit on any of the relevant health committees in the Senate, he set out to be the conservative leader on health care. It showed his force of personality," says political consul-tant and Dole ally David A. Keene. "Clearly Gramm took a smart political role for a presidential bid in 1996."

So if Gramm's so smart and such a hotshot political leader, why isn't he riveting you with his rhetoric, or mesmerizing you with the magic of his metaphors? A flip answer might be: Like George Bush, you mean? Actually, Bush *is* a good answer. He showed beyond a doubt that you don't have to be a great orator, or even a good public speaker, to be president. As for Gramm, he can on occasion give audi-ences a good emotional and intellectual ride. And there are eyewit-nesses that say, on occasion, after hitting his stride, he becomes so humorous the audience actually cries laughing. But his delivery is uneven and unpredictable from one speech to the next, and he is at times capable of making listeners see *him* as "deader than Elvis" to coin the phrase Gramm used when referring to Clinton's health-care plan. Gramm's prime-time speech at the Bush renominating conven-tion in Houston in 1992 was not, he readily admitted afterward, his finest hour. "My timing was a half-beat off," he confided. Got *that* right, Phil.

But, hey, speechifying consistency is the hobgoblin of foolish minds. Just as Gramm was the secret heartthrob of religious conserva-tive leaders and secular conservative activists going into the 1996 presidential campaigns, as was Jack Kemp their great hope eight years before. Gramm studied the Kemp fiasco and knew the whys behind it. Kemp had it all, or so it seemed. He was handsome, athletic, and a former congressman who authored the 30 percent, three-year Kemp-Roth personal and corporate income tax-rate, a cut that became the centerpiece of the first Reagan administration. He could nail an audience, have it hanging on every word and bring it to its feet, cheering and ready to follow him to the ends of the earth — but not, as it turned out, to Iowa. Kemp could also leave an audience disappointed and confused as to what he was trying to tell them, and why. Kemp can intrigue an audience for thirty minutes and after that put them to sleep. A Gramm speech at its worst bores you only sporadically, but you still come away charged up.

The question for now and the future is whether Gramm will have any more staying power than Kemp. Two years into the Clinton administration, three names topped virtually every political professional's list of the top three contenders for the 1996 Republican presidential nomination: Bob Dole, Gramm, and Kemp. But Kemp glanced up in time to wave goodbye to his Party as it shot past, well to his right on social issues like immigration, welfare, illegitimacy, and even on cutting spending and balancing the budget. Bingo! The light bulb went on — or off, in this case. Seeing that he wouldn't get the financial or popular support required, Kemp quit the race before the first declared candidacy was announced in 1995, thus saving himself a repeat of 1988.

If Gramm meets Kemp's 1988 fate (Kemp's 1988 nomination campaign had a soft landing after Super Tuesday, because it had never really gotten off the ground), it won't be because of shared errors. Kemp's "progressive conservative" line confused conservatives, failed to attract progressives, and made potential donors increasingly skeptical, leaving Kemp with the not-so-ironic fate of having to run a campaign based wholly on deficit spending (he abhorred taxes far more than spending and deficits, while Gramm's abhorrence is equal for all three).

Gramm, by contrast, has shown he can raise money like almost no one else, save for Bob Dole. Gramm raised more money in the first

****

three months of his campaign than any other Republican nomination contender, including Dole. Gramm's message, unlike Kemp's, never left any doubt as to his aspirations to progressive conservatism: he had none. Gramm is clear, consistent, and traditionally conservative on crime, spending, taxes, deficits, immigration, welfare, health care, free trade, and foreign intervention. He opposes abortion. But he is also enough of a libertarian-leaning skeptic about giving the government much power to do anything that he tends not to preach on the subject, or on the array of issues that have to do with "moral values" and "cultural wars."

His problem is a certain arrogance of place. His mother and father taught him not to try to be someone he's not, and that persons who try to portray themselves as someone else soon will be found out. Gramm is a no-nonsense economic conservative and not a cultural warrior. Never was. It's not his place. Not comfortable for him. Right up to the eve of his launching his nomination campaign, he insisted that people in the end vote their pocketbooks, and that he could win nomination just fine by sticking to the twin themes of peace and prosperity and, maybe just two or three social issues. One is crime, on which no one in his party is tougher. The other is welfare reform. Conservatives thrill to hear him divide the world into "those who ride in the wagon and those who pull the wagon," and how important it is to enact policies that get the people who are riding in the wagon out of it so they can "help the rest of us pull the wagon." Then he decided he could risk speaking his mind on affirmative action. "If by affirmative action you mean making sure people get a chance, I'm for it," he said before the 1996 nomination race started. "But I am against quotas, preferences, and set-asides. And if I become president, they're through."

Three month's into his campaign Gramm looked up to see first Dole, Buchanan, Lamar Alexander and, a little later, California Governor Pete Wilson either catch up with him, or pass him to the right, on social issues. Dole hurts him the most and quickest. Years before, Gramm had won over key Religious Right leaders. They concluded that although he wasn't about to thump any Bibles on behalf of moral-values issues or abortion, he basically was with them. He was sound on economic issues, was smarter than any other politician in the Republi-

✳✳✳

can Party, proved he could raise big money, and was therefore the man most likely to succeed.

Then Dole launched his campaign by attacking Hollywood producers, screenwriters, and the TV industry for purveying gratuitous sex and violence, and contributing to the moral decay of the culture.

This surprised Gramm, who had the distinct impression that Dole thought family values mainly referred to a husband and wife's investment portfolio.

Now the leaders of the Religious Right get on Gramm's back to do more on their issues. Get out front more on abortion, Phil. Promise a constitutional amendment banning it. Talk about the "unborn child." Go after filth and violence in the mass media, they tell him. This gets Gramm's back up. Florence Gramm didn't raise her son to take this guff from anyone. Finally, he tells one important chieftain in the family-values movement to go pound the Bible. "You're the preacher, not me," Gramm says.

Not a smart move. Gramm knows it. Gramm also knows he is uncomfortable promising the voters something he knows he can't deliver. A year ago, he was farther ahead of where the conservative Christian leadership is today on abortion. He was actually sponsoring a prolife amendment in Congress. But when it became clear that it was not remotely winnable, he went for abortion issues that will make the prolife movement bleed to death: parental notification and consent and state-set limits, no federal funding of abortion or of abortion organizations, like Planned Parenthood, and outlawing abortions for sex selection (such abortions are done primarily to eliminate female embryos). Gramm knows as President he can keep those promises.

He reminded them of this, and eventually made peace with all but the most intransigent of its leaders. He also made a series of speeches that reaffirmed his moral opposition to abortion and recognition that moral decay is a reality.

But Gramm, still a momma's boy, stays true to her faith in him, and therefore to himself and his beliefs. He focuses his speeches on the cause of the moral problems. The cause has to be something he understands and is comfortable with. What about economics? Boring! This is something Gramm can get into, and does. For too many in

✶✶

America, he opines, the welfare state's safety net has become a hammock. Welfare spawns illegitimacy, which gives birth to generations of persons born with no moral compass. It works for Gramm. Nobody on the Right disputes what he's saying, though some may wish he would go farther and say more on the subject of moral values.

Why doesn't he? He pleads "momma" the way some persons plead "the Fifth." Ask him what he thinks about violence and explicit sex not needed to advance the plot of TV dramas, or about seductively posed, half-naked teenagers selling blue jeans or soda pop in magazine ads, and he'll tell you what his mother thinks. Yes, these are examples of declining cultural standards and issues that people care about, he says. "But let me give you the example of my mother. She calls me up and says, 'Phil, I want you to get this sex off television. I watch my soap operas, and they're either getting into bed or getting out of bed.' And so I go see her, and one o'clock comes and she turns on the television. And so I say, 'Mother, if you think this stuff ought to be off television, why the hell do you watch it? Why don't you cut it off?' And she says, '*Shish*! I'm watching.'"

For the "smartest SOB in the Senate," he doesn't get his own anecdote about his momma's hushing him up in front of the TV. It doesn't illustrate what he thinks it does — that people say they deplore sex and violence but given a chance to watch it they will, and it should be their choice in any case.

It's not that Phil Gramm is too dumb to get it. He does. Or that he's too dense to have a reasonable solution. He does. It's the apparent absence of personal, moral outrage that disappoints. Gramm says, simply and coolly, that the way to deal with the problem is to "promote an environment in which advertisers will not pay to have their names associated with these programs. Ultimately, that's the solution. Like most conservatives, I'm very reluctant to put censors to work. On the other hand, the ultimate thing in society is how people feel about things and how they react to them. I encourage people who write to me about programs they don't think ought to be on television, to also write to people who paid to put the show on TV and tell them, I'm not going to buy your product."

Put the question to him directly: Would you use the bully pulpit of

the presidency to indicate your displeasure with the excesses of violence and sex in the popular media? "In extreme cases, I would," he
says. "I certainly would not do it for programs I had not watched. I
think you have to be very careful."

It's not exactly the answer of a man personally and deeply offended
by the excesses of his culture.

Gramm's reluctance to get out there and preach what religious
leaders and social conservatives believe, he thinks, may have to do
with another maxim: Don't practice hypocrisy and certainly don't get
caught at it, especially if you're going to be the goal-oriented boy your
momma and papa raised you to be.

Senator McCain of Arizona, who you'll remember is Gramm's
national campaign chairman, says most of the other fellas in the Senate don't see anything "warm and fuzzy" about Gramm, but they
admire him for other things. Although it's true that when in Gramm's
presence, colleagues feel as if someone has left the refrigerator door
open, Gramm also can give the opposite impression. He can actually
exude a personal warmth. This comes mainly through eyes that turn a
brilliant blue and dance about as if in utter elation at the pleasure of
making your acquaintance.

There is, I guess you would say, a certain diligence about this warmth
some detect in the senior senator from Texas, especially around Christmas. That's when he really opens up his big old heart to his fellow
Republican activists and state party officials in key Presidential primary
states around the country. Why, he sends every dang one of them Christmas cards, and does it in a way that assures the greeting outlasts the season — lasts, in fact, through the next year's presidential primaries.

Is Gramm embarrassed that he has so much Christmas spirit that
he left the impression with many state-party-convention delegates in
Louisiana and elsewhere that he had addressed a card to the home of
every elected Republican and every party official in a state, with a second card to the official's office, a third to the official's spouse at her
office, and a fourth addressed to the husband and wife? Of course not,
especially since the recipients see nothing cynical about it, and express
apparently honest admiration that Gramm and his organization are
so, well, diligent.

****

These delegates see him as this big-deal U.S. senator whom they've seen hundreds of times on network television but who, when he addresses their state party convention, typically comes a day early. He takes the time to sit down with some of them, one-on-one, offering advice if they're running for even the smallest elective office, and generally being so personable and attentive that when he takes his leave, his conversant is ready to walk through fire for the senator from Texas. This is no small thing, since it is just such activists and officials who vote their presidential nomination preference in straw polls at state party conventions well before the first real caucus or state primary election is held.

Christmas cards aside, Gramm's warmth comes across in his humor. If you do a critical story about Gramm, and you may hear from him directly: "Raaf," he drawls into the telephone, "I jus' wanna thawnk you for the rotten story you published about me in today's paper." He laughs, you laugh, then he gets to his real point, a list of five good reasons why he, and not Pat Buchanan, is "the real conservative in this race."

If the critical story had been written about Dole, Dole would instantly break diplomatic relations with you, and two years could pass before Dole decided to end the latest private cold war. When Dole's perceived enemy is a public figure, Dole will use the velociraptor claws of his wit to draw blood from the unfortunate creature — and win a sound bite on network television as a bonus.

Gramm rarely uses his humor to maim, except in the heat of battle. The type of battle where you go for the biggest enchilada, where a guy like Buchanan, a mere scribe and TV pundit who knows less about economics than Gramm knows about brain surgery, is actually pulling ahead of him in the polls. When Buchanan challenged Gramm to a debate on an economic policy issue, Gramm shot back, "I never duel with an unarmed man."

More typically, Gramm pulls the trigger on his wit not principally to entertain or to trash opponents, but to help drive home a policy or ideological point, and always at the same time slyly conveying the idea that when God was passing out good looks, Gramm was over getting a second helping of brains. "I'm not just another pretty face," he tells his audience, breaking out into a jack-o'-lantern grin only a mother could love. *His does.* Before declaring officially for the Republican nomination in February 1995, Gramm was promising audiences that he would provide incentives for people to work, save, and invest. "And Bill Clinton will say, my God, if people work, save, and invest, rich people will benefit," Gramm said. "And I'm going to say, great — I've had many jobs, but no poor person has ever hired me."

His presidential nomination campaign motto, "I was conservative before conservative was cool," always gets a laugh. Its real purpose is to send a reminder to GOP primary voters in search of an electible Republican who deals honestly in the currency of conservatism. Gramm's subtle reminder: A lot of three dollar bills are floating around, one of them bearing Bob Dole's picture. Imagine Gramm suggesting that Bob Dole was a Johnny-come-lately to the positions Gramm had staked out for years. Imagine Gramm suggesting that Dole's commitment to conservative positions would last only so long as it was needed to get him the nomination. Better still, imagine Gramm not suggesting that.

Gramm even tells a joke tailor-made to establish his seniority in conservatism's one big happy family. During Jimmy Carter's administration, Gramm, then a Democrat and an economics professor at Texas A&M, testified before House and Senate committees on the national hysteria of the time: the Energy Crisis. Democrats thundered that Americans were about to freeze in the dark because they were greedy about fossil fuels. Those who passed for Republicans and conservatives at the time said, "Sounds right to us, Massahs." Both sides agreed the government would have to do something drastic and, of course, very expensive.

Gramm learned from his experience what the real problem with Washington was. He said the "energy crisis" was like a piece of paper that had been blown about, affixed itself to the top of the Capitol, and blotted out the sun. The liberals' solution was to create an agency, hire a bureaucracy, and spend $60 billion to create an artificial sun. The conservatives' alternative was to build the artificial sun, but contract out the job to private industry, doing it for "only" $50. Nobody in Washington thought to simply reach up and tear the piece of paper off the Capitol dome.

****

To Gramm, silly bureaucratic solutions to unreal problems have been the basis of the political debate for the past forty years in Washington. He made fun of the liberal-dominated Democratic Party's arguing that the federal government should spend tax dollars to solve every problem, and of the centrist-dominated Republican Party's countering with a kind penny-pinching me-too-ism.

Conservative activists who were growing in strength outside the Washington Beltway were starving to hear a federal lawmaker say aloud that most problems are imagined. Gramm got such conservatives where they live, when he agreed with most free-market economists that there never was an energy crisis, only a distribution problem created by regulations imposed by the Nixon and Ford administrations. Gramm began emerging as a genuine article among conservatives in search of heroes when he began saying that the few real problems that exist are probably created by government interference in the first place. And, in any case, government-imposed solutions can be counted on to make the problem worse and/or to create new problems, at a huge cost to the taxpayers.

Okay, so maybe Gramm truly was for limiting government in a serious way before doing so was the *in* thing.

He uses his mother, a retired nurse in her eighties, as a political touchstone, which is touching at times, not to mention useful. He recalls that when he was a little boy, his mother, a poor widow struggling to make ends meet, took him to school every day. When they would pass the elegant home of a rich person on the way, she would reveal not even a hint of bitterness or envy. Instead, she would say, "If you get your education and work hard, you will live in a house like this someday."

Is he pulling your *leg* or what? Doesn't matter. It reveals something about him, because he thinks it resonates with most Americans. In his world view, they don't want to tax away the wealth of the rich; they want to join the ranks of the rich, instead, and as Americans, they believe they have a chance of doing so.

One of Gramm's greatest appeals to activists in his party who are always searching for the real McCoy is that he doesn't suffer gladly the misguided compassion and soft-headedness in general that so often comes from fellow Republicans or self-proclaimed conservatives. "Progressive conservatives" in his party, for example, long have pushed "enterprise zones" as a panacea for ills of the inner city. The idea is that if given sufficient federal tax incentives, new entrepreneurs will spring up in the crime-ridden urban ghettoes, where suburban businesses also will relocate. Thus, jobs will be created at the doorsteps of people who won't board a bus or subway to take jobs in the suburbs.

Gramm wonders why taxpayers should subsidize businesses to bring jobs to the ghetto or relocate the jobless, to bring jobs to some people when countless foreigners hungry for work and often not knowing a word of English will sail across an ocean and maybe travel over land another 1,000 miles because they heard a job may be available somewhere in the United States.

He says where he splits with enterprise zonistas is his belief that the people who pull the wagon left the inner city for reasons that had less to do with taxes and more to do with the failures of city government. "They left because the government did not provide law enforcement, public education, or even pick up the garbage. The idea that you are going to have a little tax incentive and overcome all that is laughable." He's probably right about that. But, the fact that he has to set some fellow Republicans straight on the matter is something else.

It's that sort of brutal common sense that makes so many conservatives want to hug Big Phil. Don't, however, try this at home — yours or his. He's simply not huggable. In any case, Gramm also has no illusions about why so many inner cities are populated by so many persons who don't work and either live on government handouts or on the proceeds of crime, or both.

But even "Phil the Hun" can sound a bit soft-hearted toward the wagon-riders. "We are partly responsible because we set up a welfare and entitlements system that has seduced those people," Gramm says. Still, he doesn't buy the claim that there are three generations of welfare recipients because, try as they might, they just couldn't find a single job, which the welfare industry gives as the problem. "We not only need a strong economy to ensure there are jobs out there, but we have to nudge them out of the wagon to get out there and help us pull.

Welfare reform is the way to do that." Statements like this provide a clue as to why Gramm is a favorite pinup of the liberals.

Gramm gets the wingers in his party smiling and humming when he says flatly that no amount of tax, or any other incentive, will draw business to the worst neighborhoods until they're made safe from violent crime.

And what conservative could fail to open up his heart to a man who says the growth of volent crime is the direct result not of a lack of compassion but too much of it, and almost all of it misplaced? Instead of air-conditioned cells, television, workout rooms, and far better health-care facilities than many honest, hardworking Americans have access to, Gramm wants prisons to be places where inmates work all day to pay for their keep, study for two hours nightly to improve their literacy, and live no better than Americans serving their country on submarines in the United States Navy.

Now add the story of Wendy Lee Gramm, Phil's second wife. (Gramm was divorced when he and Wendy met and fell in love while both were teaching economics at Texas A&M University.) Wendy Lee Gramm, a small, slim woman who has a Ph.D. in economics, two grown sons, a ready smile, and a love for roller-blading.

Phil Gramm's life demonstrates that you can achieve your dreams in America if you are not a quitter, even after flunking three grades. Wendy Lee Gramm's life demonstrates something else that the Gramm's regard as quintessential about America: that the descendant of poor Korean immigrants may become the First Lady of the United States. Gramm loves to tell her story. Wendy's grandfather left Korea to come to America as the indentured servant of a major sugarcane company in the then-American territory of Hawaii. He agreed to work for five more years in exchange for the company's bringing over from Korea a bride he had picked out of a picture book provided by the company. So far so good.

The grandfather spent years at hard labor in the sugarcane fields, and sacrificed so his son could go to college and become a success. The son, Wendy Lee's father, was so successful, in fact, that he eventually became the vice president of the same company that had employed his father, an indentured servant. A true story. Okay. Here's

****

where it sounds like the plot writer let his imagination go hog wild. President Reagan appoints Wendy Lee Gramm to head the Commodities Futures Exchange Commission. The granddaughter of indentured servants now has control and oversight over the whole sugarcane industry in America, including cane fields where her grandfather and grandmother labored so that their children and grandchildren would one day be successful and admired Americans.

So the Gramms are your top-of-the-line model American opportunity maximizers. But is the timing of the 1996 presidential nomination ride good for the Gramms? Couldn't be better. Their two sons, Marshall and Jeff, are in college, the elder studying economics.

And what about weaknesses? Every presidential candidate *has* to have one. That's what makes him look *human*. Gramm's greatest weakness? "Phil's zeal to achieve a goal sometimes bruises others," says Senator McCain. "But I view that as a strength," he adds. Imagine his campaign chairman saying that he sees that as a strength. Better still, imagine him not saying it.

If Phil is a bruiser in the Senate, he must be Mr. Mush at home, to balance things out and show he's a wonderful guy overall, right? Not exactly. If pushed for a softening insight about Phil, Wendy will say her husband actually *has* gotten emotional over family things "*at times.*" Like, what times? Well, she remembers the time he got "teary eyed" when he took his eldest son to first grade.

Why isn't Phil the Bruiser a Vietnam vet? College deferments. But, hey, everybody was doing it back then. Unlike Bill Clinton the student-deferred Gramm didn't oppose the war or demonstrate against it either.

Still, there are other things for which Gramm must answer. Like, if he is so conservative, why has he tried to federalize crime on everything from compulsory sentences for gun crimes, to forcing states to lock up felons for most of their sentences?

His response: "If we get provisions to put people in prison for gun crimes, states will adopt those provisions. [And] if we are going to give states money to build prisons, shouldn't we give money to states that have truth in sentencing?"

Yet conservatives may ask, why give federal tax dollars for states to build prisons in the first place? Gramm thinks that if the states don't want to stop building prisons like Holiday Inns, "they ought not to expect our help." Okay, now the Big One. How can Gramm claim to be a "real" conservative when he helped broker the 1990 budget-agreement-tax increase, first urging fellow Republicans to support it, but then opposing it? Simple. President Bush, his commander in chief, asked him to be part of a team to represent Republicans in dealing with the Democrats on the deficit. So what was Gramm to do? Say no to his commander in chief?

"I was asked by the President [George Bush] to be part of a team to represent Republicans in dealing with Democrats on the deficit," says the man who would be president and who had flunked three different grades before going on to college to win a Ph.D.

Gramm thinks the final test of his ideological soundness is that ultimately he voted no on the 1990 compromise. "I didn't go out to announce it all over the country because I had sat in on the negotiations, and in the end I couldn't support it, so I didn't think that was appropriate," he says. Not bad footwork for a guy that flunked three grades.

All right, let's try this one: Why did his health-care bill in 1994 propose compulsory coverage, threatening citizens with tax penalties if they didn't buy coverage? Hey, this is a no-brainer for Gramm. Only one thing in his bill "in any way could be called compulsory. If you were financially capable, with an income of 200 percent of poverty or more, [but] didn't buy at least a catastrophic policy, and later got sick, we were going to have the right to take your assets to pay the money back."

Compulsory is not compulsory when, in Gramm's view, it means the government won't let you get away with sticking the taxpayers with your hospital bills because you refused to take out insurance in the first place. Here Gramm comes down on the side of practical, common-sense fairness over strict adherence to the principle of individual freedom over government coercion. But, then, isn't excessive ideological consistency the hobgoblin of guys who would rather be right than president?

Gramm has been getting up every morning since he came to Congress and asking himself what he could do today to advance the cause of Gramm for President. A man *should* know where he wants to go, and how he's going to get there.

★★

So when McCain said Gramm's colleagues "may hate him" but they "pay attention to what he says," the Arizona senator may have understated the case for Gramm. The fact is, Gramm's colleagues have done more than just pay attention. They twice elected him to lead their most cherished institution, the National Republican Senatorial Committee, the mission of which is to help get them reelected through raising vast sums of money from the party faithful around the country.

Gramm wanted the NRSC chairmanship because he wanted to do well for himself by doing good for others. He wanted to be the one to preside over the NRSC in the last election cycle before the presidential elections. Every GOP senator whom he, and his fund-raising skills, helped reelect or elect for the first time in 1994 would owe him going into the 1996 presidential nomination race. Therefore, might be more successfully courted and persuaded to enlist his own state organization behind Gramm's nomination bid.

Senator Thad Cochran of Mississippi, the courtly chairman of the Senate Republican Conference, says, "Phil was reelected [in 1991] by a close margin because some people felt he was more concerned about getting elected president than in reelecting Republicans to the Senate." Southern honesty compels Cochran to add something that comes back to one of Gramm's strengths: "Phil is the first senator to be reelected chairman of the campaign committee, probably the most selfish vote Senate Republicans make collectively, because they rely on him to get them reelected."

Gramm's candidate recruitment and money-raising skills in his second two-year term as National Republican Senatorial Committee chairman helped the Grand Old Party recapture the Senate in 1994, ending eight years of minority status that had begun in the middle of Ronald Reagan's second administration. Gramm showed he could turn the committee into something more than an Incumbents' Beneficial Society.

The question is whether he will turn his own ambition into something more than being the smartest junkyard dog in the Senate. If you have to guess *his* answer, you're probably one of the poor wretches he has in mind when he says he won't duel with unarmed men."

★ ★ ★ ★ ★ ★ ★ ★ ★

KAY BAILEY HUTCHISON
Iron Lady, American Style?

KAY BAILEY HUTCHISON KNOWS that Republicans would give their eyeteeth for a woman to be their presidential nominee, or at least hold the number-two spot on the ticket. This is very exciting to her, since she is (1) a woman, (2) a Republican, and (3) available for higher office. She has hopes because she knows Republicans, despite much evidence to the contrary, can be rational human beings. They actually have, for instance, two politically *practical* reasons for wanting a female leader: (1) women are more than half the electorate; and (2) Democrats enjoyed an edge with women voters in recent years.

Hutchison, the junior United States senator from Texas, also knows her fellow Republicans, or at least the majority of them, aren't interested in trading their eyeteeth for just any Republican woman. To be the GOP presidential or vice presidential candidate, a female will have to fit two criteria. One is that she has to be a genuine, dyed-in-the-brain-cells conservative, a Margaret Thatcher with, say, a Texas accent. Calm *down*, Kay.

The other criterion is that the woman in question, must have widespread, proven voter appeal. In other words, she has to show evidence that she can beat any man, woman, or alien-planet entity the Democrats put up.

By the time she got to the United States Senate, Hutchison, who will be fifty-three on Presidential Inauguration Day 1997, already had accumulated a lifetime's experience in enough fields to qualify for just about anything she wanted to do in politics. She was a television reporter, a two-term member of the Texas legislature, acting chairman of the National Transportation Safety Board, a private sector lawyer and owner of McCraw Candies, a peanut brittle concern. She was also the treasurer of the state of Texas, a statewide elected office. Her father was a real estate developer.

Hutchison was something of a feminist. As the first Republican woman elected to the state House in the early 1970s, she pushed bills to make it easier for women to prove their claims of rape and cosponsored a bill to make it easier for women to establish credit.

Her record was not exactly what you would call rigidly orthodox or predictable or ideologically definable. As a state House member, she favored silent prayer in school, term limits on the governor, and restoration of the death penalty. She voted against limiting campaign spending, experimental community-based prisons, and voted for the abolition of the state property tax. But pro-life activists see her as having backed away from what initially was a pro-life stand. In the state legislature, she took an ambiguous position on the use of Medicaid funds for abortions for poor women, and clearly opposed abortion rights generally. She voted to make twenty-one the minimum age for abortion without parental consent.

Hutchison then began to move toward the pro-choice end of the spectrum. She said in her 1982 congressional race that she would support an antiabortion amendment to the Constitution, provided it made exceptions for rape, incest, and saving the life of the mother. But in running for the United States Senate, she switched to a basic pro-choice position, qualified by restrictions such as a mandatory twenty-four-hour waiting period and notification by a minor of at least one parent before an abortion.

Hutchison has her own version of Denis Thatcher as a mate. He is former lawmaker Ray Hutchison, a certified nice guy who made a stab at being elected governor in 1978 and missed. She became legal counsel to Republic Bank and decided to run for Congress but lost her primary bid.

In the Senate, she has not exactly been the ideological twin of Phil Gramm. Conservative on taxes and spending, she nonetheless joined a group of liberal Republicans who often provided the swing votes on legislation and nominations that President Clinton and the congressional Democrats favored.

She voted to confirm two Clinton nominees opposed by conservatives: Sheldon Hackney as head of the National Endowment for the Humanities and Thomas Payzant as assistant secretary for elementary and secondary education. She switched her vote to block renewal of a congressional patent of an insignia that incorporated the Confederate flag. She also broke with Gramm to support Clinton's national service plan that used taxpayers' money to pay college tuition in return for several years in "community service." She supported a Treasury appropriations bill that permitted federal workers to use taxpayer money to pay for abortions. But she did join Gramm in voting for a Republican amendment that would have forced workers to pay special premiums for abortion coverage.

She said she voted to confirm Hackney and Payzant because the president is entitled to appoint ideological soulmates, so long as they are not criminally incompetent. Conservatives maintained they were worse. Hackney, former president of the University of Pennsylvania, had a history of enforcing political correctness on campus. As for Payzant, as San Diego school superintendent he had banned the Boy Scouts' in-school programs because the Scouts just say no to homosexuals who want to be scoutmasters. Payzant had argued that the San Diego school board had a nondiscrimination policy on sexual orientation.

Hutchison switched from supporting the DAR's patent renewal after Senator Carol Moseley-Braun, a Left Wing Democrat from Illinois, said, in effect, that anyone who tolerated the display of the Confederate flag is a racist who condones slavery. "I just came down on the side of making a statement that we would not in any way sanction something so offensive as slavery," Hutchison said afterward.

Hutchison said she voted for the bill that lifted the decade-long ban on federal employees' health-care policies covering abortion because it contained funds for fighting drugs in Texas and contained spending cuts.

Hutchison endorsed and actively campaigned for Phil Gramm in the Republican presidential nomination race. But when Gramm was

attempting to use welfare reform to show that he is the real conservative in the GOP presidential nomination contest and Senate Majority
Leader Bob Dole is not. Hutchison kept trying to move the focus to
her argument for "equitable" funding levels of bloc grants to the states
so that those with growing welfare burdens, like Texas, would not be
underfinanced by federal taxpayers. Conservative supporters of
Gramm in Texas were not amused by Hutchison's "tin ear" on the
welfare issue as it related to presidential nomination politics. But
Hutchison had an eye on her own future standing with her constituents.

On the other hand, Hutchison supported a measure to place financial responsibility for the legal immigrant on the relative who spon-
sored the person coming into the country. And on affirmative action,
Hutchison was saying in August 1995 that Congress needed "to continue to look at the positive aspects of affirmative action. Doing away
with the goals of affirmative action would be wrong. But the goals
should help the general population and be aimed at those economi-
cally deprived and those who are discriminated against. We can fine-
tune affirmative action without killing it."

She and Gramm have differed on a few other bills. She wanted to
continue funding for the National Endowment for the Arts, even though
she was critical of some of its lapses in underwriting tastelessness and
Left Wing propaganda. She also supported an amendment to the campaign reform bill that would have limited individual contributors to $500
per election. Hutchison voted for the amendment, which was defeated
with the help of Gramm and a bipartisan coalition of senators.

She withstood some nasty artillery fire from the Clinton administration an the Democratic National Committee in her 1993 special election bid to wrest the U.S. Senate seat from Democrat Bob Krueger.
Krueger had barely had time to warm the seat after Governor Ann
Richards, a liberal Democrat, had appointed him to fill it temporarily,
after President Clinton had tapped its former occupant, Lloyd Bentsen,
for what turned out to be a brief stint as treasury secretary.

Bill Clinton, fresh from his come-from-behind victory over
George Bush, dispatched his bright and brash campaign strategists to
spank the GOP's upstart women candidates. Paul Begala headed to his

native Texas to craft Krueger's campaign. James Carville went north to New Jersey to help Governor Jim Florio snuff out Christie Whitman's challenge that would not reach the polls until the following year.

The Texas showdown, however, was the proving ground for Clinton's campaign issue arsenal. Under Begala's command, Hutchison would face the pro-choice/pro-life challenge, an issue that held the potential to divide Republicans, especially pro-life and pro-choice GOP women. George Bush's nemesis, fellow Texan Ross Perot, was a complicating factor. If she pandered to Perot, how strong would she look to Texas voters? Finally, she faced responding to the Clinton agenda and its hot issue of the day, health-care reform.

Begala looked forward to putting her through a meat grinder of his own manufacture. The Clinton administration, which Begala and his partner, Carville, worked so hard to make possible, would not be denied. After Hutchison and Whitman fell, the rest of the country's political landscape was virtually the Clintonistas' for the taking. Problem was, they underestimated Senator Hutchison.

The bloodbath expected to develop during the primaries between the rabidly pro-life contenders, Jack Fields and Joe Barton, on the one hand and Hutchison on the other, well, never happened. Compared with Jack Fields, Kay Hutchison was pro-choice. Compared with Bob Krueger, she was pro-life all the way. Kay Bailey diffused the family issue by vowing not to let the federal government dictate abortion law policy to the states and proposed a $1,000 per child tax credit to emphasize the importance of the family.

She never once courted Perot's support. Instead, she campaigned unequivocally against taxes and spending and for term limits, a balanced budget, the line-item veto, and elimination of congressional perks. These may be morally and philosophically and ideologically and theologically sound positions that any right-minded person who expects to go to heaven or at least avoid hell should adopt. They also had another virtue. Each item was warmly embraced by the good folks in Perot's United We Stand America. Her straightforward campaign style left little room for Perot to pontificate. Four days before the election, he acknowledged that 84 percent of his supporters were in the Hutchison camp.

When Begala worked with Krueger to launch the health-care missile, Kay Bailey stood her ground and announced that on health care, she wanted to "empower the people" while Krueger wanted to "empower big government," a trajectory she claimed would lead to health-care shortages.

Hutchison beat Krueger 68 to 32 percent. Crucial to her victory were Pat Robertson's Christian Coalition and its national executive director, Ralph Reed. Reed made a strategic decision to help candidates that the coalition could live with rather than only candidates that were practically one with the coalition on all major and not so major policy positions. The coalition thus would be able to expand its appeal and power within the GOP coalition, where it is already the single most powerful force. In Texas, the coalition is the major power within the GOP and it actively helped Hutchison win election to the Senate. The other factor helping her, in this case indirectly, was the powerful National Right to Life Committee, which chose not to use its formidable organizational clout and membership to oppose her at the polls.

If you want to talk historical importance, the stuff that gets recorded in the *Great Ledger of Political History*, however, it's the Christian Coalition's decision to say a prayer and pass the ammunition on her behalf. That decision represented one of the coalition's first major exercises in electoral compromise with a national focus. The coalition went out on a bit of a limb with its own supporters by electing to put its considerable energy and its legions of hard working, self-sacrificing members and friends to work on behalf of someone who does not vote 100 percent with the religious conservatives' agenda but is conservative enough and reliable enough to be worth supporting. The coalition did the same thing in supporting the election of Paul Coverdell to the Senate from Georgia. The risk is that the compromise candidates whom the coalition supports might turn their backs on the coalition's agenda, causing the trusting rank-and-file coalition members to feel as if they have been left holding the bag, thanks to the big tent strategy of Robertson and Reed. Whether the Christian Coalition would again back her if she were on the GOP presidential ticket is the question

And while Christian Coalition backing may be a central concern of Hutchison the senator, it was not even remotely on the mind of Kay

****

Bailey when, in 1972, she ran for the Texas legislature. Houston's Republican Party patrons again slammed their doors and withdrew their welcome mats to the uppity lady intent on going where nice Texas women never traveled. They refused to chip in Texas-sized contributions guaranteed to any and every male state GOP candidate. They would not finance her first run for political office.

Days after she tallied the votes to defeat Bob Krueger, Kay Bailey Hutchison found herself slapped with felony charges for claimed ethics violations while Texas state treasurer. She was accused of misusing telephones in her state office and of abusing members of her staff and forcing them to perform personal and menial tasks while on the state time card. Democrats and their allies in some of the media salivated at the prospect of skewering one of the Republican party's brightest hopes at a time when so many Clinton appointees seemed to come equipped with an independent counsel attached at the hip.

Seventeen boxes of evidence collected by the prosecutor appeared an overwhelming indication of her impending guilt. Instead, the prosecutor, a Democrat, declined to pursue the case. A Texas judge ordered a jury to find Senator Hutchison not guilty. Democrats cried "cover-up." Republicans gave her thumbs-up.

In a politically wily move in the wake of claims that she had escaped justice because of a "legal technicality," she ordered all evidence against her to be made public. A few "alternative" papers published scathing accounts of the case against her. They declined to publish her defense. But *Texas Monthly*, an iconoclastic voice on the Left, took the view that the allegations against the former state treasurer amounted to former staffers accusing her of forcing them to bring back after-dinner mints and cadge coffee creamers from local restaurants. Another staffer said Kay Bailey poked her with a planning calendar for failing to find a phone number. Yet another claimed to have been "pinched" on the arm after he was too slow to follow orders. Nobody likes the idea that she actually yelled at them for not keeping up with the pace she set for herself or her coworkers. But according to the *Texas Monthly* reporter, they were hardly felony offenses.

The most serious charge claimed she illegally stored campaign contributors on a state computer database. Hutchison says that when she was told that was not permitted, she ordered all such information removed from the state computers. In a perfect Catch-22, her detractors used the attempt to correct the problem as "proof" that she was trying to "destroy" evidence. A pinch, a poke, some mints, some creamers — not really the stuff of which national political scandals are made. When Hutchison was acquitted, Ann Richards, who you'll remember was still the Texas governor and a liberal Democrat, publicly praised Hutchison for her integrity.

Hutchison may not quite be a Margaret Thatcher in waiting, but she has proved herself to be a formidable woman in politics who has gotten herself very close to the top of the legislative heap nationally.

★ ★ ★ ★ ★ ★ ★ ★ ★ ★

JESSE JACKSON
The Left's Great Black Hope

JESSE JACKSON MAKES STRONG MEN and weak presidents weep. He had Bill Clinton crying the blues in Clinton's first run at the presidency. What could he, Governor Bill Clinton of Arkansas, *do* to keep Jesse on board? Keep him from running as an independent, messing Clinton up with the black voters. Rob him of the presidency?

Quite a lot, as it turned out.

Jackson has the highest profile of any claimant to the combined mantles of Hubert H. Humphrey, E. V. Debs, and Martin Luther King, Jr., on the American Left. That gives him a niche in the power structure of the Democratic Party. Outside that structure, he has every American who would vote a straight socialist ticket if he could. He also has every American who would vote for the late Humphrey's Americans for Democratic Action liberalism. This may be a rainbow of views, but it is *not* a lot of votes. Add to that the King legacy, meaning a goodly share of the black vote, and Jackson still doesn't have enough to win anything but the undying enmity of about a third of the electorate—people who will vote Democratic in a presidential election whether Senator Sam Nunn of Georgia and or former Senator George McGovern of Massachusetts were heading the ticket. These Democrat loyalists get royally teed-off when some darned fool renegade claiming to be a Democrat goes out and freelances, siphoning votes from The Party of Franklin D. Roosevelt and John F. Kennedy and causing a Republican to win.

Jackson talks about challenging the incumbent or going third party every year, whether there's a presidential election or not. Why? Commitment. Obligation. People's needs. The need for a tourniquet if you keep reading this. "A campaign for the presidency is such a responsibility and such a dangerous mission and carries with it the weight of so many people's needs," he told *The Nation* in the summer of 1995. "It just always strikes me in terms of responsibilities. I ran the first time in 1984 because I felt I was obligated to run."

And don't think for one minute he found any *fun* or *profit* in doing it. This running for president is *work*. Heavy lifting. " *It was no pleasure cruise,*" Jesse confided to *The Nation*. But when duty calls, it's Jesse on the spot. "I am prepared in the sense of commitment to justice and fairness in America, my commitment to inclusion, my commitment to coalition in our country — over and against polarization, my commitment to justice at home and peace in the world. It's just my public-service obligation."

Can you imagine what this country would be like if *more* men and women felt as Jesse Jackson does that it's a citizen's "public-service *obligation*" to run for president. Scary, huh?

Jackson, like Rush Limbaugh, is a TV and radio personality, besides being everything else he is always being. Jackson says, "Limbaugh is a quasi-politician entertainer who exploits gender and who race baits." Jackson says it with a straight face. This is one of several thousand reasons that Jackson is chalk scraping the blackboard for conservatives, black and white. At the same time, he is Mr. Mellifluous to those persons, black and white, who think guns cause crime. Jesse Jackson is the spokesman *without equal* for those who think the absence of jobs causes welfare rolls to grow. He is wisdom personified for those who insist that illegitimacy has nothing to do with taxpayer financing of teenage girls getting their own apartments to have children they can't steer morally because they, the mothers, have no moral compass of their own. There are enough voters in that mix to deny someone else on the Left, some regular Democrat, somebody named Clinton, the presidency in a close election, but not much else.

Clinton figured that out in the 1992 race and simply and gently nudged Jackson off into a little corner on the left side of the playground, with Sister Souljah. Clinton played a not-very-difficult game

★★

that required him not to insult Jackson and his legions too often or too blatantly; he could never kowtow to them, either.

The times had changed. The Democrats for once had a candidate who understood that. In 1988, candidate Michael Dukakis publicly kissed and made up with Jackson. Jesse Jackson liked that. The voters were underwhelmed. In 1992, Jackson invited nominee Clinton to speak before Jackson's Rainbow Coalition. Instead of showering Jackson with the praise he expected, Clinton accused rap "artist" Sister Souljah, who had appeared on a panel at Jackson's invitation, of hate talk. No one in America but the dangerously ill informed would want to take Sister Hate-Mouth's side. Captain Clinton sighted in Souljah the sub for Jackson and sank same. Put another way, Clinton "dissed" Jackson and got away with it.

Where does that leave the Reverend Jackson when it comes to future presidential nomination bids? Less well off than when he ran Operation Push as a kind of insurance business by which white corporate executives could buy themselves a little peace and tranquillity in those racially trying times? Sure. In a sense. It's harder in these more sophisticated racial times for Jackson to scare the bejeebers out of businesses that don't see eye to eye with him. What's he going to do? Threaten to picket a company because its president is Asian or white and not black? People get laughed off the American stage these days for attempting such organized whining-cum-extortion.

The truth is that Jackson is a victim of the success of the movement that he and King and other black civil rights leaders came to symbolize. Separate drinking fountains, back of the bus, Klan beatings and murders that few white police forces would do anything about, blatant disregard for the merit of black jobs and college applicants. These things are history, largely unexperienced by a generation of black Americans. Jackson helped make that happen and Americans of goodwill everywhere acknowledge a debt.

But the argument now is over quotas, preferences, guaranteed equality of outcome, not just of opportunity, no matter how poorly equipped the applicant or how poor the performance of the jobholder or student. Americans in overwhelming numbers have had it with a pendulum that had swung to the opposite end and had gotten stuck

there. Stuck there by courts, judges, civil rights bureaucracies, inter-
pretations of the law that flew in the face of the stated intentions of
their framers, including and especially Hubert Humphrey, who swore
up and down that affirmative action would *never, ever* mean quotas.

Jesse is not so good on this cutting edge stuff. He wants to fight two
kinds of battles: those that have already been won and new battles that
are unwinnable, for midnight basketball courts — used here as a
metaphor for liberal, welfare, do-good, feel-good, head-in-the-clouds
stuff.

During his "quiet" years following the '92 election, Jesse continued
to woo the poor, the displaced, and the disenfranchised, the huddled
masses yearning to be a two-welfare-check family.

Okay. That was a cheap shot. Lots of your basic huddled masses
would take a job if there was one available in their neighborhood for
really good pay and fringe benefits and that *went* someplace. Not your
dead-end job that liberals are always disparaging.

Anyway, Jackson missed no opportunity to extend his hand to
American blacks, Hispanics, Asians, gender-conscious women,
"Native Americans" (he apparently thought the natives were restless),
union rank-and-file, the elderly, the disabled, the homosexual
activists, and ideological edge-dwellers who populate the environmental and animal rights movements. Talk about a *losing* coalition.
Anyhow, Jackson's appeal as champion of the underdog was univer-
sally acknowledged. When loggers in the Pacific Northwest found
themselves threatened with unemployment because of the environ-
mentally protected spotted owl, even *they* called Jesse for help. When
Pat Buchanan and H. Ross Perot needed him for their ad hoc coalitions against NAFTA and GATT, Jesse was there. Hey, is this a great
country *or what?* (In this case, "or what" is an acceptable answer.)

With the exception of Jewish voters, who distrust him because of
his association with a certain black racist and comments he made that
could be interpreted as anti-Semitic, especially by people who speak
and understand English — except for these folks, the coalition that
Jesse Jackson built needs a tent to house it that is bigger than anything
the Big Tent Republican crowd ever imagined.

Speaking (all right, technically, it should be "writing") of tents, there is a version of Jackson's origins that has him being born to poverty, raised in a southern Jim Crow slum, and having "to steal to survive." As with so many other young black Americans, this version continues, athletics provided a ticket out of poverty for Jackson. His football scholarship to the University of Illinois brought him face-to-face with the bigotry of the North. A black quarterback had no chance. After a year, he transferred to the North Carolina Agriculture and Technical College in Greensboro. He earned a degree in sociology, played quarterback, and, stung by the racial prejudice in the world around him, joined Martin Luther King's Southern Christian Leadership Conference crusade for racial fair play. He became a respected and trusted King aide. On April 4, 1968, Jackson cradled a dying Reverend King and listened as he whispered his last words. In Dr. King's tradition, he founded Operation PUSH (People United to Save Humanity) to force corporate America to open real business opportunities for minorities. In 1984, he garnered 3.3 million primary votes. He got nearly 7 million in 1988.

Great story. Not a true story, but a great story. Jesse Jackson made up his nonexistent hardscrabble youth. He was neither born in a slum nor raised in a slum. His family wasn't rich, but they weren't impoverished, either. He was born out of wedlock to a teenage mother. His mother, his natural father, and his stepfather were all hardworking and steadily employed. They lived in a comfortable, working-class neighborhood. He studied French in high school. He would later send his own children to the poshest, most expensive, exclusive preparatory schools in Chicago and the District of Columbia, all the while championing the virtues of public education. In 1993, he and his Rainbow Coalition were hired by the California teachers' unions to go West and campaign *against* a ballot initiative that would have allowed the children of poor parents, black and white, to attend the schools of their *choice* — you know, like rich kids' schools, like the schools Jackson sent his kids to — using government vouchers. But, then, isn't consistency the hobgoblin of stupid people who don't understand how you can have your cake and eat it too?

Back to Jesse's past. If Jackson didn't play quarterback at the University of Illinois, it wasn't because of skin color. The school's starting

QB at the time was black. Jackson's ego, meanwhile, showed itself to be more than adequate in size, on campus and later. Days before his assassination, Dr. Martin Luther King, Jr., was infuriated with Jackson's self-absorbed behavior. King's colleagues were irate at Jackson's posturing the moment reporters hastened to the civil rights leader's death scene. They were outraged at his on-camera claim to have held the dying King or that he was entrusted with any last words. That a blood smear appeared on his shirt and that he wore the same stained turtleneck the next day on the nationally televised *Today* show was the last straw. King's closest advisers grumbled that Jackson was a crass exploiter and opportunist. A lot of career politicians, Democrat and Republican, would take that as a compliment. But Jesse hadn't yet gotten into politics big time. He was practically a kid.

Jesse Jackson shares a failing with much of the rest of the human race in that he doesn't always finish what he starts. He dropped out of divinity school. He got in trouble as director of the Southern Christian Leadership Conference's Operation Breadbasket.

Critics who accuse him of overweening ambition forget that he chose not to run for mayor of Washington, D.C., though this may be more of an indication of Jackson's limited capacity for self-punishment. But then he also dropped out of consideration for the top job at the National Association for the Advancement of Colored People. It was a competitive race. He did choose to run for "shadow" senator from the District of Columbia. The slot was uncontested. This is called picking your fights carefully.

Jackson must know what power he holds. It is, as the kids used to say, *awesome*. If he runs as an independent, he denies a crucial portion of the black vote to Clinton or whoever the Democrat nominee is. But Jackson also denies Republicans the votes in congressional districts across the country. Districts that the Republicans need in order to keep their new majority in the House. Why? Because Republicans and conservatives will figure that with Jackson running, Clinton or the Democrat nominee is surely a goner. So Republicans will think they don't have to put in twenty-hour days to elect the Republican at the top of their ticket. Uh-oh. With more blacks voting Democrat and fewer Republicans voting Republican, there goes the House. And very

★★★

possibly the Senate. The Senate? You bet. Sure, more Senate Democrats than Republicans decided not to seek reelection in 1996. But there are too many iffy Republican incumbents and too many vacancies in former Democrat seats to withstand an overwhelming black voter turnout for Democrats. In which case, it's bye-bye Senate, too, for the Republicans.

This Jackson will gore Clinton — ah, make that skewer Clinton — on the chance that he can make the Congress liberal again. Jesse may never run for president again. Nonetheless, he will always remain a presence. No other black leader on the Left has his charisma, his charm, his manipulative skills. His *je ne sais quoi*. He knows what that means, even if *you* don't.

☆ ☆ ☆ ☆ ☆ ☆ ☆ ☆ ☆

ALAN KEYES

A Prophet in the Political Desert

ALAN KEYES IS NOT A PRESIDENTIAL CANDIDATE. He's a radio talk show pro-life prophet haranguing the conscience of the nation from a bully electronic pulpit. He's also the reason race relations within the nation should be reevaluated.

Tune into any on-air appearance, and listen to his fawning callers. Southern drawls, western cowpoke twangs, and mountain hollow mumbles float across the air waves in acceptance and praise of Keyes' every word. Every group stereotyped by the press as intrinsically "racist" phones to tell Keyes how much they agree with his pitch and many pledge their support for his Quixotic presidential bid.

Keyes' ultraliberal critics, of course, would question whether he could attract the same crowd if he appeared on television? Is he, as liberal foes charge, a political pawn recruited by white racist conservatives to sew dissent and doubt among ethnic minorities?

Alan Keyes is a lot of things, but an easily manipulated front man for hire is not one of them. Alan Keyes can't be bought by either side, because he believes he's the intellectual superior of any one in politics. He may be right. But that attitude won't win many, if any, campaigns. In fact, Alan Keyes lost both Maryland senate races he entered, in large part because of his zero-based pander profile. His chances of being considered a serious presidential contender in this election are quite seriously...nil.

Alan Keyes is a very proud man. He's proud of his accomplishments, talents, of his family, ethnic origins, and of his nation. His view on race and families, articulated in his book *Masters of the Dream*, focuses on the major theme of his presidential campaign, the primacy of the family and its role in building the nation, and restoring order out of social and moral chaos.

Race, for Keyes, is a current running deep through his radio stump sermons. It's as much a part of his rhetorical repertoire as it is the center piece of Jesse Jackson's every waking word. Alan Keyes is black. Alan Keyes is the descendant of Maryland slaves. His family has lived in Maryland for 200 years. But Alan Keyes is no darling of traditional black political leadership, nor does he run to curry favor with it. His political genesis is worlds apart from Jackson's, or even of that perennial black congressional presence, Ron Dellums.

When black student "militants" occupied Cornell University administration buildings, serious student Keyes voiced his personal opposition to their acts and their ideology. The militants countered Keyes's intellectual challenge with a more mundane response: they threatened to kill him. Refusing to wage philosophical battle with the intellectually disarmed, Keyes beat a hasty retreat north toward Boston, where he finished his academic training at Harvard.

Keyes's post-Harvard career is what one would expect. He spun political theory at the American Enterprise Institute. Honed his diplomatic oratorical style as a member of Jeane Kirkpatrick's United Nations entourage. He was U.S. ambassador to the UN's Economic and Social Council. He spent two years with the Reagan Administration's State Department (where he opposed congressional mandated sanctions on South Africa). He was president of Citizens Against Government Waste, founded Black America's PAC, and served as interim president of Alabama's A&M University. After losing to Mikulski, he began hosting his Baltimore-based *America's Wake Up Call* radio show.

Alan Keyes identity with mainstream Americans of African descent has been strained ever since his two college years at Cornell, although it shouldn't. During his 1988 race against U.S. Senator Paul Sarbanes, Keyes polled only Maryland's base GOP vote of 40 percent and virtually none of the state's 24 percent black vote. Four years later, incumbent Barbara Mikulski took 88 percent of Maryland's black ballots.

Keyes couldn't connect with even his native Baltimore's minority population.

Keyes, like traditional black political leaders, talks of abortion with terms evoking images of slavery and genocide. Unlike liberal or radical race polemicists, Keyes believes deeply in the strength of black families. He rejects theories linking slavery to urban black crime and familial instability. Keyes blames the condescending, personal initiative and incentive-killing welfare system instead.

Alan Keyes, forty-three, is Catholic, conservative, and the nation's most articulate and intellectual antiabortion advocate. Except for his Harvard Ph.D. in government, and the fact that he's not Irish, Alan Keyes could be Bob Dornan's ideological crib twin. Both have passion and the ability to move audiences with their oratory. Both have absolutely no chance of making it to the White House except as dinner or overnight guests of the occupants. Both could be cast as 20th century John the Baptists, verbally flogging an inattentive and licentious populace to change their hedonist ways and restore moral and personal order to their lives, their communities, and the nation.

Keyes is unique to the pro-life movement. His antiabortion pitch is not cut from the same cloth as most. He carries it to a different and lofty intellectual level with a few clever talk show sound bites thrown in for good measure.

Quoting the Declaration of Independence, Keyes spins an elaborate but crystal-clear linkage between the society envisioned by the Founding Fathers and the moral "threat" of abortion and irresponsible personal behavior. With a clever omission of "liberty and the pursuit of happiness," Keyes begins his historical antiabortion analysis. The venerable document's introductory reference to the equality of man and each "inalienable right to life..." is cited as the most fundamental right from which all others logically flow. Society's focus on the latter "pursuit of happiness" phrase, is, to Alan Keyes, the root cause of the nation's "crisis of promiscuity." Such behavior, with its corresponding lack of concern for the consequences of one's acts, destroys respect for life, women, or freedom. It erodes the capability of the individual to rule him- or herself. Without individual responsibility, the entire system of government established by the Founding Fathers cannot flourish.

The moral atmosphere that condones abortion on demand, according to Keyes, is a danger to the economic and social stability of minorities, and the nation.

Keyes's style is so impressive that Ronald Reagan personally insisted that he become directly involved in Keyes's initial and foredoomed campaign against Sarbanes. After a meeting at the same time with Bob Dole, the then Senate minority leader doubled his PAC's donation to Keyes. The $5,000 was less a campaign boost than a collection-plate church acknowledgment that the preacher struck a responsive chord with parishioners.

Will Alan Keyes be at the GOP convention next year? Guaranteed. In 1988, Keyes bullied the RNC into allowing him to address the convention during prime time. He publicly chastised the Republican leadership for being "big on lip service, but short on action" in assisting black GOP candidates. True to his contrarian ways, he introduced Pat Buchanan to the gathered delegates. This go-round, chances are better than even, that Alan Keyes will again be at the podium, but as a preacher calling down divine providence and protection on the party and the nation, not as a candidate.

★ ★ ★ ★ ★ ★ ★ ★ ★ ★

RICHARD G. LUGAR

Clinton Wanted Him, But Do You?

RICHARD G. LUGAR WILL BE THREE MONTHS SHORT of sixty-five on Presidential Inauguration Day, 1997. Or if you're reading this in 1998, make that "*was* three months short of sixty-five on Inauguration Day, 1997." If you're reading this in 1998, then you *know* he didn't even win the 1996 Republican presidential *nomination* he was seeking. If you are reading this in 1995, then you didn't know that fact till you read it here, a year before *he* found out. Hey, do we give value or what?

Some of you may not know who Richard G. Lugar is. If you live in Indiana, you probably, but not necessarily, know he was your United States senator since his first election to the post in 1976. That's a long time to let yourself seep into the consciousness of the people in your own state. Not necessarily for Lugar. His friends will tell you, and they don't say it to be mean, Lugar is the kind of guy who walks into a room and blends right in. An *empty* room.

Dick Lugar looks good on paper. He is pro-life and pro-wife. He married his college sweetheart, Charlene, and has stayed married to her for almost two decades and counting. They have four children. They live and breathe family values.

He has practiced the conservative fiscal values he preaches. When he was mayor of Indianapolis, he took a stand for *fewer* federal programs for his city.

But his real interest —"passion" somehow doesn't seem the right word in Lugar's case — is foreign policy. He went up to New Hampshire and held a press conference early in 1995 and began talking about foreign policy and its importance. Try to find that story in the back-copies department of your local newspaper. It's not that he doesn't know foreign policy backward and forward. It's that when he talks about it, he has this knack for making it seem *so* serious and at the same time so *bloodless* that you start noticing tiny specks of dirt under the nail of the third finger on your right hand. But, hey, you can't take it away from this former Eagle Scout, high-school valedictorian, and naval intelligence officer. He knows his foreign policy so well that President Clinton wanted him as Secretary of State. This is not what Lugar is advertising in his GOP presidential nomination campaign handouts. Assuming he had campaign handouts, of which there were no confirmed sightings by the time this chapter went to press.

Anyhow, Lugar has something else in common with Clinton besides Clinton's finding foreign policy dull and Lugar's making it seem dull. Lugar and Clinton were both Rhodes scholars. Only Lugar went to the United States Embassy in London for far different reasons from Clinton's. Lugar went there in 1956 to volunteer for the United States Navy.

And now hear this: Lugar *is* a loyal Republican. He *did* turn Clinton down. And Lugar really is considered a wise and thoughtful independent minded earnest scholar on the subject of foreign affairs. This also is not necessarily a good thing to have said about you. An axiom of politics is that foreign policy never elected a president. Still, to show how *deep* he is about these things, he once scored points with Democrats and liberals for having bucked the Reagan administration and some Senate conservatives on a South Africa bill. But he was also a vigorous supporter of aid to the anti-Marxist forces in Nicaragua when a Commie-type of guy named Daniel Ortega had gotten hold of the place. He also has gone out of his way to annoy organized labor. He is basically a man of the Right, but not, let's say, 100 percent.

But what's he done for you lately? He said he'd help you get rid of your least favorite bureaucracy on earth: the Internal Revenue Service. He said he'd do this by replacing the income tax with a single rate national sales tax of around 17 percent, give or take a percentage point. He said this would be better than a value added tax because you can hide a lot of government taxation and therefore a lot of government beneath a VAT, which has more layers than your momma's layer cake. In 1995, he came up with this catchy line when he decided he wanted to go for the Big One in 1996: "If you have a dollar, it is yours."

Potential donors to his campaign found tremendous personal significance in this sentiment. By and large, they kept their dollars.

Too bad. What this frenetic nation needs more than a good 5-cent cigar is a good tranquilizer.

Lugar is violently opposed to gambling, except when you send a contribution to his thousand-to-one-shot presidential bid.

H. ROSS PEROT

The Bucks Begin Here

HENRY ROSS PEROT IS A BEAUTIFUL HUMAN BEING. How beautiful? About a half-billion-dollars-in-net-worth beautiful. We're talking *beauty*. You *know* it. You *love* it. You *want* it. Doesn't necessarily mean you voted for him in 1992 or will the next time, right? Maybe you did. Maybe you figured out where he is politically and said, "That's for me," and joined the 19.7 million Americans, or 19 percent of the voting electorate, that went for him. Maybe you didn't vote for him because you *sort of* knew where he was but not really? Ideologically, on the Right-Left spectrum, didn't he seem to be here, there, everywhere? At least when it comes to general policy statements. Or to specific policy promises, for that matter. Come to think of it, there aren't a whole lot of *those*, even though he has been running for president longer than any Republican except Bob Dole and Pat Buchanan, and any Democrat except Bill Clinton and Jesse Jackson.

Nothing wrong with philosophical indeterminism, of course. The Constitution doesn't say a guy running for president *has* to have a consistent, full-blown ideological worldview. This is good for Perot, because Perot doesn't have an ideology. Or, at least, not so you'd notice.

Take affirmative action. Perot thinks it's good and bad. It's good and bad for him to think it's good and bad. The upside for Perot is that at least he had the intelligence to recognize the good and the courage to mention the bad back in the spring of 1992, when most politicians wouldn't touch the issue with a you know what. Back then, Perot said of affirmative action: "It's got its pluses and its minuses. It produces

✶✶

stress in society. The plus is it cleans up the inequity...The minus is all the people who were more qualified and got passed over, who probably didn't have any negative feelings based on race, start developing them." Anybody who has a problem with *that* explanation has a *problem*. His proposed remedies, shared by Colin Powell, are another matter. "There's only one long-term solution — and that is education, education, education — and everything we can do to rebuild a moral-ethical base and a strong family unit." Right *on*, Ross. Nobody's going to get in your face for recommending the rebuilding of a strong moral-ethical base and strong family unit.

How you propose to do that, however, is what separates the libs from the wingers, the men from the boys, and the equivocators from the up-front guys. That's Perot's downside. You ask him to be up front on some specifics, and he runs out back. You can't excuse that by saying, "Well, that's a politician for you." You can't *get* more up front on this than Perot's fellow Texan, Senator Phil Gramm, who *is* a politician *by trade*. Gramm says if you make him president, by the time he takes his hand off the Bible at his swearing in, affirmative action will be history. He'd instantly issue an executive order to end all affirmative action preferences, set asides (the percentage of federal contacts set aside for minority contractors, regardless of merit or competitive pricing), and quotas based on race or sex. And what about Bob Dole? He's as professional a political as they come. He said he'd sign into law legislation making English the official language of the United States. That's the specificity Perot claims *politicians* don't have and he *does* have. Maybe Perot gets himself confused with Gramm. Understandable. Both men are real lookers.

As for Perot's making education the big part of the equation, that is itself a problem. Education may offer false hope. After spending billions of dollars for nearly fifty years on every scheme known to humankind to make public education better in this country, the federal government and the state governments have managed to make it worse, every day in every way.

One indisputable thing that the tons of data show over the years is not pleasant, but has to be addressed. It is that some members of every race do not respond fully to educational efforts, more so among whites

****

because there are more of them in the United States. But a portion of any community is not educable to the minimum work standards of the broader community as a whole. This requires a forthright discussion of the problem and of ways to accommodate the culture to it. Love to hear from you on this, Ross. Jump in anytime.

On the Big Issue of the End of the Century: *Family Values*, also known as *Moral Values* and believed to have gone under the name *Cultural Wars* in several jurisdictions, Perot is firm in favor — *generally speaking*, of course. Perot said a long time ago: "If I could do one thing, I would try to construct a strong family unit for every family on the basis of love, understanding, and encouragement. All the other problems would disappear." *All other problems would disappear?* Thinking thoughts like this *can't* be how Ross got to be a half-billionaire. There's got to be more to the man.

There *is*, and you may not like it. In Perot's world, as in everybody else's, you have, on one hand, the family values thing. On the other hand, you have some persons pumping hard for the normalization of homosexuality in this society through pushing for special rights for homosexuals. Are family values and special rights for homosexuals compatible? Maybe so. Maybe not. There are homosexuals who are also political conservatives *and* Republicans. And some who are conservative Republican activists. They tend not to be activists for homosexual "rights," however. And you *know* where most liberals and most conservatives come down on this whole issue. Where's Ross, the would-be cultural warrior?

Glad you asked. Remember when President Clinton got rebuffed by General Colin Powell and Senator Sam Nunn of Georgia on his move to open the armed forces of the United States to homosexual enlistment? Well, then and there, Perot marched right up and said, well, uh, he said he wouldn't *say* whether Clinton was right or Nunn and Powell were right. "This is a very sensitive issue in the military, whose business is fighting and dying. I hope they make a good decision." Thanks *a lot*, Ross. Good to know we can rely on a naval academy graduate like you to tell us what he *really* thinks about a public policy issue that he knows something about and that is squarely on the table and not in some theoretical realm.

****

It would be ungenerous to infer from this performance that the bucks start with Perot, but don't stop with him. It would be ungenerous to conclude that when it comes to hot issues, he prefers to let Clinton and Powell or Clinton and Gramm or Clinton and Nunn fight it out in the valley of decision making, and then come down and shoot the survivors. Ungenerous, but accurate.

When he was running the second time in 1992 for the presidency, Perot said he wouldn't appoint a homosexual to his Cabinet. The homosexual rights lobby went ballistic. *Sur-prise*. Act Up acted up. *Sur-prise*. Perot stood down. *Bummer*. He issued a statement in which he promised that any discrimination based on "sexual orientation would not be tolerated" in *his* administration.

He did more than stand down. He got on one knee. He appointed as his California civil rights coordinator a lesbian and homosexual rights activist, Debra Olson. Olson, a Beverly Hills mortgage broker, had gone with other activists to Dallas to complain to Perot about his earlier stand on homosexuals.

On abortion, Perot wants it both ways. But then so do the vast majority of Americans, who say in every poll you ever heard of and some you haven't that they basically don't like abortion but don't want the government outlawing it completely.

"It is the woman's choice," Perot once told Larry King, but added: "We are not rabbits. Each human life is precious...It is absolutely irresponsible for thinking, reasoning human beings to create a human life just because they didn't take the proper precautions." Hey, tough words. That'll make 'em shape up. And if they don't, then what? Tell 'em again that this here unwanted pregnancy stuff has got to stop? End of discussion. It's that simple. At least, it is to Perot. Talk *is* cheap, it turns out, even for a guy who's half a billionaire.

Perot thinks there are too many guns on the streets. Maybe. Certainly too many in the hands of violent criminals. Not nearly enough in the hands of the honest but unarmed persons they prey on, because they are unarmed. Perot also says gun registration laws or six-day or six-week waiting periods don't stop criminals from paying other people to buy guns *for* them. So is Perot a big Second Amendment guy or isn't he? Yes, and no.

✱✱

Perot thinks multilateral trade agreements like the North Atlantic Free Trade Agreement and the General Agreement on Tariffs and Trade create — here comes one of his famous down-home images? — a *giant sucking sound* as American jobs woosh out of the country, along with your hard-earned dollars to pay for products tumbling in, products made by foreign workers making what American workers would be making but for the way foreigners rig the game to keep American-made goods out of their markets. Pat Buchanan is with him on that. Jesse Jackson is with him on that. The AFL-CIO is with him on that. Bill Clinton, Phil Gramm, Bob Dole, Lamar Alexander, Pete Wilson aren't. They're free traders. Or pushovers for the multinationalist crowd that doesn't care where anything is made, so long as they get a piece of the action. Who is right here? Perot has a point. So do Clinton, Dole, and Gramm. Both sides can't be right, right? Wrong. On this one, Perot takes a firm stand and contributes to the dialogue, as they say. More important, he and his United We Stand America legions make the internationalists think twice before they give the store away every time they negotiate trade pacts on behalf of the United States.

Perot was against the Mexico bailout that Clinton dreamed up and got House Speaker Newt Gingrich and Senate Majority Leader Bob Dole to go along with. Perot bucked the political establishments of both parties, the media establishment, and the internationalist–New World Order establishment. So Perot is courageous? Well, let's say he knows where his troops are and sometimes it's hard to tell whether he's leading them or following them.

In fact, Perot's troops are very conservative on a host of issues, maybe more so than Perot himself. Who *are* the Perotistas?

Frank Luntz, a poll taker who worked for Perot for a while in 1992, says 95 percent of Perot voters are white (82 percent of the electorate as a whole is white). Perot voters tip toward men (58 percent). They tend not to be regular churchgoers. And they do tend to be highly suspicious of religious conservatives. Perot voters are young, in their thirties, family persons with children and modest family incomes of $40,000 to $50,000 a year. A lot of Perot's followers own their own businesses or are semiskilled. Two out of three Perot voters said they voted Republican in the 1994 elections. Perot voters are conservative in the ways the Republican Party leaders simply could not fathom until they got hit over the head by the Perot voters, the Religious Right, and others in the 1992 elections. And, true to form, the Republicans still didn't have much of a clue immediately after the '92 elections. They were scared to touch the immigration issue, scared to touch the affirmative action issue. The English-only issue. The illegitimacy-welfare issue.

Well, guess what. As *U.S. News and World Report* reported in 1995, 68 percent of Perot voters think only American citizens should be eligible for welfare and not aliens, whether legal or illegal. It is a common-sense position based on the principle that the magnet that draws foreigners to America's shores should be the opportunity to work, save, and invest, not the opportunity to go on the dole.

See. Here's the trick. Perot voters are not really Perot voters. They are Americans who voted for Perot last time but who are Republicans. Or, in fewer numbers, Democrats. Lots of them are independents. Lots of them belong to United We Stand America, which Perot founded as his nonpolitical party political party. This is not a *typographical* error. This may have been a *strategic* error on Perot's part. United We Stand members don't stand united behind Perot necessarily, or anybody else. To stay leader of the movement, he has to follow it as much as lead it at times.

The most pertinent observation to make about Perot voters as a movement is that although they are conservative in the positions they hold on immigration, on welfare, on deficits, on government spending, they are not, for the most part, *ideological* conservatives. They do not sit around thinking deeply about the philosophy of conservatism or why they hold the views they hold. They hold them because they make sense. Because their views reflect the reality they see around them. Women sometimes get pregnant when they don't want to or can't afford to; and they need to have a safe, legal way out of the problem. It's not a religious issue or a profound moral issue to Perot voters. It's a practical problem with a practical solution. If you let noncitizens get welfare and other benefits, people will abuse the system, bring their relatives over from the old country and have *them* apply for welfare and other benefits. It's that simple. Nothing to do with immigrant bashing. Certainly nothing to do with xenophobia, despite what pollster Luntz says. Lots of Perot voters are first-generation Americans themselves. They see welfare as a scam and a seduction of certain vulnerable persons to become dependent on the government. Perot voters don't feel this way because they read some conservative philosopher's warnings about the road to serfdom. It's common sense to them. They don't know a lot about Bob Dole's voting record or what goes on behind the scenes in the Senate. For one thing, they're too young to have much of a political memory. For another, they're not *that* interested. Remember Perot's United We Stand America gathering in Dallas in August 1995? The Perot folks wildly applauded Jesse Jackson and some liberal congresswoman who was a union champion and just as wildly applauded Pat Buchanan and some conservative congressman who opposes compulsory unionism. All the Perot folks cared about was that the speaker of the moment was saying things they wanted to hear about trade, immigration, welfare, government spending — the whole Perotista nine yards.

Perot voters are suspicious of the religious conservatives because media pundits and the Democrats and some liberal Republicans have created a comic book image of them. *The Religious Right: Monster or Menace?* Media commentators, Democrats in Congress, and liberal Republicans tell Perot voters that religious conservatives are out to take away their freedoms and make everyone into some sort of crazed Bible-thumper who'll shut down every bar, disco, and movie theater in the country if they ever come to power. Perot voters don't meet religious conservatives at church because they don't go to the same churches.

Perot voters are more grumpy than your average American voter. They weren't satisfied with the way the Republicans performed after Perot voters helped make them the majority in Congress. And Perot voters weren't enthralled with the performance of Clinton or the congressional Democrats. They were looking at a possible alternative. Guess who. Mr. Half-Billionaire himself. Again. Bill Clinton and the Democrats were less solicitous to Perot since the 1992 elections than the Republicans. Haley Barbour, the chairman of the Republican

✶✶

National Committee, was smart enough to invite United We Stand America picketers in for coffee and a personal chat at a summer meeting of the RNC in Chicago. Republican operatives were instructed to lay out the welcome mat for Perot voters anywhere and everywhere. After all, a big chunk of them were Republicans who wandered off the reservation in the 1992 elections. Newt Gingrich actually joined United We Stand America. So did other congressional Republicans. And by August 1995, the horde of declared GOP presidential nomination candidates accepted invitations to parade themselves before the Perotistas' all-star gathering in Dallas.

Perot himself was on his best behavior, the almost perfect host, avoiding despite his best instincts any gratuitous insults to his Democratic and Republican guest speakers, including the GOP nomination hopefuls. Perot has made himself a bit hard to take over the years. In 1986, General Motors Chairman Roger Smith gave him $700 million to go away. Perot had wanted to computerize GM into the producer of the undisputed finest cars in the world. GM bought Perot's computer system integration firm, EDS, and turned Perot loose on GM's sprawling automotive manufacturing empire. Before EDS began to streamline GM's Byzantine way of doing business, the manufacturing giant could no longer tolerate Perot the man. Thus the personal buyout.

How did he get to that point? Four years out of the Naval Academy, Perot traded a career at sea for computer sales with IBM. In 1956, at age thirty-two, he decided he'd conquered every IBM sales mountain and, with $1,000, founded his own firm, EDS, in Dallas to show IBM clients how to run the massive mainframes they bought. By 1962, EDS was an international success and Perot was a genuine rich Texan. He has used his wealth in spectacularly generous and patriotic ways. In 1969, he loaded two jet cargo planes with mail, medicine, and Christmas gifts for American prisoners of war and flew to Southeast Asia. With bullhorn in hand, he berated the Vietnamese with quotes from Chairman Mao about humane "revolutionary" treatment of captives. The Nixon White House was furious.

He sprang two EDS employees from an Iranian jail in 1978. His "direct action" approach to safeguarding his men helped create the

Perot personal mythology. Some, however, suggest that the EDS "hostages" were not so much victims of Iran's fanatical mullah-led regime as would-be chits to be held until EDS paid up the millions they owed Iran for a hastily terminated contract to run the country's Social Security system computers. After Jimmy Carter's hopelessly botched attempt to free the U.S. Embassy hostages, Perot's feat left President Carter politically embarrassed and personally livid.

During the Reagan years, Perot's penchant for clandestine public service made him a favorite recipient of furtive calls by a young and not-yet famous marine named Ollie North. In 1982, North asked Perot to foot a half-million-dollar ransom to free kidnapped Brigadier General James Dozier from Italy's Red Brigade terrorists. The Italian police sprang Dozier before the cash exchanged hands. In 1984, Perot forked over $200,000 in earnest money to the Hezboallah after the CIA's Lebanon bureau chief, Bill Buckley, was kidnapped and eventually murdered. The money vanished and so did Perot's patience with North.

After playing the dutiful citizen for the Reagan and Bush administrations, Perot decided he'd enlist White House support for his POW/MIA adventures. Every door at 1600 Pennsylvania Avenue slammed shut. Even Colin Powell snubbed him. Perot didn't just get mad at the snub by George Bush. He got even, in 1992. That is why they call him "Former President Bush," remember?

Whether Perot could do something like that to the next GOP presidential nominee is arguable. A nominee whose ideological standard is not pale and pink because he washes it in the kitchen sink every morning, a nominee who appeals credibly to enough of the conservative items on the agenda of United We Stand America — that kind of nominee could probably withstand another Perot independent candidacy. United We Stand doesn't mean Blindly We Follow.

Perot, for all his impulse to petulance, has his admirers in high places, of course. President Clinton is not one of them. Clinton is rumored not to get down on his knees at bedtime to thank the Lord for Perot's existence. As for Vice President Al Gore, he described Perot during his famous NAFTA debate on Larry King's TV show as "greedy, corrupt, an isolationist, and a fear monger." Put Gore down as a skeptic on Perot. White House adviser and political chameleon David Gergen urged Clinton and Gore to "destroy Perot's credibility and woo his voters." The advice was juvenile and could have destroyed Gergen's credibility, had he not cleverly destroyed it himself years before.

Perot's credibility will continue to live on, so long as there are men and women who dare to dream the impossible dream, who have the courage to fight the impossible fight, and who have the might to stand up for what is right. It's just that simple.

★ ★ ★ ★ ★ ★ ★ ★ ★

COLIN POWELL

Horatio Alger II or Chief of Chaff?

IS COLIN POWELL EVERY VOTER'S DREAM? Is this former Joint Chiefs of Staff chairman the "looking glass" noncandidate's candidate? Does everyone who looks at this retired four-star army general see whatever he or she wants to see? Are you *tired* of reading questions instead of getting the answers you *paid* for?

Right. Then hold tight, because you may not like the answers.

In an appearance before the Investment Company Institute, Powell gave thumbs down to parts of the *Contract with America*, the ten-point policy pledge by Newt Gingrich and his House Republicans that drove their agenda for the first 100 days of the 104th Congress. Powell said he "liked those elements of the contract that were designed to reduce the size of government and the debt, but unhappy about the parts that were aimed at eliminating affirmative-action programs and that would hurt the less fortunate," according to Scripps Howard News Service.

This is not good talk from the General for conservatives to hear. Conservatives would give their eyeteeth to have a black conservative, an honest-to-God conservative, as president. This is partly because their party has become, by default, the Republican Party, which is, after all, the party of Abraham Lincoln, the Great Emancipator. Conservatives also want a black conservative in the White House, and in just about every other office they can think of, because many of them sat on the sidelines watching the civil rights revolution march right past them. They have this lingering guilt. Almost like draft dodgers who grow up to be chickenhawks. But a guy who says he thinks Republicans set out to *hurt* the less fortunate? The *Contract with America was the one thing* conservatives agreed was okay as an opening initiative by the new Republican Congress, but only because it was a base, an absolute minimum down payment on what conservatives expected as their due for their all-out electoral support of Gingrich & Co. going into the 1994 elections.

In the same Investment Company Institute appearance, Powell explained how he fits into the conservative-liberal, Democrat-Republican context of American politics. *Not* a good fit. "I don't find I neatly fit in," he said. "I have very strong Republican leanings on economic matters and international issues, but I'm a New Deal kid from Harlem and the South Bronx. I'm in the middle. I just don't know how to make that contribution yet. I'm not sure if politics is the right thing."

Come again? In the *middle*? Between Phil Gramm and Franklin Roosevelt? Not sure politics is the *right thing*? Hoh-boy.

Everybody knows Powell is a died-in-the-wool conservative on race, ethnicity, gender, and all that jazz, that he believes the claims of "victimhood" are poor excuses for nonperformance. Right? Well, yes. Nearly everybody may believe that about Powell. But it's not true. In a Sunday *Parade* magazine story, he said: "As much as I have been disappointed in my lifetime that we didn't move as fast as we might have, or that we still have forms of institutional racism, we have an abiding faith in this country. Hurt? Yes. Disappointed? Yes. Losing faith or confidence in the nation? No."

Institutional racism, General? Where? What institutions? Are there bigots abroad in this great land? You bet. Jew haters? Absolutely. Catholic bashers? Of course. Americans who still mumble "slopeheads" in reference to Asians, and *mean* it? Denigrators of Arabs? Of course. And...well, you get the point. You can no more outlaw bigotry than you can outlaw ignorance. You can lead a jackass to the water of enlightenment on race, but you can't make him drink.

Powell told ABC-TV's *This Week with David Brinkley* that not enough has been done yet to help blacks get educated and get jobs. "Much more has to be done. It's essentially a problem of economics, education, and opportunity. I've always believed we have to work harder to educate everyone, especially those most disadvantaged, such as the blacks." Powell also said that once black Americans are educated, they must be assisted in finding jobs.

Not *enough* has been done, General? Never mind the trillions spent by the Department of Education? Head Start? The Office of Economic Opportunity? Model Cities? Special education projects, remedial reading projects, racial quotas in hiring and college admissions and college scholarships? Never mind that blacks are or have been the elected mayors of the biggest and most powerful cities in America, including New York, Los Angeles, Chicago, and Washington, D.C.

The fact is, black Americans occupy every profession and trade, own banks and chains of businesses, teach at the finest universities. Given opportunity, they have grabbed and run with it, and done spectacularly well. Others have not. Whose fault? America's, for not doing enough? Or for doing too much for those who are vulnerable to the temptations of dependency, who when offered a governmental crutch will grab and lean on it, hard, and for a lifetime?

Powell as Joint Chiefs of Staff chairman told President Clinton he was all wet on wanting to open the nation's military services to admitted homosexuals. That took a man who has the courage of his convictions. A career army officer standing up to the President of the United States on an explosive policy issue that could hurt the president politically? Unheard of, at least since General of the Army Douglas MacArthur stood up to President Harry S Truman and got fired. That act of principle by Powell told the world he had the gumption to be a good president. It was already evident he had the administrative, managerial, and "people" skills to run the country. And a good deal more intelligence than many who have run the country. But a good *conservative* president? Ah, that's another matter. Powell said no to homosexuals in the military, but he also says he has *no* objection to male homosexual couples or lesbian couples raising children. Hey, the important thing is to give kids family love and discipline. Ah, "*discipline*" might not have been the ideal word here. But, say, whatever happened to the concept of role models and how crucial they are to the development of children?

What's Powell think of the balanced budget amendment to the

****

Constitution that the *Contract with America* promised, that Ronald Reagan sought when he was president, and most conservative economic policy groups and the so-called Religious Right have endorsed? The General thinks that rather than tinkering with the Constitution, Congress ought to find the "will" to spend and tax more responsibly. General, have you ever noticed that while you were serving in all those administrations for all those presidents for all those years that the only will Congress was finding was the will to believe that pork was the only healthy diet for every member of Congress, every day, in every way?

How is the General on the issue of abortion? Conservative in thinking that there's no excuse for an unwanted pregnancy. As in, *Oh, so that's* where babies come from? Conservative in thinking once a woman is pregnant, the moral thing to do is have the baby. But libertarian in opposing the government's banning abortions.

So what else is there that's known about the Harlem-born, Bronx-raised, public-school educated, Jamaican-American with the soft voice, friendly smile? Powell will be fifty-nine on Presidential Inauguration Day, 1997. He graduated from the City College of New York, got his Master of Business Administration degree from George Washington University, married Alma V. Johnson, and has three grown children, Michael, Linda, and Annemarie. He earned his Army commission through a college Reserve Officers Training Corps program, and brings a freight car full of public adulation to the political mix.

By a hefty majority, rank-and-file Republicans and Democrats see leadership, integrity, intellect, and character as Powell's candidate strengths. ABC commentator Jeff Greenfield called him "the most compelling public speaker in the United States today. He can move a crowd with inspiration." Now, this may be a case when Jeff would rather be adulatory than right. But Powell *can* hold his own at a podium, which is more than can be said for many of the Republicans who declared for their party's 1996 presidential nomination.

Powell may feign political ignorance. Don't believe it. During the 1994 elections, Powell contributed $1,000 each to a Republican and a Democrat in the 1994 race for Chuck Robb's U.S. Senate seat. No, he didn't back his former National Security Council colleague, retired

****

Marine Lieutenant General Oliver North. Nor did he back the incumbent, Robb. Rather, Powell opened his wallet for the two candidates not endorsed by the respective parties: Democrat L. Douglas Wilder and Republican Marshall Coleman.

What about Powell, the hero of Desert Storm, as a person? Folks who've dropped over to his house because his kid and their kid were doing something together say he comes to the door to greet you in barbecue duds and a can of beer in one hand. Cheap beer. This is *not* the sign of a snob.

And don't you wish you had his résumé? He went through jump school, Ranger school. Lugged around his training squad's machine gun. *Two* Vietnam combat tours. Returns to Washington, D.C., and picks up a master's degree *and* a White House fellowship. Used the academic honor's internship to work for Caspar Weinberger and Frank Carlucci in the Nixon White House's Office of Management and Budget. Talk about fateful career choices. Ever onward and upward, he did his Jimmy Carter stint as a senior military adviser to the deputy defense secretary and then served as executive assistant to the secretary of the Department of Energy.

Hang in. We're still talking about the same man here. In 1981, Powell helped the Reagan transition team replace Carter Defense Department appointees. From 1983 to 86, he was military assistant to his old boss, Reagan Defense Secretary Weinberger. He helped plan the Grenada invasion and the bombing of Libya. The next year, he moved to the White House as assistant to Carlucci, who was then President Reagan's national security adviser. Later that year, when Carlucci replaced Weinberger as defense secretary, Powell became NSA for the remainder of Reagan's presidential tour.

George Bush knew Powell from Bush's days as vice president. They chatted during NSC meetings. In 1989, Bush appointed him Joint Chiefs chairman. Even the usual back-stabbers and constant complainers said he did a bang-up job. Unlike his consensus-building predecessors, he made decisions, including on strategic planning for Desert Shield and Desert Storm. Dissenters were free to voice their opinions — then shut up and go along with the Powell program. Powell stuck with that job through the early beginnings of the Clinton

✳✳

administration, and retired in 1993 after thirty-five years in the Army.

A modestly begun bicoastal movement called the "Exploratory Draft Colin Powell for President Committee" hoped to muster enough grass-roots clamor to convince Powell to jump into the 1996 presidential race. But some Republican conservatives and some Republican liberals were, unbeknownst to each other or to the rest of the world, getting up every morning and praying that Powell would run as a Republican. His popularity in the polls suggested invincibility. Invincibility tends, however, to evaporate like morning dew in the hot sun when the supposedly invincible starts baring his soul to the masses in an American presidential campaign.

This much can be said about Powell without exaggeration. He made it to the top by dint of hard work and an acute sense of institutional politics in both the military and civilian-governmental worlds. Lots of people have brains but can't remember where they put them. Powell never took his great gift of intelligence for granted. He used it every day in every way. His success from modest, even humble beginnings makes fat white men feel good about themselves and their country. This is no small accomplishment.

Given all that, could liberals live with him as their candidate and their president? Not easily, not if they're serious about their ideology. Powell is a small-government man and says so. But, overall, he is in the middle, neither left nor right. He has said that explicitly. Conservative Republicans say the GOP loses when it presents itself as in the middle, offering no real alternative to the Democrats. So what's the "ergo" for conservatives? Ergo, conservatives who think Colin Powell should be their party's nominee and become the first black president of the United States because he is a full-blown conservative like them, might do well to think again. And what about liberals who think *they* can get along with a black president who believes in individual responsibility, self-denial, and living within your means? They, too, should think again.

☆ ☆ ☆ ☆ ☆ ☆ ☆ ☆ ☆
ARLEN SPECTER
Lonesome Dove

DOES IT TAKE A PHILADELPHIA LAWYER to figure out how to run this country? Arlen Specter thinks so. But then—su*pr-ise* — he's a Philadelphia lawyer. How can you know for sure he's a lawyer? *You* know. No skid marks.

Actually, Arlen wasn't your run of the mill tax attorney or ambulance chaser. He was once the *district attorney of Philadelphia*. This was around the time that W. C. Fields thought of changing his epitaph. He didn't. It was too late.

It's not too late for Specter. To be president, that is. He'll be a month shy of sixty-seven on Inauguration Day, 1997. But he's not there, not the Republican Party's nominee. Not yet. Not *ever*, say his conservative Republican friends. Not many say that. He doesn't *have* many conservative Republican friends. Except in the United States Senate, where it's not who you are or what you believe that counts. It's that you're *there*, period. Hey, isn't that what clubs are for?

At the drop of a hat, Arlen Specter will tell you he is a conservative on economic issues but a bighearted, touchy-feely liberal on issues that matter, in social policy. If there's no hat to drop, he'll tell you this at the drop of an eyelid. And there's a lot of that when he starts with his spiel about being opposed to abortion personally but being personally opposed to *opposing* abortion legally and constitutionally, if you catch his nuance. To dedicated pro-lifers, that's like saying you're *personally* opposed to murder but otherwise you think murder should be a *private* matter between a murderer and his murderee.

✸✸

Sure, you can make fun of him — he got booed when Dan Quayle introduced him at the August 1995 Iowa Republican Party's octennial (the last one was in 1988) fundraiser-economic development-project-and-straw-poll, attended by more than 10,000 Republicans, including some Iowa residents. Specter got booed again by the same crowd an hour or so later when he took the stage.

He did whine about the poll being only for candidates with lots and lots of donors, candidates who could afford to fly and bus supporters in from other states and buy tickets for them to the straw poll and otherwise demonstrate that, unlike him, they have the contributors and organizations to compete seriously for the nomination, whereas he, being the party of the first part *and* from Philadelphia *and* a lawyer — and everybody *knows* lawyers, especially *Philadelphia* lawyers, won't stoop to engage in such rampant election rigging, even if the Iowa straw poll is the biggest equal-opportunity rigged election in the Western World.... Needless to say, Specter placed very low in that ten-man poll, which Phil Gramm and/or Bob Dole and/or Pat Buchanan won, more or less, given the agonized counting and creative arithmetic of the Iowa GOP sponsors who managed to take electronic ballot machines, which produce instant, accurate results if left to their own devices, and make them seem like Third World voting booths, complete with suspicious delays in counting and improbable ties.

Sure they booed Specter for trashing their straw poll, but they also booed him for saying he was in the nomination race because he is determined to move the Republican Party back to the center—where it had such spectacular success under George Bush, Arlen?

Where were we? Oh, yes. It would be easy to make fun of him, but the fact is, Arlen Specter is a major figure in the liberal wing of the Republican Party. It would be an exaggeration to say he is the *only* member of the liberal wing of the Republican Party. There are others, too few to mention here. But you know who you are.

You have an idea of how many liberals populate the GOP's ranks when Specter, whom Keystone State voters first sent to the United States Senate in 1990, announced his candidacy for the 1996 GOP nomination at a largely deserted Lincoln Memorial in the spring of

1995. This immediately raised the question of *why* he announced it, at the Lincoln Memorial or anywhere else. But before anyone could try to answer that, he took the podium and told several park workmen, a few reporters, and some of his loyal staff that he would alter the Republican Party platform's abortion plank to rid it of the abortion issue altogether.

Taking up that *other* burning issue on every American voter's mind, he vowed to relocate America's Embassy in Israel from Tel Aviv to Jerusalem. Always a gentleman, the Senator-Prosecutor from the home of the cheese steak began his presidential nomination campaign by attacking fellow Republican Pat Buchanan, who also is running for the nomination. In the same breath, he also attacked fellow Republican and Christian Coalition founder Pat Robertson, who isn't running. Robertson last ran eight years ago, which is recent enough to deserve an attack from Specter, whose wing of the Republican Party can assemble in the same phone booth to get a call from him, don't you think?

"I will lead the fight to strip the strident antichoice language from the Republican national platform and replace it with language that respects human life — but also respects the diversity of opinion within our own party on this issue," the Pennsylvania Republican said. Several workmen looked up. A plane was passing overhead.

Under a midmorning sky filled with rain clouds, Specter, who was standing in front of the Great Emancipator's memorial, quoted another Republican and fan of Lincoln's — Jack Kemp. Kemp was the Bush administration's Housing and Urban Development secretary and the pinup boy of all true-blue conservatives and neoconservatives (but not of some traditional conservatives) when he ran for the 1988 GOP nomination. That was then. Specter, announcing his nomination bid, stands there, a lonely figure at Lincoln's feet, and says Jack Kemp "put it best when he said that when it comes to moral values, we must seek to persuade rather than impose."

That was a message to the rest of the Republican Party not to give into the anti-abortion Christian conservatives in Pat Robertson's Christian Coalition, James Dobson's Focus on the Family, Beverly LeHaye's Concerned Women for America, Don Wildmon's American

Family Association, Gary Bauer's Family Research Council, the religious conservatives who were elected to head the GOP in many states and counties across the country. Specter should have talked to Wisconsin Republican Party Chairman David Opitz, who is not a religious conservative but who said in 1995: "It's no longer whether religious conservatives can get their noses under the GOP tent. They *are* the tent."

Specter has his admirers, of course, and they are where you would expect to find them. *Time* magazine called him a "fiercely independent politician who keeps his own counsel." *Time*, in a perpetual state of profound repentance for having been founded by Henry Luce and originally infused with his, *ugh*, troglodytic politics, has spent the last few decades testing to see if the left side of the spectrum has an end or just keeps going. Of *course Time* thinks Specter, who is pro-choice, is fiercely independent of, well, what? The radical feminists and the People for the American Way? Wasn't a big reason he was running for president in 1995 to ensure that he gets reelected as senator and to use the presidential nomination campaign as a vehicle for trying to make it up to the libs for having grilled that nice lady, Anita Hill, so harshly? And, of course, *Time* thinks Arlen keeps his own counsel, as opposed to, say, Bob Dole, who is what?—pathetically dependent and relies on the counsel of Trent? Lott, that is.

There is a modicum of truth in *Time*'s observation. The path of Republican liberalism can be tortuous. In 1985, Specter outraged moderates and liberals by voting money for the MX missile program. Conservatives fumed the following year when he refused to support U.S. aid to Nicaragua's anti-Communist or contra rebels. In 1987, conservatives were mumbling unpleasantries about Specter's parentage after he helped scuttle President Reagan's nomination of Robert Bork to Supreme Court. To Specter's great credit, however, he was courtly and confident enough to telephone Bork to break the news himself.

Four years later, Specter did a curious thing, an ideologically atypical thing, something which more than anything else accounts for his 1995–1996 quixotically liberal quest for the presidential nomination of what passes for the conservative party in America (the GOP). In 1991, the last full year of the Bush administration, he stoked the fires of the special Hell liberals mentally have set aside for Republican conservatives. And, what he did left even him pale and shaking from the intensity of hate mail he got. No, it didn't come from the Right Wing "fringe," a term he likes to hurl at the assortment of moral-values hawkers, pro-lifers, religious conservatives, and big-government bashers he claims has taken over *his* Republican Party, lock, stock, and Country Club.

The hellish fireballs of political and ideological threats came from liberals and feminists after Specter, deciding that this time he would play on his own party's team and try to get Senate confirmation of George Bush's nominee to the Supreme Court, Judge Clarence Thomas. The obstacle that appeared out of nowhere was a viperous lady named Anita Hill. She managed to bring the old district attorney out in Specter. He was relentless, yes, even cross, in cross-examining her. Hill's supposed nightmares over a bizarre recollection of hers that had Thomas talking about finding pubic hairs on a can of soda pop was nothing compared with the living nightmare she came to endure at the specter of Specter, seated *en banc* with the other Senate Judiciary Committee members, opening his mike and grilling her.

Somehow he had discerned in her a phony, a black woman who wore her rectitude on her sleeve, a career-climber with a hidden agenda, that agenda being to *discredit* a black man who thought he could get away with not reciting the Left Wing cant all media and establishment-recognized black leaders are supposed to spout. And to make of him an object lesson for other uppity black men. Well, Thomas got away with it, and others will follow. Conservatives and fair-minded Americans of all stripe have Specter to thank as much as anyone else.

But how did the good senator from the city with the cracked bell get *on* to this strange creature, this Miss Anita Hill, with her shadowy liberal agenda? Cynics would say it took one to know one, but such cynicism would be, well, cynical. Specter was good. Hill's obstructionism failed. The Democratic-dominated Senate confirmed Thomas, who became the first and only black conservative justice to serve on the Supreme Court of the United States.

✶✶✶

Specter is a tough law and order guy when he wants to be and he wanted to be after the bombing of the federal building in Oklahoma City in April 1995. Such tragedies always provide Congress with an opportunity to hold public hearings, the thrust of which is to display the intense opposition of members of Congress to evil in any form; in this case, mindless terrorist bombings. But if you're running for your party's presidential nomination and your party is kinda conservative and you're kinda liberal...then, hey, this is your chance to score points with what used to be your party's Right Wing but is now also its fuselage, tail section, landing gear, and engines.

Specter got to do district attorney–turned–Senator number, inviting civilian militia members to testify before the Senate Judiciary Committee's Subcommittee on Terrorism, Technology, and Government Information — yes, they gave a subcommittee that name, you can look it up — and the way he handled things didn't go over too big with your serious Left in this country. Ergo, one of the most darkly humorous attacks on Specter came from Daniel Levitas, director of the Institute for Research and Education on Human Rights, in an article he wrote for *The Nation* magazine.

Levitas's diatribe against the mid-June 1995 civilian militia hearings chaired by Senator Specter was, as they say in soft drink commercials, "classic." It made Specter out to be a running dog of the Republican Right Wing. God bless you *Nation* magazine and Daniel Levitas, Specter must have said to himself, or should have said to himself.

Among the charges Levitas leveled at Specter was his "undermining charges of white supremacy" as the core motivation behind the militia movement. What did Arlen do to put the Left in this state of high dudgeon? He let James Johnson testify. So? Well, James Johnson is black *and* a militia member. Whoa. Levitas — are you ready for this? — also accused Specter of failing to expose the militia movement's anti-Semitism. Admittedly, Levitas went a bit far, even for Specter's needs. Accusing a Jewish senator from Philadelphia of being soft on anti-Semitism? *Come* on.

"If Senator Arlen Specter had been half as hard on the militia movement as he was on Anita Hill," his hearings "might have truly discredited the radical Right" was Levitas's bottom line.

So, how does Specter see himself philosophically? He calls himself a "Goldwater" Republican, opposed to big government and for more personal freedom. To the extent the militia movement reflected similar distrust of big government by citizens guilty of no criminal offense, it got no quarrel from Specter. Specter believes every citizen, regardless of political label, has the right to assemble and demonstrate under First Amendment protection. Not exactly a revolutionary idea any longer, unless you work for the federal Bureau of Alcohol, Tobacco, and Firearms. Specter's hearing may not have been the most enlightening in the long, unenlightening history of congressional hearings, but it did allow militia members to explain their movement, at a time when militia bashing might have gone over big in some quarters.

Specter's claim to be a Goldwater conservative has merit to the extent that Barry Goldwater in his declining years has meandered all over the ideological map, mostly taking the road to the left at every fork. Something like that could be said for Specter. Take Robert Bork and gun control, for example.

The press and the two political parties treated Bork's nomination to the Supreme Court as a Right-Left struggle over ideology. The Reagan White House and Bork himself argued that Bork was a political centrist. It was and it wasn't. The National Rifle Association — not exactly your repository for stray Leninists — got Bork in its sights early and kept blasting him. Why? From the NRA's viewpoint, Bork was a sloppy constitutional scholar. Which is to say, they didn't like *his* reading of the Constitution. His claim that the Second Amendment was a collective, not individual, right made them want to Bork *him*.

Specter gave Bork a thumbs-down, as did the NRA, but there the confluence of opinion between Senator Cheese Steak and the pro-gun lobby ended. It had to. Specter soon backed a lot of provisions in President Clinton's Omnibus Crime Bill, including the ban on "assault weapons," which drove every logician bananas. Why would you ban some weapons that fire every time you pull the trigger without having to cock the hammer and manually eject a shell first? Are the weapons banned typically used by criminals in violent crimes? No. Are there far more such semiautomatic weapons not banned? Yes. Do criminals have access to banned weapons? Yes. Do honest citizens who want to defend themselves have access to banned weapons? No. It was enough to make pro-gun enthusiasts see ulterior motives, to think, if not to say aloud: Arlen, *Arlen*. Where's your logic? On loan to the same constituency that said you won't get reelected senator unless you atone for your Anita Hill sin and get with the feminist/gun-confiscating crowd? Sure looks like it.

Maybe, but Specter devoted his public career not just to setting himself up for catcalls from conservative Republicans in Iowa. He devoted himself to the rule of law. The pro-gun crowd may firmly believe that guns don't kill people, but rather that bad people with guns kill good people who don't have guns. But the gun controllers and firearm confiscators just as firmly believe that the relatively easy access to guns by people other than law enforcers undermines the rule of law.

As a former prosecutor, Specter took seriously the responsibility of bringing to justice those who trample the rights of others. The camera-dazzling Anita Hill had worked for Clarence Thomas as an enforcer of civil rights statutes and regulations. She had the responsibility of championing the rights of those who suffered the exact abuses she claimed to have endured at his hands. When his alleged transgressions occurred, she did nothing. Later, as a professor of law with the tremendous power to shape new generations of legal rights defenders, she still kept her lips zippered. A former Philly district attorney didn't need partisan or ulterior political motives of party or personal self-advancement to suspect Hill's judgment, credibility, and integrity.

To Specter, the lovely Miss Hill may have represented something more than an attempt to derail Judge Thomas's career. That something more rankled Specter, who clearly enjoyed helping turn Hill from a sympathetic figure into a suspect witness.

When Specter launched his nomination campaign long before his debacle in the Iowa GOP straw poll, he represented himself to supporters in Iowa as "Anita Hill's chief inquisitor." They stood and cheered him. But when he warned that the constitutional wall between church and state must be preserved, the audience broke into catcalls. To Specter, this made no sense. His father had trudged across Europe for a chance at a life of opportunity in America. Specter saw that opportunity threatened by anything less than what in his mind must be an arm's-length constitutional separation between government and religion. Specter's father, Harry, left a czarist Russian town where his was the sole Jewish family. The prospect of the "Christian" battalions in the GOP's revolutionary army dictating public policy conjures visions of his forebears awaiting the Cossacks.

It is beside the point that such a fear is insulting to your average fundamentalist, born-again Christian, charismatic, evangelical, or conservative Catholic who thinks of himself and his coreligionists as defenders of American constitutional freedoms, not would-be tramplers.

Specter openly defied his colleagues who "convert" for the sake of political advantage. He assailed the "Religious Right" itself as "that fringe." He chided Newt Gingrich, before he became House speaker, for his *Contract with America*. Specter proffered instead something he called the *Contract with the Constitution*.

To those who questioned Specter's ability to wage a serious campaign built upon a pro-choice or abortion rights platform, Specter responded with his version of Gingrich's ten-point contract. Specter's Ten Commitments to America include making reductions to balance the federal budget, paying down on the national debt, and stimulating economic growth by replacing the income tax with a 20 percent, single-rate, flat tax. So far sounds like your conservative's conservative ideal platform.

Specter's *Ten Commitments* also promise to reduce crime, improve education, reform health-care costs by means of the free market, to provide strong leadership in international affairs, curb weapons of mass destruction, control terrorism, and champion tolerance and freedom. Is there a freedom-loving, government-fearing conservative anywhere who wouldn't cotton to Arlen's Ten? You bet there are. It's not what his platform says, it's what his record says about how he interprets his own promises.

The American Conservative Union, one of the oldest national membership organizations around, has been rating members of Congress on their legislative voting records for years. A zero means you're so far Left you think Ted Kennedy is a moderate. A 100 percent ACU rating means you always voted for truth, justice, freedom, and capitalism and are probably qualified for sainthood or the non-Catholic equivalent (never *mind* that there isn't one — we're talking politics, not religion here anyhow). The ACU awarded a 39 percent lifetime rating, a 46 percent for his 1994 voting performance, and a 57 percent for 1993. A raving lefty he isn't. But compare his scores with other 1996 GOP presidential nomination wannabes, like Senator Phil Gramm of Texas. The ACU gave Gramm a 96 percent lifetime rating, 100 percent for 1994, and a 92 percent in 1993. Senate Majority Leader Bob Dole racked up an 82 lifetime ACU score, earned 100 percent in 1994, and 88 percent in 1993. That other would-be GOP nominee from the Senate, Richard Lugar of Indiana, got an 82 percent lifetime rating from ACU, a 76 percent in 1994, and 72 percent in 1993.

ACU to Specter: I knew a conservative. He was a friend. And *you're* no conservative. Specter to ACU: You cooked the books. You choose votes that fit *your* concept of conservatism. I'd tell you to go fly a kite if I thought you knew how to tie a string.

Specter sees a candidacy not based on pro-choice but on removing the abortion issue from the GOP platform as completely viable. It's not because there are more pro-life single issue voters than pro-choice single issue voters who 'll go to the polls and vote against a candidate who agrees with them on every other issue but abortion. Pro-lifers make up a steadily growing portion of the GOP primary and caucuses voters — the nuts who trudge through the snow to some home or fire hall on a freezing night in February to vote for a delegate to go to the Republican presidential nominating convention that summer. In August 1996, it'll be in San Diego.

Undeterred, Specter embraced what amounts to a pro-choice stand so expansively that he's recruited Planned Parenthood and the National Abortion Rights Action League (NARAL) to help him campaign. Many conservatives are pro-choice or not passionately involved with the issue, one way or the other, but from the standpoint of pro-life conservatives, enlisting Planned Parenthood and NARAL is like recruiting the Bolshevik wing of the Russian Social Democratic Party to write a five-year plan for privatizing the Russian economy. Actually, practically all conservatives think Planned Parenthood and NARAL are Left-Wing conspiracies that go well beyond the abortion issue and so are ill disposed to seeing any Republican get cozy with those outfits.

But to Specter's way of thinking, it's a smart move for two reasons, or he would not have made it. Reason 1: Well-heeled pro-choice GOP campaign donors will open their hearts and their checkbooks to him. At least, that's what they, thought, when he, with the advice and planning of sometimes GOP campaign consultant Roger Stone, decided to jump into the race in the first place. Reason 2: Specter supporters will tell you the world is full of pro-choicers and they will cite the *New York Times* poll that reported 43 percent of New Hampshire Republicans and fully 70 percent of Republicans nationally as saying they don't want the government to make abortions illegal.

In fact, less superficial readings of that and similar polls suggest that Americans who oppose outright total bans or a constitutional amendment making all abortions illegal are nonetheless conflicted about the issue. They're uncomfortable with the idea of aborting a fetus, whether they regard it as a human life at that point or not. They favor restrictions, such as parental notification or consent, spousal notification or consent, outlawing abortions in the last three months or even earlier.

Arlen Specter does have one rather sizable problem. The GOP faithful who claim to be pro-choice...do not support Specter for president.

Specter is a lonely figure who says he wants to make peace with his party but is not exactly favored by the betting in London that specializes in U.S. presidential oddsmaking. He didn't bother trying to pack the house with his voters in Ames, Iowa, in the summer of 1995, not because he didn't have a campaign kitty that could afford it (he didn't, but that's how it goes for lonesome doves). Rather, he complained that the process wasn't a "real election" — no kidding, Arlen? — and got rewarded for his observations by placing tenth out of ten Republican presidential nomination hopefuls. Of the more than 10,000 votes cast, he got exactly 67. It takes a man of courage, a man from La Mancha, a windmill tilter, to stay with it. So, march on, oh Arlen, march on. If not '96, then in 2000 or 2004. Anything is possible in the land of opportunity.

(Well, almost anything.)

★ ★ ★ ★ ★ ★ ★ ★ ★

PETE WILSON

One Man Bland or Earth Quaker?

WHEN PETE WILSON GAZES THROUGH HIS BLUE EYES into the middle distance, what does he see? Himself being sworn in as the first Republican president since George Bush.

It's *not* a pretty sight for some conservative Republicans. At a time when religious and moral-values activists have never been stronger in his party, Wilson says flat out that he wants to strip the party platform of its pro-life plank and replace it with a pro-family plank that both pro-life and pro-choice Republicans can support. Call him a California dreamer. He once signed into law a bill opponents said granted special rights to homosexuals. He said it simply ensured them the same rights as everybody else. He even has a bad ideological reputation with some on the Right who aren't personally big on the abortion or homosexual-rights issues, one way or the other. So why does Wilson, who is nothing if not a demonstrably smart man, think he has a good shot?

He'll tell you he's been elected and reelected to many things — mayor, state legislator, U.S. senator. And you'll say, So? He'll tell you he's a state governor. Again you'll say, So? He'll remind you he's the Governor of the state of California. And you'll say, Ah *so*. Suddenly, this man with short brown hair and nondescript features is not five feet ten but fifty feet tall. In American politics, California is more than a state of mind. It's a national earthquake waiting to happen.

Wilson has shown, time and again, that he knows electoral earth shakers and how to stand astride them if not cause them. He knows that somehow bland is good, when it's his bland. And that he can play Sisyphus for four years as he did in his first term, endure having the boulder tumble back down on him day after day and in the end heave it over the top and thumb his nose at history.

Hey, is that your California Pete or *what*? The comeback kid. The feisty former high-school boxer who picks himself up from the mat and continues the fight and puts the other guy down for the count. Go find a better résumé than the one owned by this man who speaks in a monotone, even when he is excited, which is never, and which also is precisely how often he displays a sense of humor.

Wilson is neither too young nor too old to be the leader of the Free World and Planet Earth. He was sixty-one when he declared for the GOP nomination in the spring of 1995. He chose to be born to an advertising father in upscale Lake Forest, Illinois, precisely in the "mid" of the Midwest, about six months after Franklin D. Roosevelt was sworn in for the first time as President of the United States.

Wilson then chose to be raised — wouldn't you know it? — in a St. Louis suburb in the Harry Truman, show-me, heartland, slightly southern state of Missouri. He picked the East Coast, north but not too far north, for undergraduate training at the prestigious, privately funded Yale University. For balance, he picked the prestigious but publicly funded University of California at Berkeley law school on the West Coast for graduate school

He served not just in the U.S. military, but in the he-man's, soul-stirring branch: the United States Marine Corps. He picked San Diego to settle in and get elected mayor of, the same city that was to be named as the Republican National Convention site for the August 1996 crowning of the Republican Presidential nominee. Does this guy plan ahead or *what*?

He could have married poor and ugly. But, *no*, Pete Wilson had to marry rich and beautiful — and tall and blonde. Nine years after Pete first greeted the world, Gayle Edlund was born in Phoenix, where she grew up across the street from department store magnate and future GOP presidential candidate Barry Goldwater. You bet he knew that decades later he would have throat surgery when everyone else would be announcing for the GOP presidential nomination and his pretty,

****

rich, blonde wife and former president of the San Diego Junior League wife would have to deliver his early campaign speeches while his throat and voice were on the mend. And don't you just know he knew when he married her that she would be wise enough to be almost as dull as he is on the stump?

And since one out of two marriages ends in divorce nationally (Californians — who brag like Texans but without the accent — claim that in their state, it's two out of every three marriages that end in divorce), it would make sense for a future presidential candidate to be a divorcée, and to marry one. He is and he did. Wilson's wife, Gayle, a Stanford University–Phi Beta Kappa alumna in biology, had first married a San Diego lawyer, breaking up with him after their two sons entered grade school. That was in the early years of the Reagan presidency. Workaholic Wilson had broken up with his first wife and he and Gayle began dating. They took their vows in 1983.

That was just after Wilson had won his first term to the U. S. Senate, in November 1982. He won reelection in 1986, but couldn't wait to grab on to the next rung on his ladder to political heaven. Instead of finishing out his second U.S. Senate term, he got himself nominated for the California governorship and then got himself elected to run this adopted state of his that boasts every thing from Hollywood to swine. That was in 1990, when it should also be noted that the Republicans desperately needed a governor of their own to offset a Democrat-dominated legislature that was determined to redistrict the Republicans out of existence. Nonetheless, Wilson managed to get himself in deep trouble in his first term, having raised taxes big time while the economy began to resemble your typical Third World basket case. He went into his reelection contest in 1994 trailing his Democrat opponent by 25 percentage points and then upset her by 15 points. That opponent, Kathleen Brown, the Democratic nominee and sister of Jerry "Moonbeam" Brown, the former governor, had been considered a shoo-in.

Once again, Wilson rose like a phoenix from the ashes of his self-inflicted destruction. How did this man do it?

More than any other Republican holding a major elected office, Wilson managed to be Big Government's best friend when needed and

Small Government's champion when required and to be both as often as not. He wanted to end federal welfare entitlements and send the federal tax money once used for them back to the states to use as they see fit to deal with their welfare problems. But he also wanted to attach federal strings to deal with the illegitimacy crisis destroying American civilization.

Like Phil Gramm — in fact, before Phil Gramm — Wilson wanted to require the states to deny benefits to girls under eighteen who have children out of wedlock. He wanted to make the states stop giving additional benefits for each child born to women already on welfare. He wanted to deny benefits to legal aliens so they would not come here seeking welfare. He wanted enforceable work requirements for the able-bodied. Score him 100 on the social conservatives' purity of essence test.

But he also wanted to compensate for the denial of these benefits by *expanding* — as in spend more dollars on—nutrition programs for women, infants, and children, for Head Start, school-lunch and breakfast and other Nanny State, feel-good, dependency-inducing welfare state programs. Your thin-lipped cynic might be tempted to say this is how your basic Big Government Republican gets to have his cake and eat it too in a party and an era that was becoming more conservative than Barry Goldwater was conservative when Goldwater was a conservative, *if* he was conservative.

Wilson's loveliest balancing act from a political technician's viewpoint was his abortion stand, which made him pro-choice but not-too-ridiculously-way-far-out for the Republican Party as a 1995 presidential nomination hopeful. Wilson averred as how he wanted to keep abortion legal but didn't want the government to pay for abortions, even for poverty-stricken, pregnant wagon-riding women who couldn't for gosh sakes *afford* your real, medical, abortion-clinic abortion. Hey, is that tough love?

Early in the summer of 1995, U.S. Senator Arlen Specter of Pennsylvania, a militant pro-choice liberal and a Wilson GOP nomination rival, even tried to nail Pete on "abandoning his pro-choice stand." Specter cited the governor's "shift" as a "sad example of politics over principle."

Specter almost sounded like a stalking horse for Wilson, as if Specter was *trying* to make Wilson sound more acceptable to national religious and antiabortion leaders. "Wilson has capitulated to [Christian Coalition founder] Pat Robertson, [Christian Coalition executive director] Ralph Reed Jr. and [conservative pundit and GOP nomination candidate] Pat Buchanan, and I think that's bad for the Republican Party and bad for America," Specter huffed at a news conference he had called in front of the U.S. Supreme Court. "This is obviously a matter of letting principle be subordinated to politics."

Wilson could not be more delighted that Specter called on all pro-choice Republicans to back Specter's efforts to remove the party's anti-abortion plank, which would change the Constitution to make abortion a crime. "I am the only pro-choice candidate running for the Republican nomination for president," Specter, a former prosecutor, boasted — in what would have amounted to perjury had he been under oath. But Wilson wasn't about to accuse the Pennsylvania Republican of anything of the sort. In fact, as if taking his cues from the Wilson campaign, Specter plunged on, saying things that Wilson, who was seriously after the nomination, would never say, attacking forces within the Republican Party's national coalition that are vital for winning the nomination and the election.

"There's no doubt about that at all," Specter yelled into the microphones in front of the Supreme Court. "The governor has run up the white flag in capitulation to Robertson, Reed and Buchanan...It's another step where the fringe is dominating the party and really trying to change the Constitution."

Wilson loved it. Let Arlen go out there and bash the fundamentalists and champions of the "unborn"and call them religious nuts and fringe-group, extremist crackpots. For his party, Specter had gotten suckered into making Wilson look better to skeptical conservatives. Specter thought he was capitalizing on a newspaper story that quoted Wilson campaign chairman Craig Fuller, as saying that Wilson, if nominated, wouldn't instruct his people on the convention's platform committee to deep-six the GOP anti-abortion plank. "We'll let it go forward," Fuller was quoted as saying. Fuller's statements, made for a Wilson temporarily silenced by throat surgery, merely reflected strategic and timing differences within the Wilson campaign organization. Wilson in fact reaffirmed his support for erasing the abortion issue from the party platform but *also* repeated his opposition to the federal government's funding abortion. Cynics might argue that Wilson was executing a tactical waffle, offering something for both sides on the abortion question. Cynics would be Right.

Wilson's problem is persuading conservatives that he can address an issue and come down on the right side of it without first being carefully scripted by hired guns on the Right. Actually, he did cut California's budget by $1.6 billion in his first term, without the help of a speech writer. He also caught the first scents of affirmative action, welfare reform and illegal immigration as the hot issues of the 1990s.

To legions of suspicious conservatives, Wilson is forever illustrating that under the skin of the hard-core Right-Winger that is running for the Republican nomination is a liberal desperately trying to break out and be heard once again. Wilson feeds this suspicion over and over. In midsummer 1995, he said that parents' involvement with their children is even more important than per-pupil spending on the schools, thus reinforcing the suspicion among Wilson-haters that he thinks there's a direct correlation between spending and quality.

In fact, Wilson has argued that letting people into public school classrooms who know something worth teaching, but have no training, is better than having unionized vacuum skulls who spent seven years learning how to teach but never learned what to teach. Letting the know-somethings replace the professional know-nothings at the head of the classroom is called *alternative credentialing*, and Peter the Bland backed it. Still, conservatives aren't comfy with Wilson's claim that he understands that public money doesn't make quality education. That, in fact, virtually every study for the past forty years has shown an inverse relationship: as public spending on primary and secondary education has kept going up, the quality has kept going down.

Wilson's paid propagandists claim he understands that the obvious reason is the education industry. Teachers' unions making sure that what future teachers must study in college involves variations on how to pass out chalk and how to teach history or English, rather than the actual study *of* history or English. "Special education" teachers requiring special supervisors in the administrative bureaucracy of the school or the school district. Principals who may be hard-working but who are former teachers who bring their union and "accreditation" biases to their jobs. And on and on.

Wilson sometimes seems to "get it," and yet he opposed the school-choice ballot initiative in 1993, claiming it was badly worded and laden with unintended financial burden for taxpayers. Then there's that lady named Maureen DiMarco. Who is she? A Democrat who pushes bilingual education and social welfare, not to mention social engineering in the public schools is who. So why should Wilson listen to this DiMarco woman? Because he appointed her as his education secretary. That tell you anything? — The school-choice initiative failed, by the way.

Two years before, Wilson once again convinced his conservative critics of what they see as his eagerness to return the GOP to its pre-Goldwater days of somnolence and liberal envy by having his organization field a slate to oppose conservatives in the GOP's legislative primaries. The Wilson fifth columnists mostly lost their primary contests but enervated the conservative victors and confused the electorate yet again as to the differences, if any, between Democrats and Republicans. It didn't help that the Bush reelection campaign, or what passed for a campaign, elected not to put a penny into get-out-the-vote drives in the most voter-rich states in the nation. Not surprisingly, the November 1992 elections dashed Republican hopes for winning a majority.

By the summer of 1995, Wilson had advanced his theretofore little noticed nomination candidacy by having his majority appointees on the University of California Board of Regents vote to end racial and sexual quotas in student admissions and in staff and academic hiring and promotion. Until then he had always supported affirmative action laws and had just signed yet another one into law for California only a few months earlier.

All told, Wilson had, however grudgingly, signed into law twenty-one bills that had tucked inside them little affirmative-action enhancing curlicues.

That sudden about face alone did not qualify Wilson to be the most suspect, self-proclaimed conservative in a highly visible public office. Just when Wilson was getting much needed publicity because of his erasing affirmative action from the University of California system, Wisconsin Governor Tommy Thompson, a pioneer in welfare reform and other measures dear to conservatives' hearts, decided to go public in opposing an end to affirmative action. Thompson thus put himself in direct opposition not only to Wilson but also to Senate Majority Leader Bob Dole, Senator Phil Gramm of Texas, and former Tennessee Governor Lamar Alexander — all GOP nomination contenders and all in favor of stripping federal affirmative action laws of racial and gender quotas and preferences.

Then Wilson publicly supported proposals to end federal welfare entitlements and turn the money over to the states to use as they saw fit with only a few federal strings attached: no benefits to girls under eighteen who bear children out of wedlock; no additional benefits to mothers on welfare who have additional children; no benefits to legal aliens and tough enforced work requirements for the able-bodied.

That appeared to put Wilson firmly in the camp of those conservatives — and some liberals, for that matter — who regarded the crisis of illegitimacy on American culture as having reached the emergency stage. One out of every three births are born to unmarried girls or women for the U.S. population as a whole, with more than seven out of ten for the black population.

For a Republican with a reputation as a social liberal — he started in politics as Richard Nixon's advance man — Wilson has taken some cutting-edge stands as Governor. He got out front on the immigration issue when other Republicans wouldn't touch it with a ten-foot pole — or Czech, for that matter. He leaped aboard Proposition 187, the ballot initiative that the whole nation watched in the 1994 elections. Designed to deny public schooling and other taxpayer-financed benefits to illegal aliens, Prop 187 passed overwhelmingly despite opposition from the Compassion Establishment, including Jack Kemp and William Bennett on the Republican side. (Think back ten years, and try to imagine Pete Wilson getting to the Right of Kemp and Bennett.)

He supported and signed into law a "three strikes" provision in February 1994 and a ballot initiative that passed in November 1994

THOSE WHO THINK THEY SHOULD BE PRESIDENT. . .

****

that made life imprisonment for violent three-time losers, part of the state constitution — thus ensuring future legislatures couldn't mess with the concept. He also signed a one-strike law for violent rapists — as opposed to the "May I please" type — and was pushing for 10-2 jury convictions in all criminal cases not involving the death penalty. But to appease liberals, as Senator, he supported gun-control legislation and as governor he supported an "assault weapons" in the apparent belief that only the criminal population should be armed.

He started talking in 1990 about reforming welfare and gets some credit for cracking down on welfare cheats and changing the old system that increased benefits to welfare mothers for each additional child. Wilson even had the brass to sue the federal government for reimbursement for benefits California had to give illegal aliens. He also put the National Guard on the border with Mexico. Wilson had an answer for everything, every charge and accusation, and stick and stone your unforgiving, squint-eyed, hard-nosed conservatives threw at him.

So what if he swore up and down during his 1994 reelection campaign that he wouldn't skip out on his state and run for president in 1996? And, if elected, leave California to the tender mercies of that awful, liberal Democrat, the lieutenant governor, who would automatically finish out what would have been Wilson's last two years as governor?

So what, indeed. There he was, barely having been sworn in for a second term as governor, with a ready answer. "I am able to help my state and the country even more by running for president and by winning than by remaining as governor for the last two years," he said. Why? Because — and now follow the answer man closely—in the last two years of "my term, I would be struggling to wrench concessions from a hostile [Clinton] administration [which] does not share my values or California's, or frankly, I don't think America's values." Geez, Guv, when you put it that way, it's clear you kinda got a civic *duty* to skip out on your promise and run for president.

And, sure, in seeking his first term as governor, Wilson promised he wouldn't raise taxes. But he never said *income* taxes. Okay, so he ended up raising taxes by record amounts, but he had to. He inherited the largest deficit in the history of time, in the history of the universe; well, certainly in the history of the state of California. And he had this liberal Democratic Assembly that refused to let him balance the budget that year solely through spending cuts, even though that's what he really wanted to do, don't you know?

Okay, so you confront him with a clip from a story at the time by a San Francisco reporter and it has him saying he won't raise income taxes and, well, yes he says he did raise income taxes, but he *had* to. And so he *did* twist many a Republican assemblyman's arm to get him to vote with the Democrats for the income tax hike. In California, you needed a two-thirds majority to pass a budget and, naturally, damned few Republicans wanted a recorded vote for an income tax hike. Like the Constitutions of most states, the California Constitution requires a balanced budget every year. As governor, he did the only thing he could do, despite his deep loathing for taxes, don't you know? Plus, he'll tell you, he's cut more state spending than any governor in the country. He'll pull out charts till your eyes glaze over to show you California was spending $1.6 billion less at the end of his first term than in his first year on the job.

There is more than a patina of plausibility here, and no politician makes the case for it more soberly, doggedly, humorlessly than bland-faced Pete Wilson. You begin to understand why he never lost an election, from the San Diego mayoralty to the California Assembly, to the U.S. Senate and the governorship. Okay, he lost the 1978 Republican gubernatorial primary. Give him a break. The man's a winner.

But is California a winner? In the electoral scheme of things, how important is this sunshine, nut-case, moonbeam, looney-tunes state? This state with a bigger economy than most countries have. This state with a great climate and lifestyle practically everybody else would trade theirs for in a heartbeat. (Except, that is, the hundreds of thousands of residents who have been fleeing the state's high taxes, crime, and bad air.) How important electorally is this state? Awesomely. Fifty-four electoral votes. That's twenty percent of what you need for a four-year lease at 1600 Pennsylvania Avenue. But you've got to get enough convention delegates to grab the nomination first. Guess what? Donald Duck Land has 201 of them. That's 16 percent of the total at the 1996 Republican National Convention in San Diego, which just happens to be Wilson's hometown.

What's more, California stopped smoking and inhaling long enough to move its presidential primary election up from June, where for years it came too late to matter, to March 26, 1996, which could make it decisive.

Compare California's delegation with the 121 from Texas and the 100 from New York, the second and third biggest delegations. Yep, you get it. *Californ-I-a* is the closest thing to an 800-pound gorilla you're going to find in America the Beautiful's election process. So it doesn't take a Boalt Hall (University of California at Berkeley) law degree to figure out it's to Wilson's advantage to be from the biggest-delegate state if you want to win your party's nomination. And it doesn't take a Missouri-born Yalie to figure out that it's to the GOP's advantage to virtually assure that Republicans take California by having a Californian heading their presidential ticket.

A major concern of California Republicans is that under their states' law, Lieutenant Governor Gray Davis, a Democrat, would automatically become governor if Wilson wins the presidency. That's not why California Republicans dug deep into their pockets to support his reelection in 1994. Not why many conservatives overlooked his faults to make sure he defeated one liberal Democrat, Kathleen Brown, just to have another liberal Democrat take over the state.

If Wilson has an answer to everything, did he have one to this little problem of succession? You bet. He got three former California GOP chairmen to help him out by promising to cosponsor a November 1996 ballot initiative calling for a special election in case of a gubernatorial vacancy. The initiative would be virtually assured of passage if Mr. Wilson were the nominee and won California in the general election.

Wilson has his admirers among religious conservative leaders, but the Reverend Lou Sheldon, a Californian who is chairman of the Washington-based Traditional Values Coalition, a grass roots lobbying organization of 31,000 churches, had some reservations about that solution. Sheldon told *The Washington Times* in the spring of 1995 that he had "worked hard" for Wilson's reelection in 1994.

✶✶

"We like Wilson, but can we be assured that the [special-election] proposition will qualify, be on the ballot and pass, so we would not end up with Davis as governor?" Sheldon said. Be assured? Get real, Lou. Give Pete a break. He wouldn't have gone into this thing if he thought there were any loose ends he couldn't take care of. The man's a *winner*.

Okay. So what if he dropped out in September? People weren't giving him money. His campaign manager and campaign chairman were giving each other grief. California Republicans were getting ready to pitch eggs and tomatos at their governor for going back on his promise to stick out his second term. Nobody was buying his sudden conversion to red-meat conservatism. *Not his* fault. He gave it a shot. His best shot. Like a winner who is, well, a loser. But, hey, the Dole people were there, even before the decision, secretly offering to buy up the Wilson campaign debt in exchange for Dole's getting important pieces of the Wilson California organization, including the finance end, and some help with the Wilson people in Florida where an all-important November straw poll was to take place. Gramm's campaign organization wasn't far behind, scrambling to pick up the best pieces of the Wilson operation. Nasty-minded people said there wasn't a lot to pick up. *Dole-Wilson '96* bumper stickers began to appear. Mainly in Pete's mind.

Following is a letter that began circulating among California Republicans the day Governor Wilson announced he was quitting the race. (It is of course a satirical letter, and not written by Wilson.)

Dear Californians:

It is with deep regret that I announce that I am withdrawing from the race for president.

Over the past few months, I have learned that I have no friends and realized that I am an incredibly arrogant, self-centered, and philosophically bankrupt politician who constantly lies. It has become obvious that I have no appeal to voters in, or outside, California except when I run against Jerry Brown's little sister. Unfortunately, Jerry's sister isn't running for president.

I am dismayed to learn that most of you never understood

★★★

my message — whatever it was, or would, or could have been tomorrow. If only you had given me a chance. If only I could have raised money. If only I could have made it through at least one primary. If only I had supported Ronald Reagan in 1976. If only I hadn't made such an ass of myself.

In closing, I would just like to say that I am not the loser that you think I am. Those of you who didn't support me, which would include just about everyone except Tom Metzger who was my only major endorsement, can go straight to Hell.

Sincerely,

Pete Wilson

PS: I support abortion funding again.

PART II
★ ★ ★ ★ ★ ★ ★ ★ ★ ★ ★ ★ ★ ★ ★★ ★ ★★ ★ ★★ ★ ★ ★ ★ ★

Dark Horses (or Lightweights?)

★ ★ ★ ★ ★ ★ ★ ★ ★ ★

GEORGE ALLEN

Why's This Man Smiling and Smiling and Smiling?

GEORGE ALLEN, THE GOVERNOR OF VIRGINIA, and Ronald Reagan, the former governor of California, are a lot alike. This observation is good for George Allen and should make him smile.

How are he and the Gipper alike? Both are tall. Allen stands at six feet four inches. Tall is good, in politics and everything else. Studies show that tall persons get better jobs than short persons. The presidency is a good job.

Allen and Reagan have dark hair, rosy cheeks, an aura of sincerity, a flash of humbleness, and do good work on the stump.

Like Reagan, Allen has a warm, friendly smile. Unlike Reagan, Allen wears his nice smile a *lot.* You might say perpetually. Allen smiles when you just *know* his feet are killing him. He smiles when the Virginia legislature hands him his head, as it has at times. He smiles when he ultimately prevails with that same legislature, as he often has. Smiling does not seem to be a strong indicator of George Allen's emotional state at any given time.

Still, this perpetual-grin business is probably a good trait in a man who some want to be the Republican presidential nominee *now*, but will settle for sometime down the road. There's lots of folks lined up ahead of him.

So what entitles this tall smile, this son of the late, revered Washington Redskins coach, George H. Allen, even to *think* about a GOP presidential nomination in his future? That he lived in Whittier, California, same as Richard M. Nixon? That's a coincidence, not a qualification.

Allen is a lawyer, but then so are some other nice people. Okay, not many. But some. He served in the Virginia legislature and was a congressman for one term before seeking and winning the governorship. So he has legislative experience.

All right, try this. Like Reagan, he shows signs of internal fortitude, even stubbornness, in fact, far more so than Reagan or Richard M. Nixon. Nixon who was forever compromising with Democrats. On budget cuts, on wage and price controls, on recognizing Commie China over non-Commie China. As for Reagan, he stuck to his guns a lot, but not always. He wanted and got the biggest tax cut in history in his first year as president and then signed into law the largest tax increase in history in his second year. He fired the illegally striking air traffic controllers, but flinched in confrontations with the Democrats and liberal Republicans in Congress when they opposed his proposals to eliminate useless and even harmful departments, agencies, and programs.

Allen is such a hard-core ideologue that, rather than take half a loaf, rather than accept settling for less than he believes, he let the Democrat-run General Assembly kill his proposed $2.1 billion tax cut, his budget cuts, his education initiatives, most of his prison construction program, and his plan to return $300 million in annual lottery profits to local governments.

He smiled, but once the Democrats made clear they weren't going to give him what he said the voters of Virginia wanted, he did not go to the Democrats in the legislature with a deck of compromises in his pockets. He did not, in the time-honored tradition of politics everywhere, say: "Look, fellas, let's make a deal. You get to look good with your constituents, and I get to look good with mine." No, what he did instead was jump on a passing airwave and tell folks listening to their radios how the Democrats were obstructing the people's *will*.

Not nice behavior on a governor's part. Not traditional. Not clubby. Not the way the game is played. Or was played. He's well-known for his convictions and internal fortitude to make a promise and keep it. Smiling George's idea of compromise is to put what he wants on the table and let it sit there till the other side decides either to take it *all* or drops dead waiting for him to negotiate. He did that to the Democratically-controlled legislature with welfare and they finally gave in, gave him the welfare reform he wanted. Allen also persuaded the Virginia General Assembly to go along with a plan to abolish parole.

Conservatives, in fact, were thrilled when he got a "conceal and carry" provision enacted. What this basically says is that unless you've been convicted of a crime, you can pay a fee to the state and recieve a permit to carry a concealed weapon.

What's absolutely beyond the pale for his liberal critics is that Allen will grab any conservative idea that isn't nailed down and make it his own. Shameless. When Christie Todd Whitman, the socially liberal, fiscally conservative governor of New Jersey, got national headlines for cutting taxes, you *know* what George Allen came up with for Virginia: tax cuts that he never even *promised* in his campaign.

And when William F. Weld, the socially liberal, fiscally conservative governor — yes, another one of those — of Massachusetts, got his state to enact a welfare change to put recipients to work after sixty days on the dole, Allen had to get him some of that good stuff. He even went Weld one better. Allen said welfare recipients in Virginia would have to get a job in thirty days.

This did not enhance his chances to win the Annual Compassion in Public Office Award from the Americans for Democratic Action. But good soldier George smiled on.

To show how shamelessly imitative conservatives can be, Allen even jumped on the anti-reverse discrimination bandwagon. He announced that he wanted to end hiring and admissions based on racial goals or quotas at state colleges.

He says he is neither pro-life nor pro-choice. It sounds as if he wants to have it both ways. *Sur-prise*. A politician who straddles. But this both ways business is also where the overwhelming majority of Americans come down, more or less. Like them, he thinks no restrictions should apply in the first trimester, except for a twenty-four-hour waiting period for a pregnant woman to rethink her decision. And like most Americans, he also supports parental and spousal notification and consent. It's not a clean position if you think life begins at conception and abortion is therefore murder. Nor is it a clean position if you think

★★

life doesn't begin at birth and therefore think any restrictions are statist and intrusive.

Some feel Allen can play Avis to the GOP presidential ticket's Hertz in 1996? Since the chances of Virginia not voting Republican no matter who heads the slate are approximately the same as Bill Clinton's kicking Al Gore off the Democratic ticket to make room for Jesse Jackson, Allen's visions of imminent veephood would seem absurd. Virginia is not, as they say, a "battleground state." But what if there is a chaotic GOP nominating convention, with everything and everybody up for, you'll excuse the expression, *grabs*?

Still, even a man who smiles this much knows there are a lot of folks lined up ahead of him for number two, let alone number one. On the other hand, he can wait them out. Allen will be only forty-four when the presidential inauguration takes place in January 1997.

Yes, there *are* people that young who think they should be president. Reason enough for Allen to smile away the miles on the road to his destiny.

★ ★ ★ ★ ★ ★ ★ ★ ★

JOHN ENGLER
Able and Available

I F CENTRAL CASTING SENT JOHN ENGLER to play the part of president, you'd send him back. He doesn't even look like the Governor of Michigan. Except he *is* the Governor of Michigan. He doesn't look as if he grew up on a farm fifty miles south of Michigan State University. What he looks like more than anything else is a triggerman, as they used to call the short, stalky, bullet-headed, beady-eyed tough guys in the gangster flicks.

It didn't help that Engler, who will be a tender forty-eight years of age on Presidential Inauguration Day in January 1997, rarely let a smile cross his face, even when he relaxed with fellow conservatives for an intellectual jam session. Or came to Washington with other governors to huddle with the Republican leadership in Congress or meet with the president. But since his second wife, Michelle, gave birth to triplet girls five days after his 1994 reelection victory, he smiles a lot more. And it's amazing what that smile does, especially if you know what *he* has done as governor of a Rust Belt state that everybody thought had seen its best days.

In a relaxed environment, Engler tells marvelously humorous stories about this, that, and everything else, including the absurdities of the regulations and bureaucracy he still runs into in government. He is more at ease personally. The more readily evident smile reflects a level of self-confidence that comes from an accumulation of certified successes.

These weren't easy to come by. Engler had served in the Michigan legislature for twenty years, most of those years under the heel of liberals who controlled the legislature or, when he became Senate majority leader, the bureaucracy of government. He didn't get his freedom, so to speak, until he won election as governor. He did that by barely defeating the young, handsome incumbent and once-commanding figure in Michigan politics, James Blanchard. Engler's victory margin was a narrow 50 percent to 49 percent. Even after he got used to being the governor, Engler found he was still a Michigan boy, a heartlander not all that comfortable in the big wide world beyond its borders.

He was a very bright man who went into politics with a certain feeling of inferiority, a suspicion that out-of-staters, especially from Washington, D.C. or New York, would see in him the hayseed that they could make fun of. Therefore, those dark, suspicious looks that used to cross his face more often than a smile did. One problem was that, in a sense, he never left home. He has worked all his life as a law-maker drawing a taxpayer-financed government salary and then as chief executive, drawing a salary from the same source. He was comfortable in the milieu he had come to know, day in and day out, year in and year out. His first marriage was to a fellow state lawmaker. It ended in 1986 with a divorce.

Once installed in his state's highest executive office, however, he did something that distinguished him from a lot of other politicians drawing government salaries. He kept his campaign promises. Engler, in fact, quickly developed a national reputation, especially among policy wonks on the Right, as a conservative welfare slasher, privatizer of public services, including the public schools — he likes charter schools — and man who made Michigan the leader among industrial states in reducing unemployment.

The victories began with some unpleasantness. Engler no sooner got into office as governor than he began to irritate organized labor. This is a very big deal in the land of the United Auto Workers. Governor Engler managed to tee off the trial lawyers, the public school teachers and education establishment, not to mention the social welfare bureaucracy. He alienated the leadership but not necessarily the membership of these groups. In fact, he did things in office that caused many UAW *members* to defect from the Democratic Party and come over to this radical Republican conservative. This alone entitles him to an honored place in the Pantheon of Conservative Heroes, at least in the view of your basic Right wing, Adam Smith lover.

Engler ended Michigan's $250-million-a-year general assistance program, which was handing out welfare checks to single adults who had no children to care for and who were healthy enough to work. The liberals, the Democrats, and the press called him mean-spirited. He claims he didn't have to pay them a red cent for calling him that. The voters, meanwhile, called him their kind of guy.

Engler also sought and got federal permission to reform the federal-state Aid for Families with Dependent Children program. As a result, recipients are required to do twenty hours of paid or volunteer work. This has cut the welfare rolls and would do still better, Engler complained, but for the fact that welfare recipients who are allergic to work are able to run to the federal housing subsidy and food stamp programs for compensation when their AFDC benefits are cut.

Engler wasn't born the conservative he has become. He wasn't even the conservative he is when he was a Republican state legislator. He opposed Ronald Reagan's GOP presidential nomination bids in 1976 and 1980. He was a Gerald Ford loyalist *and* a George Bush loyalist. Oddly enough, what started him on the road to the Right was the liberal Republican Governor William Milliken, who, Engler says, made deals with Democrats and cut fellow Republicans out of the process. That's when he started his glacial movement eastward on the ideological continuum.

One indicator of how far Right he has come is taxes. Engler now may be the tax-cuttingest governor around. All told, he was responsible for fourteen tax cuts for individuals and businesses from the time he took office in his first term to the first two months of his second term.

Engler's biggest self-assurance boost came when he beat liberal Democrat and former seven-term Congressman Howard Volpe in 1994 by a decisive margin of 61 percent to 38 percent. Now Engler is enjoying the reputation of being, along with fellow Republican Governor Tommy Thompson, a conservative in *heart and mind* and a successful second-term chief executive of a substantial state. And you know what that means. Before summer's heat crept over Michigan in 1995, Engler found himself courted by the two leading contenders for the Republican presidential nomination, Senate Majority Leader Bob Dole of Kansas and Senator Phil Gramm of Texas, as a possible running mate. Catholic, pro-life, midwestern, conservative on economics and social policy, Engler talks *publicly* about moral values and brings to the ticket a state and region that *matter*. What more could a GOP presidential nominee ask for? Okay, maybe a conservative Hispanic woman from California would bring even more to the ticket. But Engler is good.

The main obstacle to higher office, or any future elected office, was thought to be Michelle who, when she was pregnant with the triplets, said she hoped John's 1994 campaign would be his last. She wanted him at home more, and he was on board for that. Or so it was said.

After her husband's reelection, however, Michelle Engler began to talk about John's possibly being offered a spot on the national ticket as a "heady experience" and "difficult" to turn down. Put Engler down as available for 1996, 2000, and who knows what else.

★ ★ ★ ★ ★ ★ ★ ★ ★ ★

TOMMY G. THOMPSON
Before Welfare Reform Was Cool

TOMMY G. THOMPSON IS THE CONSERVATIVE-FROM-THE-START governor of that liberal-from-the-start state of Wisconsin. Thompson sort of looks that part, but he definitely doesn't look any more like a *President* of the United States than does John Engler, the governor of Michigan.

Thompson is too rough-hewn. Too burly. A certain goofiness to his smile. When Thompson shakes your hand, your hand knows it has been shaken. He has bear-sized paws. Looks a bit like a bear, too. He could be the president's bodyguard, if American presidents had Latin American style bodyguards instead of svelte, disciplined young suits who talk into their sleeves and wear buttons on their lapels advertising that they are members of the SECRET SERVICE! *Sssh.*

Thompson *could* be what he doesn't look like if Phil Gramm or Bob Dole or Pat Buchanan were to win the Republican presidential nomination, pick him as running mate and then go on to win the presidency in November 1996.

Thompson had been flirting with a run for the GOP presidential nomination right up until June 1995, when he shocked a state party convention by officially taking himself out of a race he had never officially entered. The real reason, of course, he was going to run is the same reason he has his closet adviser, James Klauser, doing high-level volunteer advising for Dole's Wisconsin campaign. And the same reason his former communications director, Mark Liedl, was a volunteer adviser to the Wisconsin campaign organization of Gramm, the senior senator from Texas.

✸✸✸

And the same reason Thompson has Liedl writing a book about Thompson. Thompson knows about the only road to the presidency for a non-presidential-looking conservative Midwest governor who is not a household word outside his state is through the vice presidency.

Thompson knows what he is doing. He took over as head of the National Governors Association in 1995, just in time to cut a secret deal with Dole. The Senate majority leader and President Clinton were the only 1996 presidential candidates invited — let's be frank here, the only ones *permitted* — to address the governors' conference in Burlington, Vermont. This was in the summer of 1995, just at the height of a fight between Dole and Gramm over who was more conservative on welfare reform. Both Dole and Gramm wanted to turn federal tax money collected for the federal portion of welfare back to the states to use as they choose. Dole wanted no strings attached. Gramm wanted several restrictions, including disincentives for teenage mothers to bear illegitimate children and mandatory work requirements for the able-bodied.

These were almost exactly the restrictions Thompson pushed in Wisconsin. Yet, at the governor's conference he went out of his way to side with Dole's position. Somewhere there exists a rocket scientist who doesn't see the connection between all of this and a very prominent role for Thompson in a Dole administration, if there is a Dole administration. What kind of rocket scientist doesn't see this connection? The kind of rocket scientist who couldn't hit the bright side of the moon on a clear night.

Thompson may have cut a deal with a man who over the years has been less consistently conservative than Thompson, but Thompson has shown he can stand up to his party's hierarchy when principle is involved. Just after George Bush's loss to Bill Clinton in the 1992 presidential elections, the Republican Governors Association convened in Lake Geneva, Wisconsin, and Thompson was the host. One of the governors briefing the press at the closing news conference was Kirk Fordice of Mississippi. Fordice had it up to the eyeballs with Republican pollsters and strategists who lectured the governors to the effect that the Republicans lost the presidency because the GOP nominating convention that August in Houston had presented too conservative a face to the nation, scaring voters off with talk of cultural wars and Christian values.

Fordice, in response to a press question, said the United States is a Christian nation with certain moral values worth preserving. Fordice went out of his way to add that he did not mean that "Christianity or any other religion should be shoved down the throats" of any American, but only that the moral standards were worth recognizing as America's cultural heritage and worth resurrecting.

The Left went bonkers when the press reported some of what Fordice had said — the Christian nation part — and almost immediately the enforcers of political correctness, led by Rich Bond, in charge of the national Republican Party at the time, swung into action. They ordered Fordice to hand them a written apology for having said America is a Christian nation, when, as everybody *knows*, America is a, well, never mind, just apologize, Fordice, *now*. Never mind that Orthodox Jews came to Fordice's defense.

Fordice refused to go to his knees, but eventually was forced to face the humiliation of saying he didn't mean to hurt anybody's feelings, when in fact he had already made that clear in his initial statement. Only Tommy Thompson was willing to stand up and be quoted several days running to the effect that Fordice was entitled to his opinion, there was nothing wrong with saying America is a Christian nation, and the Republican Party had no business ordering the Governor of Mississippi or any other state to change his views.

Thompson had years of experience dealing with a hostile environment, and not always from the opposition party. Like Governor John Engler of Michigan, Thompson had spent twenty years in the state legislature, in his case beginning in 1960, before his election as governor.

Like Engler, he was a lawyer, having earned his undergraduate and law degrees at the University of Wisconsin in Madison, where he rebelled against what he saw as infantile campus Marxism and liberalism. He became a Barry Goldwater conservative.

Like Engler, Thompson is basically shy and had to force himself to be outgoing in college. Even in 1994, he would come to Washington with other Republican governors and meet with GOP congressional leaders and then the governors would hold a press conference. Thompson was about the only one too shy or gentlemanly or both to elbow his way to the microphone to answer a question from the press corps. This is a nice attribute if you are running for gentleman but not if you are running for president, a race in which shy guys finish last.

He has been married since 1968 to Sue Ann Mashak, a teacher, and the Thompsons have three children.

Unlike Engler, Thompson didn't move from the Republican Left to the Republican Right. He started on the Right. Thompson was Mr. Welfare Reform before welfare reform was cool. Haley Barbour, chairman of the Republican National Committee, often calls Thompson the Republican "pathfinder" on welfare reform. In fact, as governor, Thompson had fought an eight-year war on welfare until the voters of Wisconsin gave him a third term in November 1994. He's still fighting the war and steadily winning, if winning means getting Wisconsin citizens off the welfare rolls and discouraging non-Wisconsin welfare-benefits seekers from migrating there. Welfare rolls dropped 19 percent in his state, while climbing 32 percent nationally.

The fact is, Tommy Thompson does well for himself by doing good for his state's economy. It saw a net increase of 382,000 jobs in the last year of his second term. And the University of Wisconsin won the Rose Bowl. Thompson wasn't responsible for that. But he'll take the credit if you want to give it to him as part of the overall good times he has brought to the state.

His cutting-edge conservatism is so popular that last November 1994, a whopping 67 percent of the voters said yes to a third term for him.

When Thompson was sworn in as governor, he immediately cut welfare benefits 6 percent and froze them permanently at that level. He was still complaining last year that the level is still too high, still attracting welfare families from Chicago. "For an $8 bus ride, you can get $200 more a month by coming here [to Wisconsin]," he complained.

Over the years, Thompson's common sense politics and policies have won him affection from virtually every segment of the population, except one — this group is major, though shrinking: the Democrats. You could say Thompson has an ability to appeal to people who aren't supposed to vote Republican. In 1986, he won 10 percent of the African American vote; in 1990, 20 percent; and in 1994, he claims more than 40 percent. At the same time, he cornered the vote on white so-called Reagan Democrats.

He has gone all out to bring school choice to Wisconsin. Thompson has fathered a list of initiatives longer than your arm. His Children First plan, which the legislature enacted, offers deadbeat dads the choice of supporting the children they fathered or going to jail. That then became a big deal nationally. Bridefare, begun in July 1994, offers a welfare benefits boost to encourage teenage parents to get married. Novel idea. Married teenage welfare parents? In this day and age? Now everybody's grabbing on to it. And Thompson's Family Cap tells welfare mothers they won't get a cent more for having more children. His Two Years and You're Out plan, begun as a two-county experiment, limits anyone's welfare to two years, period. Thompson is realistic in acknowledging that some welfare recipients are going to have trouble finding and holding jobs, no matter how plentiful jobs are. But you have to start somewhere in reversing the dependency cycle welfare begun, and Thompson is willing to ride the experiment out and see where it goes.

Thompson has a form of the line-item veto that is more powerful than most other governors have and he has used it with a vengeance. In eight years, he used it almost 1,500 times to pare about $800 million in proposed spending. As of January 1995, he had a Republican legislature to deal with for a change and it will be of historical interest to chronicle how many fewer times he will need to wield the veto.

In Wisconsin, it's show time for Republicans.

Thompson is not your sophisticated speechifier, and he goes on too long, but there is a nice, genuinely homespun quality to his delivery that works to his advantage, Wisconsin accent and all.

Gramm or Dole or whoever the nominee is could do a lot worse in choosing Thompson, but not any better.

PART III

★ ★

Agenda Setters (the Big Two)

★ ★ ★ ★ ★ ★ ★ ★ ★

So many similarities and related differences leap to mind regarding Bill Clinton and Newt Gingrich that you *know* it's going to be challenging and fun to try to sort them out. Bill Clinton has already achieved the highest and most respected political office in the land, the leadership of the world's only remaining superpower. The one country in the world where more persons over more generations have been prepared to do almost anything for the privilege of coming to it in order to reside within its borders than is true for any other country and nation and political system in the history of the planet.

Newt Gingrich already has achieved the second most powerful political office in the land, the Speakership of the United States House of Representatives. He attracts more crowds, more attention, more comment, more criticism, more praise, more jokes, more everything than anybody else in political life in the country, including the President of the United States.

Both Clinton and Gingrich have an agenda for the future of the country. Clinton's, though outlined in his *covenant*, has turned out to be vague, in flux, as responsive as a feather in the wind to polls and surveys and headlines and daily developments at home and abroad. Clinton's agenda of the moment, whatever the moment is, draws criticism from his supporters on the Left as too conservative or ill defined and from his supporters on what passes for the Democratic Right as too liberal or ill defined or both.

Newt Gingrich has an agenda that he explicitly says is conserva-

✳✳

tive, that he laid out in the *Contract with America* and in pronounce-ments after the stunning electoral sweep by Republicans in Novem-ber 1994 and periodically through the early days of his tenure as Speaker. Gingrich's agenda is not vague. The Left attacks it, item by item, every moment of every day, or so it would seem. The difference is that Gingrich's supporters on his left and his right do not try to tear him down the way the president's supporters on his left and his right try to tear him down.

This is not evidence that conservatism is good and liberalism bad or vice versa. Or that the electorate has stopped thinking like Clinton, if it ever did, and started thinking like Gingrich, however he actually thinks. Nobody held a gun to the electorate's head to make the New Deal the longest deal in America's relatively short history.

The electorate does seem to care more about finding ways to restore moral values than Clinton and the Democrats care about, so long as no one group or religion gets to shove its narrow set of behav-ioral standards down the collective throat of the nation. The Democ-rats and the liberals in the Republican Party say that shoving values down people's throats is the aim of the Christian fundamentalists and others associated with the religious conservative movement that has moved big time into the Republican Party's Big Tent. The "fundies" and evangelicals and conservative Catholics say, publicly and privately, that such allegations are unutterable nonsense, that they understand and cherish the principles of a free, non-theocratic Republican democ-racy as much as anybody staffing the Democratic National Committee or the folks over at People for the American Way. What some persons forget is that nothing in the Constitution or the Bill of Rights man-dates a separation of church and state. Rather, the founding docu-ments, like the founding fathers who wrote them, openly embraced religion, though *not* any official religion that the government would be permitted to show preference for over any other religion.

Gingrich lines up with the religious conservatives and with the government shrinkers on the economic, free-enterprise Right. The choice is clear. If you like where he is, he's your man — moral and intellectual and ideological warts and all. For the presidency, or long-term Speakership, or simply to admire and quote. If you loathe where

Gingrich is ideologically and operationally, then Clinton still may not be your man, regardless of his moral and ideological warts. You many want someone who is clearer on policy directions and prescriptions and who knows better how to get things done, at home and abroad.

Have we made ourselves *clear* on this or what? Look, if you're seeking saints, they're not between the covers of this book, and certainly not in the person of either Clinton or Gingrich, as influential and accomplished as both men are.

Face it. These two guys are so similar in ways we've yet to mention that it's scary. And so different it's a relief. Start with the obvious: two southerners with big hair. But wait. Except for the big hair, the similarity is more apparent than real. Gingrich's mother likes to recall that he was conceived over a gas station in Harrisburg, Pennsylvania. He was an Army brat who traveled with his family in Western Europe and the United States before happening to settle in Georgia. Clinton was born in Arkansas and spent virtually all his working life there until he got a four-year lease on a big house on Pennsylvania Avenue in Washington, D.C.

Clinton, unlike Gingrich, had to build from without. Gingrich was introspective from the beginning, and read a lot for enjoyment and fantasied about what he was reading. Thus, Gingrich was able to use his fantasy life to build, from within himself, the man he was to become. As a kid, Gingrich was the contradiction in terms, the popular nerd. For his part, Clinton was popular in a facile way. Clinton was more "other directed" than Gingich, more dependent on signals and approval and direction from those around him. Newt was the flip side of that record, more "inner directed" than Clinton. His old schoolmates and friends recall him as being popular. They liked him, liked being with him. This was always a surprise to Gingrich, who looked back on himself as the nerd.

The Speaker of the House of Representatives is the stepson of a disciplinarian. Gingrich's natural father, Newton C. McPherson, Jr., was a carouser who slapped his wife, Kathleen Gingrich, around. She left him. Kathleen bore his child and namesake, Newt, and then three years later married Bob Gingrich, who had been an Army corporal in World War II. Bob Gingrich was the role model Bill Clinton never had. Bob Gingrich, after marrying Newt's mother, worked his way through college as a bellhop. Through his enrollment in the Reserve Officers Training Corps, Bob Gingrich earned a commission as a second lieutenant in time to be shipped off to serve in America's undeclared war against the Commie hordes overrunning Korea.

Newt Gingrich found his stepfather, Bob Gingrich, the veteran of real shooting wars, to be an authoritarian who occasionally slapped his son around but who was also a heroic figure, strong and determined, and a family man who did not say "I love you" to his wife or his stepson or the three children he had with Kathleen, but clearly did love them. Bob Gingrich's tough love crossed the line into abusiveness at times. A contradiction of a man, Bob Gingrich was stable, reliable, accomplished, courageous and *there* for his family.

Unlike Clinton, Gingrich has a half-sister, Candace, who is a lesbian activist. Yet, it was Clinton, not Gingrich, who went after the homosexual vote. Newt says his position is that homosexuals deserve neither to be singled out for attacks nor to be accorded special rights and protections. Gingrich says he believes their sexual desires are real and different from those of heterosexuals and make them unsuitable *in that respect* for military service, period. Clinton argued that homosexuals would, could, and should have no problems serving with straight men in foxholes or barracks or straight women wherever they end up serving in the armed services. Common sense and thousands of years of human history defeated Rhodes Scholar Clinton on that one.

What may be most important about the ways Clinton and Gingrich stack up against each other is that Clinton came from an alcoholic family life. Children from alcoholic families always have that life as *their* secret. So from the first moment of their lives, they try to make sure no one else knows they are different. And this is one of the reasons why Clinton can't make decisions and is forever seeking consensus.

Gingrich, by contrast or comparison — it's unclear which is the appropriate word in this case — had emotional needs that led him in somewhat different directions. Gingrich's first marriage was to his high school geometry teacher. When he got into politics, Gingrich showed more than a brotherly affinity for female campaign workers. Good traits? Bad traits? Mixed bag? Relevant to the ability to govern well? You decide — unless you want *us* to decide. Okay. We *categorically* reject the victimhood that is so fashionable and dangerous in American culture today. We'll judge you by your actions. They are your individual responsibility. Regardless of how loud and long you may be inclined to whine about all the reasons and factors beyond your control that prevented you from doing what you said you'd do, what you contracted to do, what you set out to do, what you longed to do. Whatever.

So, that's the playing field we set up. Put Clinton on it. Put Gingrich on it. Clinton had a worse upbringing than Gingrich. He has more excuses, more justification, for growing up to be the imperfect adult he is, than Gingrich had for being the imperfect adult *he* is. Yet Clinton's moral character has come in for harsher questioning on more fronts than has Gingrich's. On this playing field on these pages, however, you either score the goals you promised or were expected to score, or you lose. No excuses. We award the game so far to Newt. The game, not the series. That goes on. We'll be watching and judging and won't keep it to ourselves, God willing.

★ ★ ★ ★ ★ ★ ★ ★ ★

NEWT GINGRICH
The Hair Apparent

IF YOU WANT TO KNOW WHO NEWT GINGRICH IS and what he means to the Republican Party, think of it this way:

In August 1995, the Iowa GOP held a Presidential nomination preference straw poll and fund-raiser at the Hilton Coliseum on the Iowa State University campus in Ames. It was the biggest, openly rigged election in the Western World, but it was an equal opportunity rigging.

A ticket to get you in to vote cost $25. Every Republican presidential nomination candidate could buy blocs of the tickets and pass them out to whomever he wanted. Every candidate could airlift and bus in as many attendees from out of state as his campaign organization budget and ability to find out-of-staters permitted. Phil Gramm, Lamar Alexander, Bob Dole, Pat Buchanan, and others spent hundreds of thousands of dollars in direct-mail advertising, bus and plane charters, and ticket purchases. All told, the ten GOP nomination candidates managed to fill the Hilton Coliseum in Ames, Iowa, with a total of 10,500 persons. No one got a majority, or anything close. Gramm and Dole each got exactly 2,582 votes or 24.36 percent of the total, for a first place tie. The cash-poor conservative commentator Buchanan was next with 1,922 votes, or 18.14 percent of the total. Most political operatives working for the various candidates agreed privately that had Gingrich alone made an appearance in the coliseum that day, 10,000 Iowans would have lined up to pay $25 to see and hear him. He wouldn't have to spend a penny to attract them. All this for a congres-

✶✶

sional leader? Tom Foley and George Mitchell, eat your hearts out. Ditto, for that matter, Bob Dole and Phil Gramm.

Throughout much of the summer, he was the politician who was on a book tour, signing his *own* book, and being mobbed in virtually every bookstore where he showed up. He attracted record-size crowds in some cases, and the book was on its way to selling a million copies. Put another way, the book was on its way to having a million Americans spend twenty-five bucks a copy to find out what some Republican politician from Georgia thinks about the future of the country. And when you total up the number of contributors to the campaigns of the Republican nomination candidates and to Clinton, you still have fewer persons than the total number expected to buy Gingrich's book. The largest number of campaign contributors was the 170,000 donors recorded for Reagan. Clinton came in second with 130,000 contributors.

Who *is* this Newt Gingrich they're lining up for?

A week after Pete Wilson, governor of California, a state with more population and economic output than most nations on the planet, was on day two of his GOP presidential nomination campaign kickoff tour, he flew to Philadelphia where he addressed an almost empty room at the Fraternal Order of Police hall. It was empty except for the FOP head, the candidate's family, the campaign staff and a few reporters. Had Gingrich made that same appearance, Philadelphians would have filled the hall to legal capacity, and been lined up twenty deep outside on the street.

That's who Newt Gingrich is now. When Gingrich came to Congress in 1978, he had big hair, coiffured like a television anchorman's. The hair is still big, but has grown older and grayer *with* him. In January 1997, when the winner of the 1996 presidential elections is sworn in, he'll be fifty-two. And like many other men with visions of greatness, he admires the late Winston Churchill. This is good. Winnie is a better role model than, say, Ivan the Terrible. Newt desires mightily to emulate him (the British prime minister, not the Russian czar). Newt has succeeded in emulating Churchill, in leadership as well as girth.

Churchill wrote magnificent histories. Gingrich has yet to. But he writes prolifically. And he and Winnie share a certain intellectual self-assuredness. Gingrich has never been more convinced that he knows *how* to know it all. It's just a matter of time till he *does* know it all.

Meanwhile, as he progresses inevitably to political apotheosis, his brown eyes can project warmth, friendliness, and good-listener attentiveness. Or they can just as easily turn beady and menacing, when their owner walks into a large room full of people sweeping over the crowd 100-megahertz speed, picking out and mentally filing the troublemakers, the hostile questioners, the potential opponents, the boring idiots, the sycophants, the potentially useful, the ones who owe *him* and the ones *he* owes.

Although he has a pedestrian taste in ties, he is becoming a more careful dresser, sweeping through the halls of Congress in dark suits that try to keep up with his expanding girth. Looking kempt is *de rigueur*, given his political mega-stellar status. But what turns him on is ideas and power, and maybe one or two other things, but *not* clothes.

Gingrich is everything an admiring conservative may say about him, and everything a *suspicious* conservative may say about him as well. A purist he is not. "Reform conservatism means taking government seriously," he once wrote. "If there is going to be a Department of Labor, conservatives have to know how to run it." He has also said the point of conservatives taking power is to dismantle the "corrupt welfare state," not learn how to run it better than the Democrats and liberal Republicans who created it and helped expand it.

Candid at times he is, even when it means identifying himself with conservatives' worst nightmare. "You have to understand that leaders, including Presidents, will always sell you out," Gingrich said at a private gathering of conservatives before he became Speaker. It is a statement so prophetic it makes chills run down the spine.

All that said, Gingrich is the most formidable Republican in memory to talk conservative ideas, draw up broad legislative agendas, concoct grand strategies for winning elections, and *make all this work*. Gingrich's formidableness can be measured by not just what his enemies on the Left say about him, but to what artful lengths they will go to say it. He is a Republican leader of such potential stature, that he drives the gatekeepers of the dominant media culture to fits of public retching over him. This was best evidenced by a profile in *Vanity Fair* barely eight months after Gingrich was sworn in as Speaker. This glossy monthly magazine is one of several examples in the contemporary American magazine culture that has replaced the radical chic of the 1960s and 1970s, with radical-psycho-porno-glitzy chic of the 1990s. Like so many other "upscale" glossies littering the American landscape, the advertising that appears on its pages is the sort that has girls barely in their teens hustling blue jeans, in ultrasophisticated poses, that are as provocative and subtle as your average 14th Street whore in Washington, D.C. on any night of the week. The editorial content is usually Left–wing. It always boasts a definite "with it" flair.

To do the job on Gingrich, the magazine commissioned Gail Sheehy, a superbly gifted writer, who has figured out that there is immense fun and even more immense profit to be had in savaging fellow human beings, as long as they are famous or rich or conservative. Ergo, Sheehy savaged famous and conservative Newt Gingrich in one of the most lurid pieces of writing ever to appear in *Vanity Fair*. She reported his alleged infidelity to his first wife. She recounted a vow by his second and current wife, Marianne, that she'll go on television to "undermine" him if he dares run for president without first getting her okay. And she recited examples of Gingrich's own wackiness and says it is a result of having been an orphan, after being rejected by his biological father and then his adoptive father. Sheehy concluded that Gingrich sees himself as a John Wayne hero who will save the Republic from cultural chaos, thanks to his "narcissistic vision of global glory." Sheehy clearly is *pissed* that Churchill defied her by living and dying too early for her to grind *his* psyche through her laptop.

How formidable is Newt Gingrich? Finding him campaigning for you in your district is better than finding a four-leaf clover. He's his party's Joltin' Joe DiMaggio and then some. Gingrich batted 575 in the 1994 season. Of the 127 Republican candidates he campaigned for in 127 congressional districts across America, seventy-three won election to the House that year.

Next, he took the oath as Speaker, then immediately mounted up, uttered a deep-throated "Forward, *ho*-oh," and drove more major internal House reforms to adoption, and more major legislation to the floor for a final vote in three months, than past Speakers got enacted in a lifetime. Gingrich began with bang that made the Democrats whimper. Then, House Speaker for only five months, he pulled off one of the great political coups of modern American political history. He went to New Hampshire when Clinton was also visiting, and conned him into a public televised debate on the Great Issues of the Day.

Newt's New Hampshire triumph was also Newt's revenge. Virtually from the day he arrived in Congress, Gingrich was to journalists in Washington, what Christians were to lions in Rome. The press ignored him and his words, except at feeding time, when they continued to ignore his words but instead took huge chunks out of his flesh. Then came his ascendancy to House Speaker, a position that most reporters had thought was reserved by the Constitution for a liberal Democrat. Almost no working journalist had covered a Republican Speaker, *ever*. Now comes Newtrino, The Bomb Thrower–Jim Wright Dethroner–Thomas S. Foley Slayer, and Crusher of the Democrats' Corrupt Welfare State. Gingrich, the man who first figured out that C-Span's hungry eye could be turned to an advantage by the Gingrich Conservative Opportunity Society gang members who were willing to stay after hours, go to the floor of the House, and rip the living excrement out of the Democrats. While C-Span lenses and microphones broadcast the educational monologues to millions of viewers around the country. The Democrats, smug in their then thirty-year possession of the Speakership and control of all the committees, sat there, using their thumbs as orificial plugs, and watched, uncomprehending, as Newt laid the foundation for their ultimate overthrow.

Throughout his New Hampshire visit, the press hungered after his every *word*. The ladies and gentlemen of the Fourth Estate who dared nip at his flesh found that he nipped back. This is not the way to make the press like you. Grudgingly respect you, maybe, but not *like* you. Curiously, for all his star quality that would make a revivified Elvis envious, Gingrich still is thought poorly of by a large proportion of respondents in national telephone surveys of public opinion. Democrats and labor unions and all kinds of other special interests on the Left, grow absolutely apoplectic at the mention of his name. They carry picket signs damning the day that he was born and blaming him for every evil that befell, is befalling, or is about to befall anyone anywhere on the planet. They despise him so much, they show up with these rabid anti-Gingrich signs at campaign appearances of Dole,

✶✶

Gramm, Wilson, and you name it. Gingrich gives them one of his
beady-eye specials when he sees them, while smiling on the inside.
Here's why: It is a historic fact that Gingrich managed to draw far
more press — from all over the world — than President Clinton
attracted on the same visit, or than any of the declared Republican
presidential nomination candidates had ever drawn in New Hampshire. *And* Gingrich maneuvered successfully for a live televised discussion of America's problems with the big guy himself, the prez,
mano a mano, as they say.

Not in the lifetimes of most Americans have the chief executive
from one Party, and the highest-ranking member of Congress from
the other Party, shared a stage to discuss the great issues of the day.
And take questions from a citizen audience. *Let alone* fourteen months
before a presidential election. Can you think of a "more perfect
union," as they say in preambles, than Gingrich-Clinton? Two men of
the same generation, both of whom inhaled — you just *know* they did.

Gingrich played his "Superstar visits Granite State" role to the hilt.
Cecil B. DeMille couldn't have produced a better show. Opening
scene, day two of The New Hampshire Visit, on the farm of conservative icon and former New Hampshire Governor Meldrid Thompson.
The stooped, eighty-four year-old Thompson and his wife, stand just
outside the front door of their red-brick and white clapboard home,
awaiting the arrival of The Great Man. Gingrich, in one of three heli-
copters that appear over the mountain to the east, lands behind the
house. We hear *Hail to the Chief* in our ears, even though nobody's
playing it. As Gingrich and Thompson stand shaking hands, the first
words out of the governor's mouth are, "You're the ideal man." This is
a historic *fact*. Thompson *said* that. It is a moment for a presidential
candidate media adviser to *die* for.

After meeting privately, the two men reemerge and Thompson
allows that he can think of no other Republican who has Gingrich's
ability to talk about moral and social issues with the same ease and
authority that he addresses economic issues. "If there is [such a
Republican], I haven't met him," says old Meldrid Thompson, who
had formally endorsed Senator Phil Gramm of Texas for the GOP
nomination, and was sticking with that endorsement.

In fact, like a number of Republicans who came to see Gingrich at other, more public stops that day in New Hampshire, Thompson said Gingrich's "skills and intellect" are needed in the House for the next few years, and that Newt's time for the presidency "will come later."

The Thompson encounter showed off Gingrich's extraordinary ability to meet politicos who have seen it all and turn them into awed admirers. Because they see his inner goodness and humanity and love for all things both great and small? Yeah, sure. Try: Because they see in him what they had hoped the world would see in them, and other things they hoped the world would never find out was in them. Could it be ruthlessness and cunning, combined with superior intellect and strategic acuity, not to mention a tactical awareness best evidenced in trained killers who fight in jungles for the "special forces" of advanced industrial democracies? Could it be otherwise?

Whatever it is, he leaves them wishing he could be cloned, so he could be Speaker, and President, and Majority Leader, *and* give the sermon in the church down the street on Sunday.

Gingrich accomplished something else of potentially more value than the Clinton coup, and the mass media fawning in New Hampshire. Combining moral values and economic analysis in speeches given to gatherings of nearly 1,000 persons or groups of fewer than 200, he showed he could grab and hold their attention better than any other Republican. Others may have more presence than Gingrich, but he was *Papabile* — had the stuff of which popes and leaders of that ilk are made.

Even Nackey Loeb, the powerful publisher of the *Manchester Union Leader*, betrayed a longing for Gingrich to run, even though she told him in a private meeting that he is too valuable as Speaker to leave the job. Clearly, Gingrich tapped into something important in New Hampshire during the summer of 1995.

So what was all that about? Upstaging the Democratic president *and* all nine declared presidential nomination candidates from Gingrich's own party? There was much teeth-gnashing among the latter group over Newt's vanity extravaganza. Wasn't the man satisfied with the Speakership and all the attention anyone could ask for? Did he have to butt in on the presidential race, too? Wasn't it a bit egomaniacal and contemptible to bare an ankle to the Republican electorate, saying, in effect, "Hey, if those other boys haven't shown you something you like by Christmas 1995, well, just look me up. I just might be available."

Well, yes, there's *that* Gingrich, always climbing, never satisfied, write a novel, write a book, write three books, run the House, run the nation. And there's another Gingrich. The high-techie futurist former history professor, who, it turns out, knows Hollywood and cinematic image making like you wouldn't believe. It was, as they say, a certain delicious irony about to reveal itself. No sooner was he in office than the Democrat in the White House, and the Democrats in Congress, and the Democrat newsies, were criticizing the new Speaker as not being ready for prime time. They were *all over* him for accepting (and later rejecting) a $4.5 million book advance from media tycoon Rupert Murdoch. They made Newt out to be a Dickensian troglodyte for touting — sensitive readers may want to skip to the next paragraph — *orphanages* like Boys Town, for God's sake. Why, Newt the Grinch was touting orphanages as possibly *better* places in which to bring up children than in the "homes" of their unmarried, thirteen year-old, third-generation welfare mothers. Are we talking your quintessential frozen-hearted, kid-hating, widow-starving, animal-beating Republican or *what*?

Since no sensible suggestion, no adult statement by a living politician, ever goes unpunished in the world's greatest democracy, Gingrich came under the kind of attack the survivors of the Dresden fire-bombing might recognize. So where did Newtrino turn for help? To Michael Deaver, a loathsome figure to many conservatives who remembered him as the guy who handled President Reagan's image-making, largely by sheltering Reagan from having to take positions that might upset the Washington establishment. Deaver knows his business, and Gingrich is an eager student. Things got better.

Gingrich, philosophical conservative or not, is learning the actor's trade pretty well, and showing he knows how to make the graybeards of the conservative movement second-guess themselves. At a dinner at the Heritage Foundation, Washington's most prodigious conservative research institute, syndicated columnist Cal Thomas bets Heritage founder and president, Edwin Feulner, that Speaker Gingrich will seek the Republican nomination for *President* in 1996, probably in December 1995.

Gingrich doesn't know about Thomas' bet with Feulner, of course, when he gets up to address the dinner. But Gingrich knows what he wants for Gingrich, and how to build roads that take him where he wants to go. So he gets up and gives an extemporaneous tribute to Jack Kemp, the former tax-cutting congressman from New York, and hero of the supply-side, "progressive conservative" crowd in the Republican Party. Gingrich pays heartfelt homage to the ideas that Kemp and Gingrich had forged from the early years of the first Reagan administration on. Gingrich says the "conservative revolution" Republicans, long plagued with revolution envy, love to apply these words to every act and event with which a Republican is associated, with only a few exceptions. Anyhow, Gingrich says the "conservative revolution" couldn't have happened without Jack Kemp leading the way. Gingrich, playing this crowd like a Stradivarius, gets choked up with emotion and abruptly ends his remarks. The dinner guests break out in thunderous applause. Feulner turns to Thomas and says, "I withdraw my bet." Feulner understands what the crowds in New Hampshire understood. Feulner is looking at the one Republican *who really* has it, whatever *it* is, and is unstoppable as a result.

Gingrich has something else. A temper. Sometimes, it's the sort of thing that makes conservatives bless him and bless themselves for having him. Example: Whenever a reporter asks him a question that is so heavily laden with liberal bias that even the most Potomac-hardened conservative would want to punch the reporter's lights out, Gingrich jumps down the reporter's throat instead. As in: How *dare* you ask such an imbecilic question? You ought to be *ashamed* of yourself.

Before Gingrich, virtually no one in Washington talked to the press that way.

Gingrich doesn't have to huddle for three days with advisers and pollsters every .me he gets hit with a shotgun blast out of ideological left field. He returns fire before the opposition has a chance to reload. Phil Gramm and Pat Buchanan come closest to also having that intellectual quick-load-and-fire mechanism. In Gingrich's case, the same quality has gotten him in trouble, but then he is not the first politico to talk before he thinks. It just gets stickier when you're Speaker.

Gingrich always looked like one of the brightest young back-benchers in the House, and he really was the pedant of the lot. He was the natural leader of the fresh-faced conservative Republicans, the "young Turks" who wanted to change the way the House was run, the way America was run and the way the world was run, and do it *yesterday*. Which was a *bit* ambitious of them, given Republicans were the minority party in the House.

No matter. Gingrich, beady eyes, big hair and all, joined with five other young Turk Republicans to found the Conservative Opportunity Society in the House. This outfit was the militantly anti a lot of things, but most of all militantly anti-racist and anti-welfare state. The young Turks wanted the COS to be their in-house think tank, strategic planning group, legislation mill, and vision producer. It *was* all of that and less. More it couldn't be so long as the young Turks and their party were in the minority. Nonetheless, their COS brainchild attracted wave after wave of the brightest and the best young conservative Republicans to ever hit the House. But the vision thing was all Newt's. He produced it, he taught it, he led it.

Neither the House nor the GOP had ever seen anything quite like it before, or since. Its leading House members, including Gingrich, Vin Weber of Minnesota, Bob Walker of Pennsylvania, and Duncan Hunter of California, had several things in common. First, and what may prove most enduring, was that they were actively, even vociferously anti-racist, as opposed to being quietly disdainful or even grudgingly tolerant of it.

The Conservative Opportunity Society revolutionists understood, thanks to Gingrich, the wonderful uses to which they could put the omnipresent eye of C-Span. So these GOP youngsters defied decorum and tradition to charge to the floor on an instant's notice, after hours, to speak extemporaneously on virtually any issue, always with the purpose of drawing sharp ideological differences with the Democrats, even when neither Democrats nor other Republicans were present in the otherwise empty chamber.

The Gingrich "guerrillas in a TV box" tactics were aimed to end-run the gentlemanly "Let's Make a Deal" approach to the Democratic majority of the Republican's titular general at the time, the aging, pleasant, noncombative Minority Leader Bob Michel of Illinois.

Gingrich's band of young Turks believed that the road to becoming a majority party in the House lay not in continuing the Republican habit of saying no to every Democrat initiative for spawning or expanding a government program to benefit some interest group, and expanding government and its intrusiveness in the process.

Rather, they sought to preempt the liberals with proposals to create and expand opportunities in the private sector for all Americans, weaning them away from the "corrupt liberal welfare state." But when conservatives attempted to offer positive alternatives to the liberal Democrats' ideas, they risked sounding like the government-expanding "statists"* they supposedly oppose.

Gingrich's embrace, at one time, of a "conservative war on poverty," of special tax breaks and other government-financed incentives for inner-city business, and for federally subsidizing tenant ownership of public housing, naturally inspires suspicions that he is a closet "big government conservative," like his good friend Jack Kemp. Nonetheless, Gingrich's Conservative Opportunity Society defined conservative politics and ideas, certainly in Washington and most certainly for the Washington press corps, throughout the Reagan era.

How did Gingrich work his will throughout all of this? Imagine it's 1982, and there is Gingrich, younger and thinner than the man you know now, standing at the front of the "class," boxes of books at his feet and on nearby chairs, waiting to be handed out — Alvin and Heidi Toffler's *Third Wave*, Pete F. Drucker's *The Effective Executive*, and who remembers what else.

Several dozen Conservative Opportunity Society members, all GOP congressmen, were gathered in that "classroom" at the Capitol, on that Friday morning, with their bags packed and their wives and children waiting outside, ready to board buses bound for the Conservative

---

*Statists have this sick belief that the state, rather than voluntary associations of individuals, should be the venue of *first* resort for addressing problems and that groups' rights are more important than the rights of the individual.

Opportunity Society's first weekend study-and-strategy retreat in a hotel outside of Baltimore. But before he boards the buses with them, he is telling them what they should be reading, and scolding them for not reading. And they're *taking* it. They go on their three-day retreat, and there's lots of speakers and "seminar" leaders, but, hey, it's Newt's show all the way.

After a few years, he got bored with it — the Conservative Opportunity Society, not the vision or the leadership. Others became the society's leaders, but by then COS was just part of Newt's growing empire of intellectual institutions and power centers.

Gingrich also decided to do something your typical rank-and-file Republican, even the ones with the most hyperactive gonads, did not think of doing, even when in an altered mind state: go after and bring *down* that Lord of Creation, the Speaker of the House, whose every step made the earth tremble, at least on the House side of the Capitol. The Speaker of the moment happened to be a corrupt Democrat from Texas named Jim Wright. No other Republican was so suicidal, or self-confident, as to risk even associating himself with Gingrich's kamikaze mission. So, incredibly, single-handedly, Gingrich brought Wright down, forced his resignation. This act alone, of killing the biggest lion in the jungle, and one that had also been marauding the village, would have, in simpler times, entitled the lion-slayer to be chief of the tribe. Republicans as a tribe, however, tend to sniff at valor, especially another Republican's, and say things like, Yeah, but he used a number eight spear, and I could have done the job with a number seven spear.

So when an even more fateful event happened, the sudden opening up of the House minority whip's job, Gingrich was not the automatic choice, even though he had launched his lonesome attack on Wright. The House minority whip is the guy in charge of counting the probable votes for, and against, a bill he and his party's leader are supporting or opposing — and of cajoling or coercing fellow members of the House into voting the "right" way. It's an okay job, entertaining for the manager, deal-cutter, and body-mover in Newt, but nothing that challenged, to the hilt, the intellectual side of him. Still, if you want to be Speaker of the House of Representatives, the next most powerful office after President of the United States, you have to be top-ranked in your party, if and when, it becomes the majority in the House. That means if you want someday to be Speaker, you better be minority leader when your party takes over, and the Speaker's job opens up. But if you want to be minority leader, you have to be whip first. Newt won the whip's job, by one vote, because he outhustled and outmaneuvered his rivals, and because he got more liberal Republicans to vote for him than common sense would dictate. Yes, there were *quid pro quos*. You bet. Why not. Price of leadership. Of getting to join guys at the helm, the afterguard — the skipper and his tactician and his chief navigator — so you can do some of the steering exercising leadership.

Gingrich can be a kind and gentle political killer, and he'll do the job himself if he can. Like Czar Ivan the Terrible, who, when he decided he had to kill his own son for treason, did it himself instead of hiring someone else to do it. Newt maneuvered a nice old man, Bob Michel of Illinois, who had been minority leader for too long and for all the wrong reasons, into announcing before the 1994 elections that he would retire right after the 1994 elections. Gingrich not only knew before, *long* before, that his party would finally, after forty years, win back the House. He knew and predicted, on the record, it would be a huge, unprecedented victory for Republicans. A *sweep*, no less. He *had* to be at the helm as soon as the new Congress was sworn in, or the Republicans would muff it again. It's not for nothing that, among themselves, they sometimes refer to the GOP as the "Stupid Party." Anyhow, Michel was a gentleman and helped young members get their ears wet and get committee assignments, but he would smile at you with a blank look if you talked about *vision*, and he knew as much about strategy as he knew about brain surgery. *Zilch* might be overstating what he knew. He had to *go*, and everybody knew it. But, gee, thirty-eight years in the House. An old man. How nice to be Speaker for two years and then quit, even one year. Newt could have made sure the old guy had that at least. No. It wasn't good for the party or the country. He had to go. He went. Newt was the man.

Actually, in 1994, Newt was really running the show for the Republicans in the House. Every victory they had as the minority party over Clinton and the majority Democrats was Newt's strategic doing, Newt's enforcing and coercing and cajoling unity to an unprecedented extent. It was his Contract with America that took them into the stunning victory of the 1994 elections, and his leadership as Speaker that got it all done in the first hundred days of the new Congress, as promised.

It was then that it began to dawn on all but the most rabid Republican-phobes and Gingrich haters, that Gingrich just might have the right stuff eventually to take his place among the Titans of history, men who had both extraordinary vision and ability to infuse enthusiasm for that vision in others. And lead them to the fulfillment of that vision. A Churchill comes to mind. But Gingrich is also afflicted with the diseases great men are heir to: growing intoxication with the exquisiteness of their own ideas; a creeping belief that they are what the sycophants around them say they are; and that they are entitled to a *break* from the carping of lesser beings with whom they must out of necessity surround themselves, being there is a critical shortage of great beings like themselves at the moment.

Sometimes, Gingrich's temper is a personal embarrassment to himself, and to conservatives. Take one July night in 1995, when R. Emmett Tyrrell Jr., the editor of the *American Spectator*, had a private dinner for press pundits on the Right and a few politicos, including Gingrich.

The talk of the town was Gingrich's having just pulled one of his tactical retreats — to Newt, of course, he's not retreating. He's just fighting in another direction. This particular retreat came when Newt decided that House Republicans wouldn't lunge ahead after all with their promise to consign affirmative action laws and programs to the junk heap of history.

This was one of those occasions when Gingrich had bought into the conventional wisdom and pollster palaver about how Republicans are on the edge of making a historic breakthrough with black voters (in the 1992 presidential elections, the GOP got 11 percent of the black vote, and 12 percent in the House elections in 1994) and so shouldn't push to discard affirmative action quotas, preferences, and set sides, until the GOP comes up with a "positive alternative," probably not until the next year. He bought into Jack Kemp's latest line that the black community is just *dying* to come home to the party of Lincoln, if only the party of Lincoln and Gingrich will show its *compassion*. Now this really ticked off a lot of fellow Republicans in the House. They had gone out on a limb pushing for an end to affirmative action in the mistaken belief that this was going to be one of those issues where Speaker Newt would take the helm. Lash himself to the mast if necessary. Make the case eloquently, comprehensibly, and comprehensively as only he could. Demonstrating irrefutably that in the long run, blacks would benefit as much as whites from ending reverse discrimination. All the while enforcing party discipline and unity, so that House Republicans could sail off into the sunset, victorious and hailed as such.

A Republican from Connecticut who was particularly teed-off was Gary Franks, who kind of stood out among those who had been leading the charge to dump federal affirmative action. Franks is a black man who represents a white majority district in Connecticut. He thought he had a promise from Newt. Newt pulled the rug out from under him, without warning. Franks was *not* amused by Gingrich's sudden abandonment and said so publicly.

So here's Gingrich at this private dinner, in an upstairs room at the Brasserie, where some years earlier a waitress had found Senator Edward M. Kennedy having sexual relations with a female lobbyist under a table. That was then. Now it's twenty-four conservative thinkers, writers, talkers, and doers seated at a longer table. One of the guests is syndicated columnist Bob Novak, who had written a devastating column about Gingrich's strategic abandonment of the effort to knock off affirmative action. Another guest is Bill Schultz, a *Reader's Digest* news executive. Schultz makes the mistake of asking Newt what gives with this affirmative action stuff. Gingrich transmogrifies into Newtrino, and does a nuclear fission number. "I'm sick and tired of being questioned and second-guessed by conservatives who *just don't get* it," he says. He's shouting.

Anyhow, here's Gingrich, glaring and shouting across the dinner table, jabbing his finger mostly at Novak, and sounding a bit like Captain Queeg. "I've gotten us to where we are. I have a seven year plan, and I cannot accomplish everything today. Given my track record, you ought to give me the benefit of the doubt, because I know what I am doing and have proven it."

Gingrich, the words coming fast even for him, the original machine-gun mouth, asserted that as bad as affirmative action is, it would be foolish to do anything about it until, and unless, the Republicans advance an alternative urban plan that can gain them the support of the black ministers who control the vote in their communities.

Gingrich thundered that anyone who doubted his philosophical opposition to quotas and racial preferences had never read his work or sat through his televised college course. But, he said, Republicans would be "crazy" to make affirmative action an issue, given the nervousness about the Republican Party within the black community.

Out of control, his eyes sweeping up and down the table like the muzzles of twin machine guns, he told the two dozen assembled conservatives that "conservatives" were taking an essentially *racist* position in opposing affirmative action at this time.

When asked by a guest who he, Newt Gingrich, considered guilty of using the issue for racist reasons, Gingrich pulled the trigger instantly. "Pete Wilson," he barked.

A moment of stunned silence, broken by American Conservative Union chairman David A. Keene: "*You* must be the only person at this table, Newt, who believes Wilson is a conservative," Keene shot back.

Gingrich, without even a wince, proceeded to cajole the dinner assemblage to be *patient*. Wait until Newt Gingrich is *ready* to articulate the conservative urban policy of the future. He assured all present that it was being developed by one of his top intellectual henchmen, Jeff Eisenach, who heads one of Gingrich's many intellectual front groups, the Progress and Freedom Foundation. And by Gingrich's guru of that summer, Marvin Olasky, author of a seminal and readable work called *The Tragedy of American Compassion*. Gingrich thundered that he would be able to *use* this new conservative urban policy he was hatching. How would he use it? To split the Congressional Black Caucus "right down the middle."

Keene had Gingrich's number years before Gingrich's ascension to the Speakership. "Newt is not and never was a philosophical conservative. But he has done more for the cause of conservatism than anyone else in Congress," Keene once observed. Keene got it just right. Gingrich is too eclectic intellectually, to be a philosophical anything. Or too ambitious. He is a coalition builder, and his goal is to lead not just conservatives, but everyone in his party, the liberals included. And everyone in the *nation*, liberals and Democrats included.

He had won the whip's job by a one-vote, 87 to 85 margin over his Republican rival. The rival's 85 votes were made up of a coalition of liberal Republicans and conservative Republicans. Newt's 87 were libs and wingers, too. Hey, that's principle and philosophy in Congress. It's the way the world works. Or that part of it at least, that sits on the fevered banks of the Potomac. Seven years later, Gingrich led the House Republicans from his official whip position and his *de facto* minority leader's position in a stunning setback for President Clinton and the House Democrats on a 33 billion omnibus crime bill. He claimed the bill was chock full of useless social welfare spending. Such as "midnight basketball courts" that the brain-dead in Congress said would prevent inner-city kids from robbing and killing. As in, "Geez, I wuz gonna go rob and kill the McDonald's staff and manager until I remembered there's a basketball court open all night down the street, so I said, why don't I do *that* instead?"

Gingrich said the bill's ban on certain kinds of semi-automatic guns, the bill's Democrat authors designated as "assault weapons," was as stupidly useless as the social spending, while also abridging the rights of law-abiding citizens to gun ownership. He held his Republican minority together, along with enough conservative Democrats to stop the bill cold. But then he shocked conservatives, and just about everybody else when he sent a team of liberal Republican House members into negotiations with the Democratic leadership and, not surprisingly, the liberal Republicans gave the store away. Clinton got a lot of his social spending *and* his gun ban. And the liberal Republicans got to look "moderate" for their liberal Republican districts and constituencies. Gingrich had shown them that he was *their* leader, as much as he was the conservatives' leader. The following January, he was elected House Speaker by a unanimous vote of his fellow Republicans, and he passed out rewards in committee chairmanships across the ideological board.

✶✶✶

He has his good friends, Alvin and Heidi Toffler, the husband-and-wife futurists and old-time Lefties who have drifted away from the Trotskyite-Social Democrat-labor union-We Shall Overcome world, but are self-avowedly *not conservatives*. He appointed liberal Democrat Jane Fortson to spearhead his National Cities Project, which has the District of Columbia as its first project. He had her named as a senior fellow at the Progress and Freedom Foundation, one of his intellectual front groups. Miss Fortson is a Jimmy Carter friend and former Atlanta Housing Authority board member — appointed by the liberal Democrat, and then-mayor Andrew Young. She has proved very useful to Newt in establishing diplomatic relations with the Left-wing black Democratic establishment and its white business, real estate and contractor allies that have relentlessly, and successfully, run the District into the ground and several miles underground. Newt believes he must work with, coalesce with, them, in order to save the nation's capital.

Coalitions. That's the thing. The key. The Password to Greatness for Newt Gingrich. We're talking about the Newtrino who helped engineer one of the most sweeping political victories of a political party in American history, what even former liberal Republican pollster Fred Steeper, after intensive analysis of massive exit-polling data and voter interviews, concluded was the first genuinely ideological election in a long time, and one driven by, of all things, moral values as much as by economic self-interest.

So what name did this man Gingrich then invoke following that election, in his nationally televised "inauguration" speech on being elevated to House Speaker? The hero of the 1980 conservative revolution in Washington, Ronald Reagan? Uh-uh. Barry Goldwater, the hero of the "conservative" — or so it was thought at the time — takeover of the Republican Party from its Eisenhower-Rockefeller Country Club care takers in 1964? Nope. Newt Gingrich, who on his way up from backbencher to superstar used habitually to refer to the "corrupt Democrat liberal welfare state," invoked on the crowning day of Republican conservatism, the name of none other than that icon of American socialism and liberalism, Franklin Delano Roosevelt, the father of the corrupt liberal Democrat welfare state. Newt was broadening the tent, don't you see? To include whom? All those Reagan Democrats who had

★★

already come over in 1968? The Republican tent? It already housed a majority in the U.S. Senate, the U.S. House of Representatives, thirty governorships out of fifty, parity in state legislatures. Major gains at local levels. Whose tent, then? Ah, now *that* is an interesting question.

Newt Gingrich, big hair and all, thinks — change that to *knows* — that he is the heir apparent to the Reagan mantle of leadership of the conservative movement and the Republican Party. He *will* lead. If not now, later. If not the United States, then the universe. And why not? He's a *futurist*. It's really just a matter of time and planning. Newt Gingrich is supremely good at both.

✮ ✮ ✮ ✮ ✮ ✮ ✮ ✮ ✮

BILL CLINTON
The First Latchkey President

IF YOU BUY INTO THE NURTURE SIDE of the nature-nurture argument over why and how individual human beings turn out the way they do, then President Clinton deserves much admiration for turning out as well as he has turned out. He did not have the relative familial advantages enjoyed by Newt Gingrich, the other dominant political figure of the last decade of the twentieth century in America. This is *not* the highest compliment available on the planet to pay someone, let alone to the President of the United States, the former governor of the great state of Arkansas, *and* the close personal friend of Webster Hubbell. But Clinton deserves his due, and often gets it, which is why he is so often in a bad humor, snarling at the press, snarling at the Congress — and that was when it was controlled by Democrats — and snarling at the world for creating foreign policy problems for him, when he was trying to concentrate on creating domestic policy problems for himself right here in the good old U.S. of A.

It would be totally unfair to say that his first term showed that he can function only in the chaos he creates, that he is completely indecisive and engages in the dissemination of blatant dissemblance, not to mention dissimulation. It would show a lack of respect to say that he was almost always indecisive on any matter before him, at any time, for any reason, and that he preceded to dismantle public trust normally accorded to a president, and that he did this virtually before the ink was dry on newspapers reporting his election as president.

So let the word go forth that, in the pages of this book, those accusations *will not be made*. As for the possible hyperbole that no deputy chief counsel to a President of the United States had ever committed suicide until Vincent W. Foster, Jr., bosom buddy to Bill and Hillary

****

Rodham Clinton and senior partner with Mrs. Clinton in the Rose law firm, decided to make it a first.

One must remember that many millions of Americans voted for Bill Clinton for president, and will vote for him again if they have the opportunity. They *like* Bill Clinton. They *respect* Bill Clinton. Deporting *that* many Americans on the grounds of mental midgetry is simply not a legal option. Besides, Republicans would object on the grounds that it would *cost* too much.

And if you think you're going to find the kind of titillation you probably got from reading about Gennifer Flowers and "bimbo eruptions" or Clinton "containment squads" allegedly paying off women not to tell about their supposed affairs with Clinton before he was president in this book, think again. *All that is ancient history.*

As for his not serving in the United States armed forces during that unpleasantness in Indochina awhile back, it will be beneath the dignity of this exposition to regurgitate the feloniously irresponsible speculation about, and accusations of, so-called "draft dodging" on Clinton's part. So he didn't serve? So can't a man get *lucky*, for goodness sake, without people accusing him of being the moral equivalent of Hanoi Jane Fonda?

Nor will it be argued in these pages that William Jefferson Clinton purposely, not to mention artfully, has created a sense of dependence among the poor, the alienated, and those who have come from dysfunctional families like his. Bill Clinton probably did not set out to make his actions as president such as to force much of America, and almost all of his administration, to behave in a dysfunctional way, thus contributing to the creation of a dysfunctional nation. It just, well, *happened.*

If would be simplistic and too easy to argue that Clinton has deceived the American people so often that they have come to accept these deceptions as normal behavior, just like the lies told by the drunkard who was his abusive father. It would be a doubtless exaggeration to say that some Americans, perhaps the 43 percent of the votes he got from those who voted in the 1992 presidential elections, no longer recognize the lies, and this places much of the nation in a state of confusion. This state is not, after all, unique to Democratic administrations or even to Bill Clinton. There was considerable speculation that the state of confusion could become the fifty-first in the nation if the Bush administration continued in office much longer. But under Clinton, it did seem to immobilize more Americans' abilities, and drive more of them into dysfunctional dependency.

Back to the nurture over nature premise. Accept for the moment the supremely important impact of psychological conditioning, or enculturation, or familial upbringing, or whatever they're calling it this month. That accepted, it might seem to follow that if Bill Clinton allowed himself to be treated by any psychiatrist, he would be diagnosed, based just on his family values and family background, as a patient who is in total denial about the pain he suffered as a child, the pain of complete abandonment by his mother and his father.

Because of the lies his mother and his father told him during his childhood, has Clinton come to accept lying as normal behavior? Is that why he cannot make decisions? Is that the origin of his torturous self-doubt? If you come down on the side of environment over genetics, or even *vice versa*, then it may not be a stretch to conclude that this lack of self-worth stems from having a stepfather who came home drunk most of the time and abused his family most of *that* time.

Anybody remember a test used by some psychiatrists after Dr. Harvey Cleckley published it in his 1964 book, *The Mask of Sanity*? Just for fun, you understand, you might want to put a check mark (see next page) next to the traits you think describe Bill Clinton (or the politician of your choice). Too many check marks indicate too many problems in character. Beware.

Remember the family values "thing" Republican Presidential nomination candidates began falling all over themselves and each other to claim as their own when the nomination race began in 1995?

These were the same Republican characters who, with one or two exceptions, wouldn't touch the moral-values issues with a ten-foot pole in 1992, and 1993, and 1994. Certainly not after the media dumped all over the Bush-Quayle '92 campaign's brief brush with values as an issue, through the awkward device of *Murphy Brown*. Remember when the media and liberal Democrats and liberal Republicans told you that Quayle's *Murphy Brown* speech and Pat Buchanan's "cultural wars" speech represented a mean-spirited, Hitlerite, Protestant fundamentalist, Papist plot to delegitimize bastardy? The media and liberals in both

✯✯

Character Trait	Clinton, or the Politician of Your Choice
Glibness/superficial charm	
Grandiose sense of self-worth	
Need for stimulation/proneness to boredom	
Pathological lying	
Cunning/manipulative	
Lack of remorse or guilt	
Shallow affect	
Callous/lack of empathy	
Parasitic lifestyle	
Poor behavioral controls	
Promiscuous sexual behavior	
Early behavior problems	
Indecisive, cannot carry out long-term plans	
Impulsiveness	
Irresponsibility	
Failure to accept responsibility for own actions	
Many short-term marital or sexual relationships	
Juvenile delinquency	
Revocation of conditional release	
Criminal versatility	

Chart from the book *Mask of Sanity* by Harvey Milton Cleckley, published by C.V. Mosby Co., 1964.

parties said Quayle and Buchanan were part of a moralistic, Bible-thumping, Torah-spouting, Koran-emulating plot to return America to the past? Which past? To the *unenlightened* past when fourteen year-old girls did *not* walk down the street, or ride public transportation with an infant in one hand, a welfare check in the other, a wedding band on the fingers of neither hand, and even a hint of shame nowhere to be seen.

Legend, memory, and the political image-makers did a lot to rewrite the history and impact of the Quayle and Buchanan speeches, just as they have done a lot to touch up Bill Clinton's childhood and youth. Many of the stories told completely disregard verifiable events that tell a very different story.

In fact, if you wanted to look at Bill Clinton's relationship with his parents in the purely clinical terms of a child psychologist, you might see a recipe for disaster. You might see a sad, sympathetic figure in Clinton the child. You might see in the child all the makings of what later becomes disturbed, troubled, and oppressed by the horrible feeling of abandonment that comes when you lose your natural parents for any reason.

Fact: Bill Clinton's father was the type of man that every family dreads its daughter will fall for: a good-looking, sweet-talking salesman who had trouble with the truth, and trouble with all of the women in his life, all his life. Indeed, Bill could be a "chip off the old block." His father, William Jefferson Blythe, was the living, breathing definition of a deadbeat. And this guy never even *made* it to Congress. In his dealings with others, he often used phony names and dates of birth. This was nowhere more apparent than in his relationships with women. He was married the first time to a seventeen-year-old girl named Adele Cofelt. Before a year was out, he divorced her, left her pregnant with a baby boy, and in December of 1940, married Adele's sister, Faye. Gave a special meaning to "keeping it all in the family," Blythe did.

In yet another marriage, he abandoned the woman in Los Angeles after two weeks and was divorced from her within nine months. An Oklahoma judge stated that William Jefferson Blythe was guilty of "extreme cruelty and gross neglect of duty."

More than one young woman claimed to be carrying Blythe's baby and, indeed, at the age of twenty-three, he was listed as the father of a baby girl born to a Missouri waitress to whom he may or may not have been briefly married. No one can be sure. He married yet again, at the age of twenty-three. This time the lucky woman was Winneta Ellen Alexander, who gave birth to his daughter eight days after the wedding. She did not divorce him until April 1944, eight months after he had married Virginia Cassidy, who would become the mother of President Bill Clinton.

Blythe met Virginia at a hospital when he was taking one of his girlfriends or wives to the emergency room. Virginia Cassidy was spared the fate of the others thanks to the man who was uncle to us all. Five weeks after they were married (and while he was still married to Winneta Ellen Alexander), Uncle Sam shipped Blythe overseas to become part of the American forces in World War II. Virginia Cassidy was to spend the first of many Thanksgivings and Christmases alone. She was not to see him again until December 7, 1945.

As for Virginia Cassidy, she spent those war years away from Bill's father as the subject of unkind but endless gossip and rumors. She was supposedly the town's wild one. With a husband overseas, it was said that she exercised the freedom to go out and party till dawn.

A few months after Blythe returned from the war, he met his death in an automobile accident. Eight months after Virginia Cassidy had her reunion with William Jefferson Blythe, she gave birth to Bill. Fairly or not, tongues wagged.

In any event, the baby was born to an already shattered family. Children feel a sense of abandonment when a parent is missing, whether it's caused by divorce, death, war, or personal tragedy.

Virginia Cassidy, after the birth of Bill, found herself psychologically deserted because of her husband's death. She had to live with her parents, with a father whom she loved and a mother whom she could not stand. Not ideal. But altogether part of what is so often the human tragedy. Maybe one of the reasons she fled home as a teenager was that, by all accounts, she had an abusive mother.

Edith Cassidy, Virginia's mother, constantly criticized her husband. She constantly criticized Virginia. Edith played martinet, ordering them about. And when things weren't done her way, she would shout and scream and throw things.

Virginia Cassidy would physically abandon her son, leaving him with this woman barely five months after his birth. There were many who believed Virginia Cassidy abandoned young Bill before that, partly because of her appetites, and partly because her domineering mother demanded to take control of her grandson and to dominate their lives.

Young Bill Clinton was to be raised in a household filled with conflict, and argument, and lacking consistent love. Less than five months after his birth, Virginia Cassidy left him. He would not return to her care until he was four years old.

She was not your conventional, *Saturday Evening Post*–type mom. Busy-bodies questioned whether she was fit to raise Bill or any child. They said that all of her life she had a fondness for alcohol. That she frequented the most disreputable bars in Little Rock. That she was addicted to gambling, and even used the racing form to teach her children to read. Whatever the truth, she did have a history of choosing men who would abuse her. And by any conventional standard, she failed to concern herself with the effects her lifestyle might have on Bill Clinton or later on his brother.

Three years after being reunited with Bill, Virginia Cassidy determined to marry his stepfather, Raymond Clinton. In doing this she condemned Bill Clinton to a childhood that was to be filled with violence, fear, and chaos. Raymond Clinton was a man who physically and mentally abused and terrorized his family. He came home drunk most of the time. Raymond Clinton had already been married before and was divorced by his first wife in 1948 because he had abused her.

Children subjected to, for want of a better term, "parental deprivation" are not necessarily deprived of their parents' physical presence. Rather, they may suffer from inadequate or distorted care at home. Regardless of its specific nature or intensity, parental negligence has been associated with a more or less specific pattern of development in children. They often have a tendency to be overly aggressive and prone to impulsive behavior, such as cheating, overeating, lying, and so on. The presence of a strong sibling or stepparent can often prevent, or even reverse, some of the damage created in the dysfunctional family.

✱✱

Raymond Clinton was a father who would see his son only after he had had several drinks, never spend any time with him, would constantly argue with the boy's mother, had an addiction for gambling just like Virginia's, delighted in terrorizing the boy, and exploded into fits of jealous rage, which Virginia gave him many opportunities to do, both real and imagined.

This was definitely not your Norman Rockwell–type American family. It wasn't even your Lincoln Rockwell–type family.

Dr. Paul Fick, in his book *The Dysfunctional President*, writes that "in an alcoholic home, truth is of little value. For a time, a child in the home believes the word of the alcoholic parent, only to be hurt and disappointed repeatedly. The hurt resides inside the child because in the alcoholic home there is not an effective communication structure to express the pain. The hurt turns into anger over time. Withholding the anger results in a lowering of the child's self-worth. The child ultimately learns that telling the truth is not only of little value in the home, but also that lying is acceptable." Dr. Fick further observes that "the child learns not only to lie, but also to distort reality in such a fashion that at times he even deceives himself. The child begins to believe his own lies."

It is sad to think of Bill Clinton being raised this way. In the 1940s and early 1950s, it also was far more rare for anyone to be raised that way than in the 1990s, when psychiatrists and clinical psychologists are becoming all too common.

Bill Clinton has paid a price for the upbringing that was not his fault. Almost never during his presidency did a majority of Americans polled give him a thumbs up. The electronic and print media, cartoonists, stand-up comics, and late-night television hosts have dwelled on Clinton's "moral character." It has not been pretty to watch or hear, for the most part, if you are a Clinton fan or a Clinton family member.

He is routinely written about as a man who cannot tell the truth, whether it is about the files of Vince Foster, his $200 haircut, Whitewater, his wife's commodities investments, "Travel-gate" or his relationships with Gennifer Flowers and Paula Corbin Jones.

He is looked upon as someone who would easily betray his closest supporters if it became politically expedient to do so.

✶✶

The media aside, he has created, on his own, the image of a man who would sooner jump off a cliff than make a decision, *any* decision. Bill Clinton makes Hamlet look decisive. Nor has he ever met a decision of his that he likes after having made it. He is utterly ruthless and heartless in second-guessing his own decisions as on Bosnia, Haiti, North Korea, balancing the budget, tax cuts for the middle class, health care, and on and on. You sometimes wish he would cut *himself* some slack. Then you review the decisions and you say, no, he *should* second-guess himself.

It was thus from the very beginning. You have to wonder at the political acuity of this man, at the degree to which he is in touch with ordinary citizens and not just with the liberal elite, when you recall that long before he put his hand on the Bible to be sworn in as president, he told the nation his first priority was to open the door of military service to homosexuals. They had voted for him and he owed them, right? Maybe. But as the first act of a man not even yet sworn in as president? Who didn't bother to find out if the chairman of the Joint Chiefs of Staff, a man who has known his own share of discrimination, would dump on his idea publicly?

The president, any president, is always the butt of humor. It goes with the turf. The humor that surrounds Bill Clinton, whether it is created by a conservative activist, a Jay Leno, a David Letterman, or lesser-known comedians who play in towns and cities throughout America, goes a bit beyond the norm, however, and calls into question his character. The not-very-funny fact of life is that Bill Clinton, as president, quickly went from the man from Hope to the clown from Little Rock's red-light district who picked up prostitutes in Arkansas' "Hookers' Row" and took them to his mother's vacation cabin outside Hot Springs.

This is not good for the nation, for the president, or his family and friends. Yet whose fault is it? The humor that surrounds Bill Clinton works, gets laughs, because it assumes the audience, the nation, more or less agrees, that the subject of the humor is a man with no moral compass, no backbone, and no rock-solid, core values. Whose fault? *Not* a pleasant question.

The press and the comics and the cartoonists have been tough on others. They got laughs out of painting Ronald Reagan as a stupid old man and dumb old reactionary. But Reagan used to laugh at anything that was ever said about him, and could tell more jokes about himself than any of his enemies or harshest critics could tell about him.

The humor that George Bush elicited was mostly kinder and gentler, and when it was harsh, it was to suggest that he was an upper-class twit with a fatal inability to understand the average American. Then there was Jimmy Carter, who was looked upon as a school teacher so out of touch with the reality of the real world that the nation could spend recess laughing at his pious pronouncements.

Other chapters in this book are devoted to candidates who are basically unknown to the broad American electorate, or not known so well as Clinton, even though he has been on the national stage only a relatively short time. The problem for him is that Americans — the admirers, the uninterested, the disinterested, and the haters alike — know him all too well.

Okay. So why is he different from these other presidents? And have the changes in American society made him what he is today?

Bill Clinton is the first president of the United States who was ever raised without the support and guidance of a father. He is our first "latchkey" president, and our first president not to have had the physical presence of a mother in the home during the first two critical years of his development.

The "parental deprivation" referred to earlier is one of those psycho-babble terms that give most sensible humans a severe case of the yawns. But, hey, an absence of adequate care from, and interaction with, parents or step-parents or a strong sibling during a kid's formative years is *not a good thing*. And you don't need a psycho-quack to tell you which way that wind blows.

Like it or not, the victims of such experiences may get their cognitive maps fouled up. On such maps, the basic stability, trustworthiness, and affection of the world and of relationships are represented, if at all, to be uncertain and thus unworthy of serious commitment. Cheating on a spouse comes to mind.

Psychologists and psychiatrists talk about children who grow up unattached, without compassion from a mother, and without loving, tender guidance from a father. The claim is that these children can grow up to be arrogant, shameless, irreverent, and cunning. So can children brought up by their natural parents in a stable environment. But you sort of instinctively want to bet that the kids from a dysfunctional home are more likely, as children and adults, to find denial easy and to reflect no remorse when caught in wrongdoing.

Make no mistake that Clinton reflects today's America, where 40 percent of all children are raised in a home where there is no father. Never before in our history have so many children grown up not knowing what it is like to have a father. Indeed, many Americans have suffered the same loss as Bill Clinton, and felt the same pain that he felt. There is no question that Bill Clinton and this group of children have been denied physiological, social, economic, and moral assets that the other 60 percent of American children take as their birthright.

Is this why members of the nut wing of the feminist movement, the men haters, are so committed to Bill Clinton, assuming there *is* a nut wing of the feminist movement, which we know is *not true*? But if there were, would they be just dizzy with delight to have a man in the Oval Office who shows that fathers are expendable? Or, in the case of Bill Clinton's cruel and abusive stepfather, that fathers are the *problem*? From the first settlement of America until well into the nineteenth century, most of our leaders were raised in homes according to law and custom. Fathers bore the ultimate *responsibility* for care and rearing of children in the *policy-setting* sense. In fact, the child rearing manuals of that time were addressed to the fathers, not the mothers. Blame for children who turned out wrong was placed solely on fathers. Religious and moral education was the responsibility of the father. Never mind a good argument can be made that mothers — then, before then, now, always and *ad infinitum* in both directions on the temporal continuum — have done the real, day-to-day woman's work in child rearing, while the *presence* of a father figure provided a useful, even vital balance.

As America entered into the conflict of the Civil War, urbanization and industrialization had begun to create a household that recognized a more joint responsibility for both parents. But, starting with Bill Clinton's generation, responsibility shifted toward the mother in a

★★

single-parent household. This does not make for bad kids necessarily or for unsuccessful grownups. William Bennett, the former education secretary and drug policy administrator in the Bush administration, and author of a best-selling book about virtue, was raised by his mother in a single-parent household. But Bennett recognizes that the chances for a healthy childhood and success in adulthood are measurably better with a mom and dad at home.

Highly educated persons with "ologists" at the end of their professional titles and ordinary folks who have only their common-sense observations to go on agree on one point. It is that the absence of a father is a leading cause of drug use, violent juvenile crime, and the boundless self-gratification that comes from riding the welfare merry-go-round for generation after generation. It is not Bill Clinton's fault that he is the first latchkey president and brings to the job whatever character-trait baggage that may have caused.

Nonetheless, in deciding on whether to accord him a second term, Americans will judge Bill Clinton by the traits of character he has shown as president, as well as his concrete accomplishments in office. In order to get re-elected, Bill Clinton will have to talk about family values and what they really mean to him. He will have to draw on the values he learned from his childhood. This could be a problem. He will have to say that in bringing up his own daughter, Chelsea, he relied on parental example and not just pietistic speeches to her. *This* could be a problem. As Dr. James Dobson, founder of Focus on the Family, has noted: "There is no substitute for parental modeling of the attitudes we wish to teach. Someone once wrote, 'The footsteps a child follows are most likely to be the ones his parents thought they covered up.'"

Bill Clinton also will have to talk about *keeping* promises. He promised no new taxes when he ran for his first term in the White House, and then proceeded cheerfully to sign into law the largest nominal-dollar tax increase in the nation's history.*

---

*It was the second largest, corrected for inflation. In inflation-corrected dollars, the largest was Ronald Readan's 1983 tax hike, but that came after the most sweeping tax cut he had sought and got enacted the year before.

Clinton promised a middle-class tax cut. He will have to explain why that promise went the way of the dodo bird. He will have to explain why his support of two consecutive measures that made it more difficult for honest citizens to buy firearms is not simply a prelude to the banning of all firearms except for law enforcers and the military. This, of course, would mean the government is armed, criminals are armed, and only the great mass of law-abiding citizens are unarmed and helpless to defend themselves and their liberties.

Clinton will also have to explain an executive order that he quietly signed that gave organized labor a major victory that most voters won't like when they hear about it. Clinton's executive order forbids anyone with a federal contract from hiring permanent replacements for workers who walk off the job because they are demanding more money from their employer, including an employer who may have only two or three employees, thus totally shutting down small businesses.

He will have to explain to the labor union members who benefited from this striker-replacement ban why he supported the North Atlantic Free Trade Agreement and the latest General Agreement on Tariffs and Trade, which organized labor said would permanently cost Americans, whether labor union members or not, far more jobs than might be preserved with a striker replacement ban.

He will have to explain why he led the way in insisting on the American taxpayer bailout of Mexico, which is just the down payment on the next bailout of Mexico.

He will have to explain why as president he kept changing his story about whether, how well, and under what circumstances he knew Paula Jones when he was governor of Arkansas.

There are other things he will be asked to explain. Every president who wants a second term has to defend his record, and justify his asking the electorate to entrust their lives, their future, and that of the nation to him yet again.

And when he answers these questions, will he tell the truth or will he even recognize the truth?

Fair question?

PART IV

★★★★ ★★★★★★★★★★★★★★★★★★★★★★★★

Special Interest Groups: The Meat in the Electoral Sausage

☆ ☆ ☆ ☆ ☆ ☆ ☆ ☆ ☆

How do candidates reach voters in America? Who besides the candidates influences those voters? Good questions, if we do say so ourselves.

The answers, like American politics, have evolved over the years, but if you want to understand who's got the clout now and why and how he plans to use it, it's useful, even fun, to recall how we got here from back there.

In the beginning, there was the beginning. That's when Americans began regarding voting not as a privilege, and therefore revocable, but as a fundamental right. Let's call the beginning 1789. Since then, America led the way in extending the franchise, first to propertied white males, then to propertied white and black males in the North, then to all males everywhere and finally to women.

While the basic principles of democracy and America's commitment to free elections have remained fairly constant, social changes have dramatically altered the way we campaign for public office. Oh boy have they.

Hand-wringing pundits and professional worriers aside, political campaigns in the nineteenth century were no less intense and emotionally charged than they are today. However, the operating framework was considerably less complicated, just as the ability to reach voters more limited. A hundred years ago, the candidate spoke to the voter directly, bad breath and all, even shook his hand (how many Californians can say they shook a presidential candidate's hand in the last forty years?). In the old days, candidates marched in just about every parade they could find. And attended rallies. Lots of rallies. Sure, there was mass communication. Newspapers and pamphlets you had to stick in people's hands. That was about it.

In the early 1920s, women achieved suffrage and doubled the number of voters. At roughly the same time, radio added a new dimension to political communication. A great communicator like Franklin D. Roosevelt could mobilize the masses, speaking his message to all corners of the country simultaneously, and making himself heard, if not necessarily understood, even by your occasional illiterate voter.

Television created the next communications revolution. The continuously evolving television medium has had the most visible impact on the way we conduct political campaigns.

Then, in the 1960s, the civil rights movement began with a new emphasis on voter registration, voter turnout, and organization of new voter segments through institutions such as churches. In some cases, a candidate who didn't have prayers didn't have a prayer, if you catch the drift.

Anyhow, in the 1970s, the development of cost-effective computer technology enabled candidates to carefully isolate, identify, and target individual voters. *Ugh.* Sounds a bit premeditated and calculating. But, hey, it worked.

For the first time, lifestyle, family structure, and a whole host of demographic data were incorporated into campaign strategies and appeals. Millions of targeted letters and telephone calls could now be completed in days, even hours. Voter responses could be polled, monitored, analyzed, dissected, tracked, and then incorporated into the next day's campaign strategy.

Before World War II, Americans were likely to live in the same neighborhoods as their parents. They really did. This is historical *fact*. We would *not* lie to you about this. Anyhow, in today's society, a lot of people don't know their neighbors. Some who do, wish they didn't. During the campaigns of the 1950s and 1960s, when working wives and single households were not the norm, there were volunteers readily available. Today, this is not the case. Campaign headquarters soon went out and bought computers to compensate for the low volunteer turnout.

Political operatives developed this targeting technology at a time when the constant movement of families dramatically altered the foundations of the traditional campaign strategy, which revolved around the geographically drawn precinct. Candidates unable to rely on a stable geographic base had to search out and identify supporters in social, economic, and behavioral clusters, which transcended geographic lines. Getting the picture of how complex this whole business of electoral politics and electioneering is becoming? Soon it will require an electoral engineering degree.

Then came federal campaign finance law restricting how much an individual could contribute directly to someone's candidacy. This didn't eliminate the influence of money on campaign politics, but it sure changed the way it was collected, both by whom and from whom.

In the old days, major candidates endorsed by their parties found few obstacles in acquiring campaign donations. Money was not a problem because there were no limits and no reporting requirements. The post-Watergate-reform movement changed that and prevented billionaires from giving hundreds of thousands of dollars, even millions of dollars, to deserving candidates. What good is it to be a billionaire if the law says you can give, say, only one grand to the guy you want to see in the White House? Doesn't mean you can't buy his attention in other ways, but it sure cuts down on one billionaire's influence.

State after state began to adopt similar limits and reporting requirements for candidates for state office. Professional fund-raising experts were no longer panting audibly over just the richest men and women in America. Campaign managers, used to custom-tailoring their suits, now had to custom-tailor events and direct mail solicitations toward anyone, anywhere, who believed strongly enough in the candidate's ideology.

As a result of the increased marketing efforts of the 1970s, national party donors now numbered in the millions, with at least one national committee having a base of 2 million donors.

The creation of that *Pow! Wow!* phenomenon, the Political Action Committee, has fostered a furor, not to mention controversy, by switching the emphasis for campaigners away from affiliation with political parties to affiliation with special interests.

Today, those so-called special interests and their voting patterns play the most profound role in American politics. Indeed, they have become a rallying point for those voters who no longer feel their views are represented by the two major parties. These groups and their political action committees entitled to channel donations to candidates and political parties range from the mega-member retirees' association, the teachers' lobbies, the gun controllers and the anti-gun controllers, the pro-lifers and the pro-choicers and the morality mongers. Then there are the pushers of amoral relativism and the pushers of civil libertarians (often thought to be one and the same). The farm lobby, the welfare lobby, the association for federally subsidized electricity users, and on and on. Each with a niche, a targeted segment of the electorate to serve or go after.

At the same time, the Democratic and Republican parties have suffered a decline in voter identification with their positions. The Democratic Party has made it clear that pro-prayer, antiabortion Democrats are not so welcome anymore. But then the Democratic Party also made its organized racist segments unwelcome two or three decades ago. The GOP, party of Lincoln, was never keen on organized racists but hasn't made great strides with blacks, either. The party of FDR made it clear that Democrats who think that government is too big and that organizations like the teachers' unions are out of control have no place in the Democratic Party's ranks. The Democratic Party has made it clear, too, that it is sometimes at odds with itself over whether to worry more about criminals getting a fair shake or victims' rights, but it clearly has no room for pro-second amendment types.

While many of these constituents have moved out of the Democratic Party, they have not all moved into the Republican Party. Some of the Republican Party structure is still controlled by the wealthy, elitist, old-boy network. It still thinks in such quaint terms as the supreme need for geographic-and-ideological ticket-balancing. This is *no joke*. There are leading Republicans who continue to talk like this.

Some powerful forces in the Republican Party still fail to grasp fully — or don't like what they see — the fact that the party's growing strength comes from voters who were not born Republican, and probably cast their first votes as Democrats. These are the same voters who stayed home in 1976, and stayed home or voted for Perot in 1992.

What has become obvious in the elections of today is that although these former Democrats are willing to listen to the likes of

Ralph Reed, Wayne LaPierre, William Dobson, Gary Bauer, Phyllis Schlafly, and others, they will not blindly follow the lead of any of them or of polls or statistics that run counter to personal conviction and moral commitment.

Probably the best example of this was the case of House Majority Leader Tom Foley and Congressman Jack Brooks, chairman of the Judiciary Committee. Both were longtime National Rifle Association supporters. Not only had they received rewards and accolades from the organization, they were indeed principally responsible for stopping the Democrat-controlled Congresses from passing gun control legislation. But in 1993 and 1994, Foley and Brooks voted for the five-day waiting period for gun purchases and the semi-automatic assault weapons ban. They had been supplied by the Clinton administration with polling information that showed these proposals were so popular among the American people that the 80 million gun owners in America would not possibly vote against them.

However, this was incorrect information, and to the 80 million American gun owners, this was outright betrayal. "Betrayal" was an easy message to sell because the average American doesn't believe that political leaders have their best interests at heart. Poll after poll shows Americans distrust their government and even feel betrayed by their leaders, who they believe will say anything to get elected and then treat their campaign promises like dirt under their feet.

Foley and Brooks are no longer members of Congress. In fact, it is worth noting that in the 1994 elections, not a single congressman who voted against the two big gun control measures, the Brady Bill and the ban on semi-automatic weapons, was defeated. President Clinton himself claimed in a vent-the-anger speech in Cleveland after the elections that the gun owners' lobby and political action arm had single-handedly defeated his party's candidates in Senate and House elections in 1994, thereby raising speculation that Clinton was on the board of directors of the National Rifle Association and just never told anybody.

The power of special-interest groups today rivals the power of the political parties in earlier years. Indeed, as a group, they have become more powerful than the parties themselves. These groups distribute information, not just to their members, but also through a grass-roots communication network that rivals television and radio as a source of information. When candidates seek volunteers or money, they seek them from the members or supporters of these groups. They are committed to their beliefs, responding with more loyalty, contributions, and volunteer time than the loyalists in either political party.

Most Americans who support the views of special interest groups, whether they are members or not, both seek and find information on how their group feels about a candidate *before* they vote. Candidates have become aware of this and will often supply this information to prospective voters.

In order to dramatize how voter interest in supporting special-interest groups has matched support of the two political parties, a number of national pollsters in the 1994 election asked the questions below in twenty-five states.

The pollsters included such nationally known firms as: Mason-Dixon, which polled almost exclusively for news services; and two Democratic firms, Dresner, Sykes, Jordan & Wickers and Penn & Schoen, whom President Clinton has chosen to be his official polling firm in the upcoming elections. They also include two university polling firms, the Institute for Social Science Research at the University of Alabama, and the Roper Center at the University of Kentucky, and three Republican firms, Luntz Research Co., Moore Information and Marketing Research Group. All of these are nationally known firms.

These polling numbers matched the Republican and Democratic parties with two national special interest groups, the National Rifle Association and United We Stand America. These were selected because they are the largest two organizations, both in membership and in actual money available to develop a political communication delivery system to get their message out. United We Stand America at the time had two million dues-paying members and the National Rifle Association had 3.5 million.

The question that was asked in all these states was: I am going to name a number of organizations, and I want you to tell me if this organization speaks for you (1) all of the time, (2) most of the time, (3) some of the time, or (4) never. For this comparison, the most important number to use is from respondents who stated — all of the time —

because those are the individuals who will be totally motivated by either the Republican or Democratic parties or by the special interest groups.

State	Pollster	Date	GOP	DEM	UWS	NRA
AL	ISSR	6/95	5.9%	7.2%	8.5%	9.6%
AK	P&S	10/94	5.0%	5.0%	7.0%	17.0%
CA	LRC	7/94	7.0%	8.0%	5.0%	6.0%
CT	RC	11/94	3.0%	2.0%	2.0%	6.0%
FL	M-D and P/MR	5/94	4.0%	3.0%	2.0%	8.0%
GA	M-D and P/MR	5/94	5.0%	6.0%	2.0%	8.0%
ID	MI	5/94	3.0%	4.0%	2.0%	13.0%
IL	P/MR	10/94	8.0%	7.0%	4.0%	4.0%
IA	M-D	9/94	3.0%	3.0%	4.0%	2.0%
MA	M-D and P/MR	10/94	7.0%	7.0%	5.0%	9.0%
MI	MRG	10/94	5.0%	5.0%	3.0%	8.0%
MN	M-D	6/94	6.0%	8.0%	4.0%	8.0%
MO	M-D and P/MR	7/94	7.0%	5.0%	2.0%	9.0%
MT	MI	5/94	4.0%	5.0%	3.0%	14.0%
NV	P&S	10/94	7.0%	5.0%	5.0%	12.0%
NJ	LRC	7/94	5.0%	3.0%	4.0%	6.0%
NY	P&S	10/94	4.0%	4.0%	5.0%	6.0%
OK	LRC	7/94	4.0%	5.0%	6.0%	10.0%
OR	MI	5/94	6.0%	6.0%	1.0%	8.0%
PA	LRC	7/94	6.0%	11.0%	7.0%	10.0%
SC	M-D and P/MR	6/94	5.0%	4.0%	2.0%	8.0%
TN	M-D and P/MR	9/94	9.0%	10.0%	2.0%	13.0%
TX	M-D and P/MR	9/94	5.0%	4.0%	5.0%	4.0%
VT	DSJW	10/94	5.0%	6.0%	3.0%	7.0%
VA	M-D and P/MR	10/94	7.0%	7.0%	2.0%	14.0%

KEY
ISSR=Institute for Social Science Research at University of Alabama; P&S=Penn & Schoen; LRC=Luntz Research Co.; RC=Roper Center; M-D=Mason-Dixon; P/MR=Polit-ical/Media Research, Inc.; MI=Moore Information; MRG=Marketing Research Group; DSJW=Dresner, Sykes, Jordan & Wickers.

✶✶✶

As you can see in most states, in order for supporters of a political party to win, they need to recruit the supporters of other groups, like United We Stand America, the National Rifle Association, and the Christian Coalition. In previous elections, Democrats have made a concerted effort to fashion their base by attracting special-interest group supporters of organized labor, of the National Organization for Women, of the gay alliance, and of the labor union representing teachers, the NEA.

When studying the political system, it's important to note that the men and women who lead these special-interest groups can inform members about an issue or candidate and even persuade members *up to a point*. Special-interest group leaders cannot, however, *make* members work hard on behalf of, or even bother to vote for, someone these members think is a phony on their issues. You would expect most Christian Coalition members to pay a bit more attention to Pat Robertson's judgment of a candidate than Bill Clinton's. But a Robertson endorsement has to have plausibility. Coalition members will walk away from a Robertson-endorsed candidate who, they believe, opposes any display of religion in public places or any restrictions on abortion. These are their issues, and to be wrong on them is to mess with profound convictions shared by this interest group. No matter *what* Pat Robertson may say.

Given all this background, we thought it would be fun and just possibly useful to know how selected interest groups on the Right feel about certain famous Americans who may think they want to be president — and who in some cases should think again. So we went to extensive trouble — and expect extensive thanks — to prepare for you an analysis of the grass-roots feelings among the major political groups. What you are about to read — calm down, we're getting to it — rates the grass-roots feelings of twenty (count them, *twenty*) declared, potential, probable, and, as it turns out, improbable Republican or independent candidates for president or vice president.

We asked special-interest group leaders to rate the desirability of the following men and women as potential candidates for president and vice president, now or in the future, this century or next: Lamar Alexander, George Allen, William Bennett, Patrick J. Buchanan, Robert J. Dole, Robert Dornan, John Engler, Newt Gingrich, Phil Gramm, Kay Bailey Hutchison, Jack Kemp, Alan Keyes, Richard Lugar, Dan Lungren, Ross

✱✱

Perot, Colin Powell, Arlen Specter, Bill Weld, Christine Todd Whitman, and Pete Wilson.

Respondents had the following options to describe their feelings toward each potential candidate:

10 Completely supportive.
 9 Strongly supportive and leads on the issue.
 8 Votes Right or is always there when you need the support.
 7 Has a record of support, but has been reluctant in the past to speak out on the issue.
 6 Seems to support the principles of the issues.
 5 Has not taken a stand for or against.
 4 Usually against the issue.
 3 Votes against the issue almost all the time.
 2 Is a leader against the key issues supported by the group.
 1 Is totally opposed to the principles and will do everything to defeat them.

A rating of 6 or better means active and almost complete support is likely from that group's *members*. Remember, the leadership may have different views on that candidate.

A rating of 4 or 5 means that the likelihood is that a majority of the grassroots will base their decision to support a candidate on other issues.

A rating of 1, 2, or 3 means that if you're thinking about being the candidate, your chances of winning grass-roots support from that group range from slim to none.

Here's something else: If you're the voter and are that type of voter who regards a single issue as the main reason for voting, polling shows you're highly unlikely to vote for a candidate who holds the opposite view from yours on that issue, even though the candidate may agree with you on virtually every other issue.

If you're part of the far more numerous segment of the electorate whose members believe there are other reasons that are just as important to them, you will probably base your decision on a variety of issues, but even then it will be a difficult task to garner your support.

Candidate	A	B	C	D	E	F	G	H
Lamar Alexander	6	4	7	7	7	7	6	6
George Allen	9	10	10	9	10	9	8	9
William Bennett	7	6	10	9	2	8	9	6
Patrick J. Buchanan	9	10	10	9	10	8	8	10
Robert J. Dole	7	4	9	8	9	8	7	8
Robert Dornan	9	8	10		9	10	10	9
John Engler	9	5	9	5		7	8	9
Newt Gingrich	9	4	10	9	10	8	9	8
Phil Gramm	10	8	9	8	10	8	9	9
Kay Bailey Hutchison	6	6	6	7	10		7	4
Jack Kemp	6	4	8	8	6	8	6	6
Alan Keyes	8	9	10	9	9	10	9	9
Richard Lugar	5	1	9	7	6	5	5	4
Dan Lungren	8	5	10	6	4	7	9	6
H. Ross Perot	5	2	5	5	7	4	5	3
Colin Powell	5	5	7	8	5	2	5	5
Arlen Specter	2	1	1	2	6	2	2	6
Bill Weld	5	2	1	3	4	1	2	2
Christine Todd Whitman	4	2	1	6	5	3	3	2
Pete Wilson	5	1	4	6	2	3	3	5

J	K	L	M	N	O	P	Q	R	S	T	U
5	7	9	7	6	8	5	3	7	8	4	5
7	8	9	8	9	9	7	8	8	9	10	8
8	7	9	10	3	5	8	8	10	10	9	9
10	9	8	6	8	8	8	10	8	10	9	9
6	5	8	9	8	6	9	9	6	9	8	6
10	9	8	9	8	9	10	10	10	9	10	9
9	9	9	9	8	4	9	10	8	6	10	
7	8	10	10	8	4	8	8	9	10	9	9
8	7	9	10	9	8	9	10	6	5	9	9
6	6	5	9	8	7	8	2	8	5	6	7
7	6	7	9	6	1	9	10	10	5	8	7
9	8	8	9	9	7	8	10	10	8	10	9
6	7	7	9	6	6	7	9	5	9	7	6
10	8	10	10	2	4	7	9	5	9	9	9
4	4	6	7	5	4	6	3	3	8	3	5
4	5	5	8	5	5	5	5	5	5	5	5
1	2	5	7	6	1	4	1	2	3	5	1
1	2	8	8	2	1	3	1	4	5	3	1
1	2	5	8	5	2	7	1	4	4	3	1
1	4	7	7	2	2	2	1	2	9	7	2

✶✶✶

Key of Special Interest Groups:

A **American Conservative Union**. Chairman: David Keene. Oldest national membership organization on Right. Lobbies Congress on traditional conservative issues such as individual freedom and devolving power to local government and voluntary citizen associations.

B **American Policy Center**. President: Thomas DeWeese. Citizens' group. Lobbies Congress on the environment and education. Presented evidence against claims of global warming. Advocates ending federal involvement in education.

C **Christian Coalition**. Founder: Pat Robertson. Executive Director: Ralph Reed. Fifty-state grass-roots organization claiming 1.7 million members dedicated to promoting moral and family values through the political process from local school boards and city councils to Congress and the Presidency. Distributes voters guides about candidates and their positions.

D **Christian Voice**. President: Robert Grant. Oldest national religious conservative organization. First to provide voters guides about candidates and their stands.

E **Citizens Committee for the Right to Keep and Bear Arms.** Executive Director: Paul M. Williams. Fifty-state membership organization. More than 150 members of Congress on advisory board. Advocates Second-Amendment rights.

F **Citizens United**. President: Floyd Brown. Does research and informational direct mail on officeholders it suspects of violating the public's trust.

G **Conservative Leadership Political Action Committee.** Chairman: Morton C. Blackwell. Non-membership PAC. Helps elect conservative congressional candidates.

H **Eagle Forum**. President: Phyllis Schlafly. National women's membership organization. Promotes traditional morality, private enterprise and national defense.

I **Federation for American Immigration Reform (FAIR)**. Executive Director: Daniel Stein. Advocates excluding illegal aliens from census, comprehensive reform of immigration laws and enforcement of laws against illegal enforcement of laws against illegal immigration, employment of illegal immigrants, visa abuses.

J **Family Research Council.** President: Gary Bauer. 200,000 members. Public policy research group. Issues policy studies to policy makers, lawmakers and media. Focuses on parental autonomy, impact of parental absence, community support for single parents, adolescent pregnancy, alternative education, sanctity of life. Issues voters guides.

K **Free Congress Foundation.** President: Paul M. Weyrich. Influential public policy research group with close ties to conservative leaders in Congress.

L **GOPAC.** Chairman: Gay Hart Gaines. Political Action Committee. Recruits, trains candidates to run as Republicans for elective office. Formerly headed by Newt Gingrich.

M **Heritage Foundation.** President: Edwin J. Feulner, Jr. Largest conservative public research organization in the nation. Issues timely policy papers to members of Congress, their staffs and the media regarding legislation that Congress is debating and issues that the White House and executive branch are grappling with.

N **National Rifle Association.** Chief Executive Officer: Wayne LaPierre. Three-million member organization. Promotes gun-owners' rights, trains members in the safe use of guns, organizes amateur and professional shooting contests, helps train local police and other law enforcers.

O **National Right to Work Committee.** President: Reed E. Larson. Opposes compulsory union membership in the workplace. Lobbies lawmakers, maintains speakers bureau and conducts research and education programs.

P **National Tax Limitation Committee.** President: Lewis K. Uhler. Promotes a constitutional amendment requiring a balanced federal budget and a super-majority in Congress to raise taxes.

Q **National Republican Coalition for Life.** President: Phyllis Schlafly. National grass-roots group promoting pro-life positions within the Republican Party.

****

R   **Toward Tradition**. President: Rabbi Daniel Lapin. National organization of Jewish conservatives.

S   **U.S. English**. Chairman: Mauro E. Mujica. Works to designate English as the official governmental language of the United States.

T   **Young America's Foundation**. President: Ron Robinson. Service organization for conservative high school and college students. Gives annual awards to teachers who oppose political correctness.

U   **Concerned Women for America**. President: Beverly LaHaye. National conservative women's organization with chapters in 50 states. Advocates family values and women's issues.

✶✶✶

WHO SPEAKS FOR YOU?
ALABAMA STATE POLL

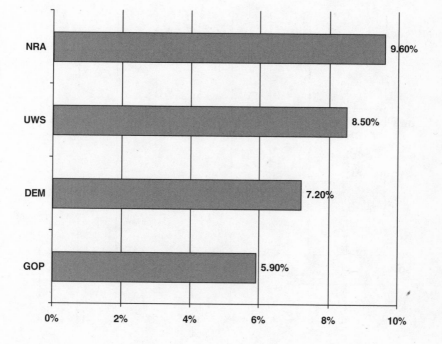

Source: Institute For Social Science Research - University of Alabama
June, 1995

WHO SPEAKS FOR YOU?
ARKANSAS STATE POLL

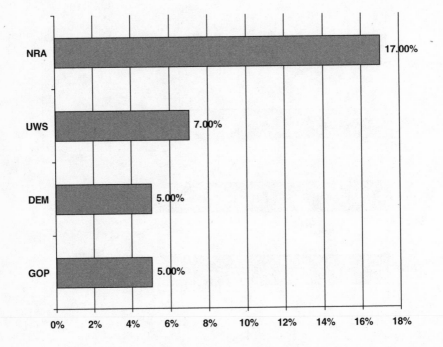

Source: Penn & Schoen Associates, Inc.
October, 1994

****

WHO SPEAKS FOR YOU?
CALIFORNIA STATE POLL

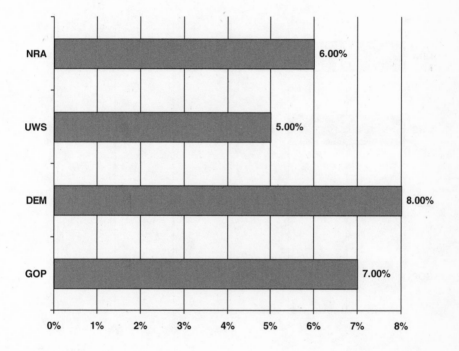

Source: Luntz Research Co.
July, 1994

✳✳

WHO SPEAKS FOR YOU?
CONNECTICUT STATE POLL

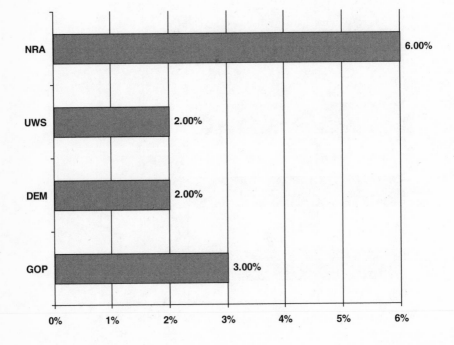

Source: Roper Center
November, 1994

****

WHO SPEAKS FOR YOU?
FLORIDA STATE POLL

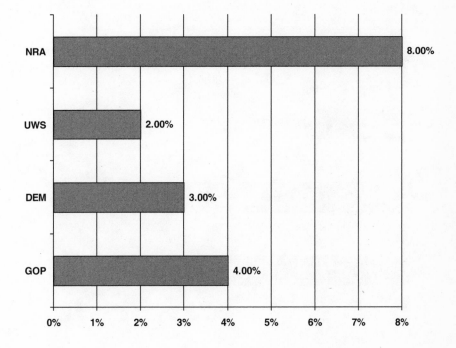

Source: Mason-Dixon and Political/Media Research, Inc.
May, 1994

WHO SPEAKS FOR YOU?
GEORGIA STATE POLL

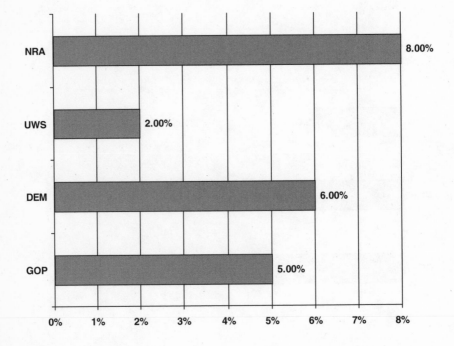

Source: Mason-Dixon and Political/Media Research, Inc.
May, 1994

✶✶

WHO SPEAKS FOR YOU?
IDAHO STATE POLL

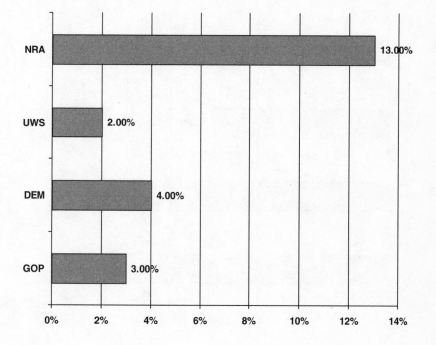

Source: Moore Information
May, 1994

✷✷

WHO SPEAKS FOR YOU?
ILLINOIS STATE POLL

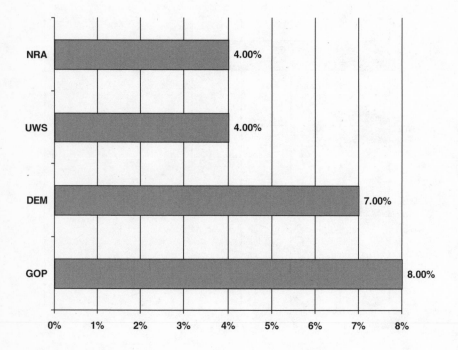

Source: Political/Media Research, Inc.
October, 1994

✶✶

WHO SPEAKS FOR YOU?
IOWA STATE POLL

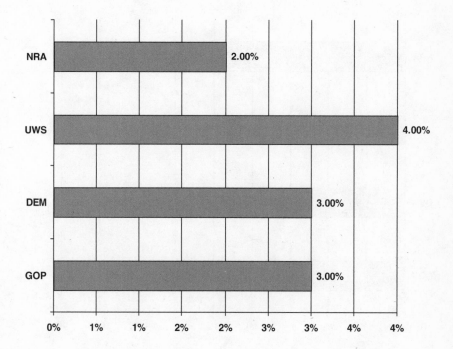

Source: Mason-Dixon
September, 1994

✶✶✶

WHO SPEAKS FOR YOU?
MAINE STATE POLL

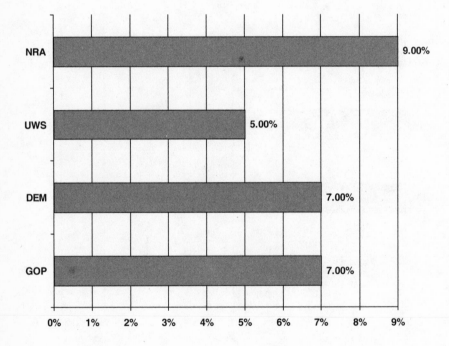

Source: Mason-Dixon and Political/Media Research, Inc.
October, 1994

****

WHO SPEAKS FOR YOU?
MICHIGAN STATE POLL

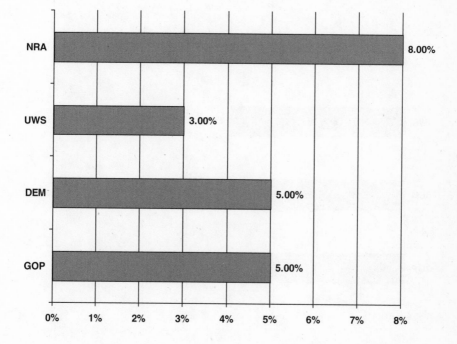

Source: Marketing Research Group
October, 1994

****

WHO SPEAKS FOR YOU?
MINNESOTA STATE POLL

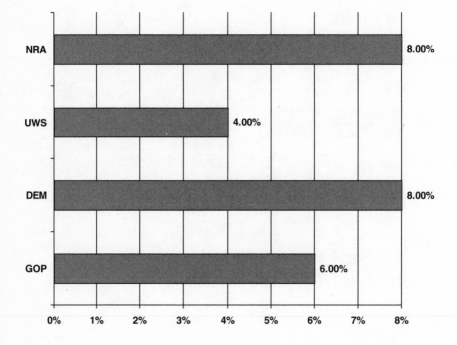

Source: Mason-Dixon
June, 1994

****

WHO SPEAKS FOR YOU?
MISSOURI STATE POLL

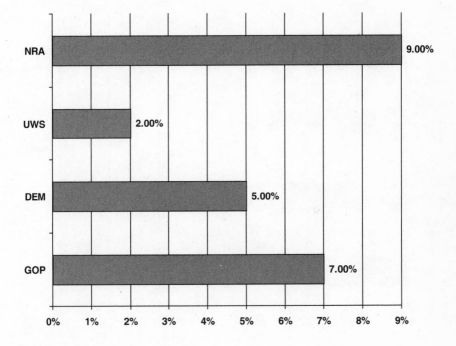

Source: Mason-Dixon and Political/Media Research, Inc.
July, 1994

✶✶

WHO SPEAKS FOR YOU?
MONTANA STATE POLL

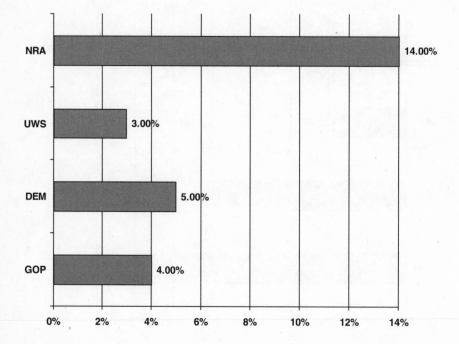

Source: Moore Information
May, 1994

WHO SPEAKS FOR YOU?
NEVADA STATE POLL

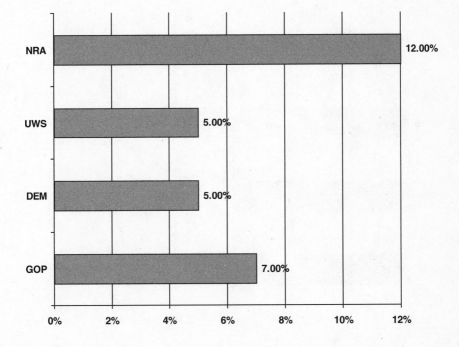

Source: Penn & Schoen Associates, Inc.
October, 1994

✶✶✶

WHO SPEAKS FOR YOU?
NEW JERSEY STATE POLL

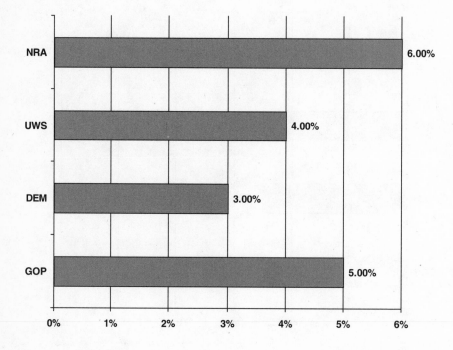

Source: Luntz Research Co.
July, 1994

WHO SPEAKS FOR YOU?
NEW YORK STATE POLL

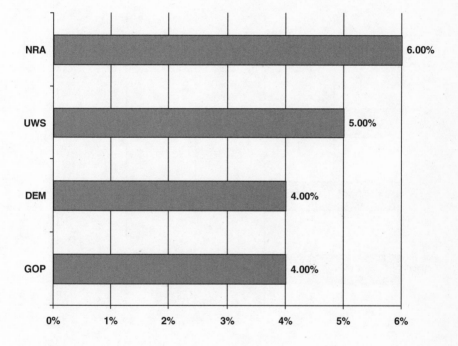

Source: Penn & Schoen Associates, Inc.
October, 1994

****

WHO SPEAKS FOR YOU?
OKLAHOMA STATE POLL

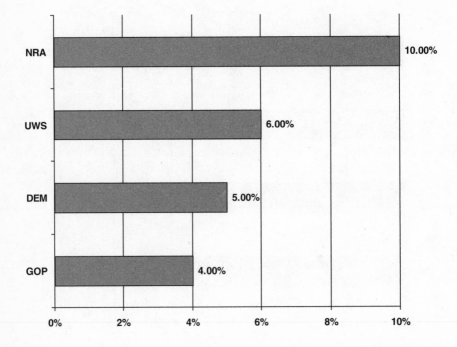

Source: Luntz Research Co.
July, 1994

WHO SPEAKS FOR YOU?
OREGON STATE POLL

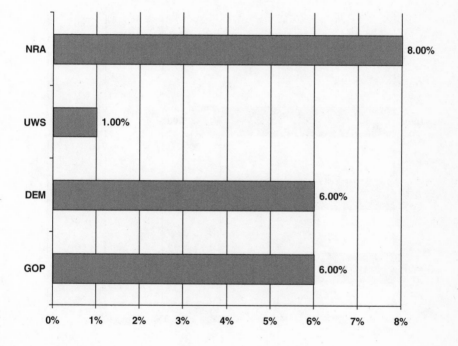

Source: Moore Information
May, 1994

****

WHO SPEAKS FOR YOU?
PENNSYLVANIA STATE POLL

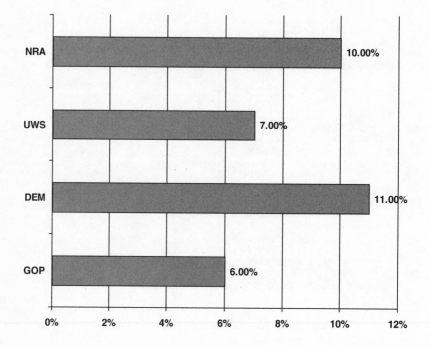

Source: Luntz Research Co.
July, 1994

****

WHO SPEAKS FOR YOU?
SOUTH CAROLINA STATE POLL

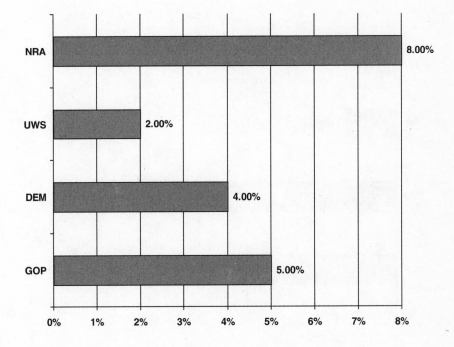

Source: Mason-Dixon and Political/Media Research, Inc.
June, 1994

✳✳

WHO SPEAKS FOR YOU?
TENNESSEE STATE POLL

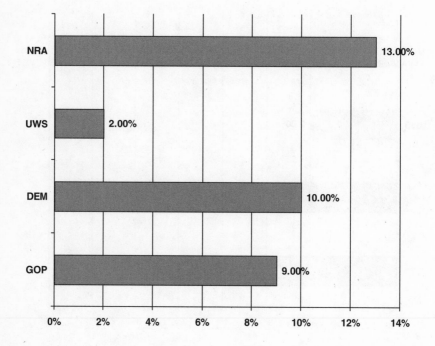

Source: Mason-Dixon and Political/Media Research, Inc.
September, 1994

✶✶

WHO SPEAKS FOR YOU?
TEXAS STATE POLL

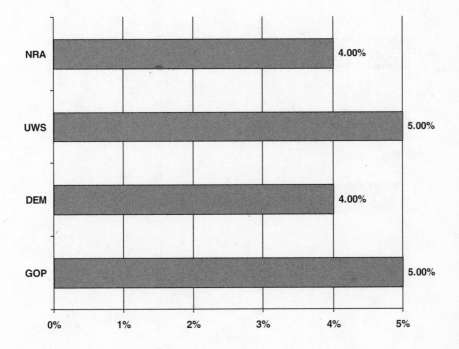

Source: Mason-Dixon and Political/Media Research, Inc.
September, 1994

****

WHO SPEAKS FOR YOU?
VERMONT STATE POLL

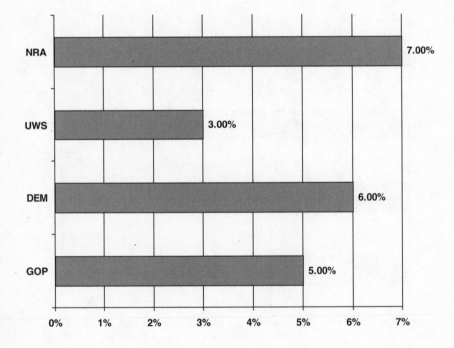

Source: Dresner, Sykes, Jordan & Wickers, Inc.
October, 1994

✫✫

WHO SPEAKS FOR YOU?
VIRGINIA STATE POLL

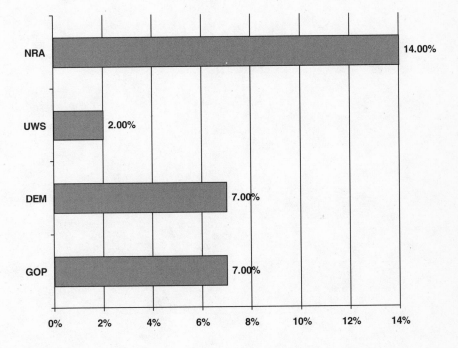

Source: Mason-Dixon and Political/Media Research, Inc.
October, 1994

About the Authors

Ralph Z. Hallow, the senior national correspondent for the *Washington Times* and former editorial writer for the *Chicago Tribune*, is frequent guest analyst on television and radio. A thirty-year veteran of daily journalism, he also has contributed to national magazines on the Right and Left, including *National Review*, the *Nation*, and the *Progressive*. He has reported from around the world on war and peace, economic summits, NATO, SALT talks and dictatorships of the Left and Right. For the last decade, he focused his analysis on the White House, Congressional politics, and presidential campaigns, traveling with the candidates across the United States.

* * *

Bradley S. O'Leary is a political feature writer with articles appearing in the national Sunday magazine *USA Weekend* with over 39 million readers. His newsletter, the *O'Leary Political Report*, is one of the top political news reports in the country. He can be heard weekly on the point/counterpoint NBC mutual network show "The O'Leary/Kamber Report" with nearly 1.5 million listeners. In 1996, he will join the ranks of the weekly syndicated NBC mutual broadcast network. Former chairman of the American Political Consultants. As a twenty-seven-year veteran of politics, he's acquainted with many of the politicians he writes about. He cut his political teeth in Texas working with former Governor John Connally, Senator John Tower, and Ross Perot. He grew up in St. Louis with Pat Buchanan. His client list has included Bob Dole, Newt Gingrich, Phil Gramm, Jack Kemp, and Richard Lugar.